WE FIGHT M(

Wisdom and Inspiration that spea

Michael Kurcina

Spotter Up LLC.

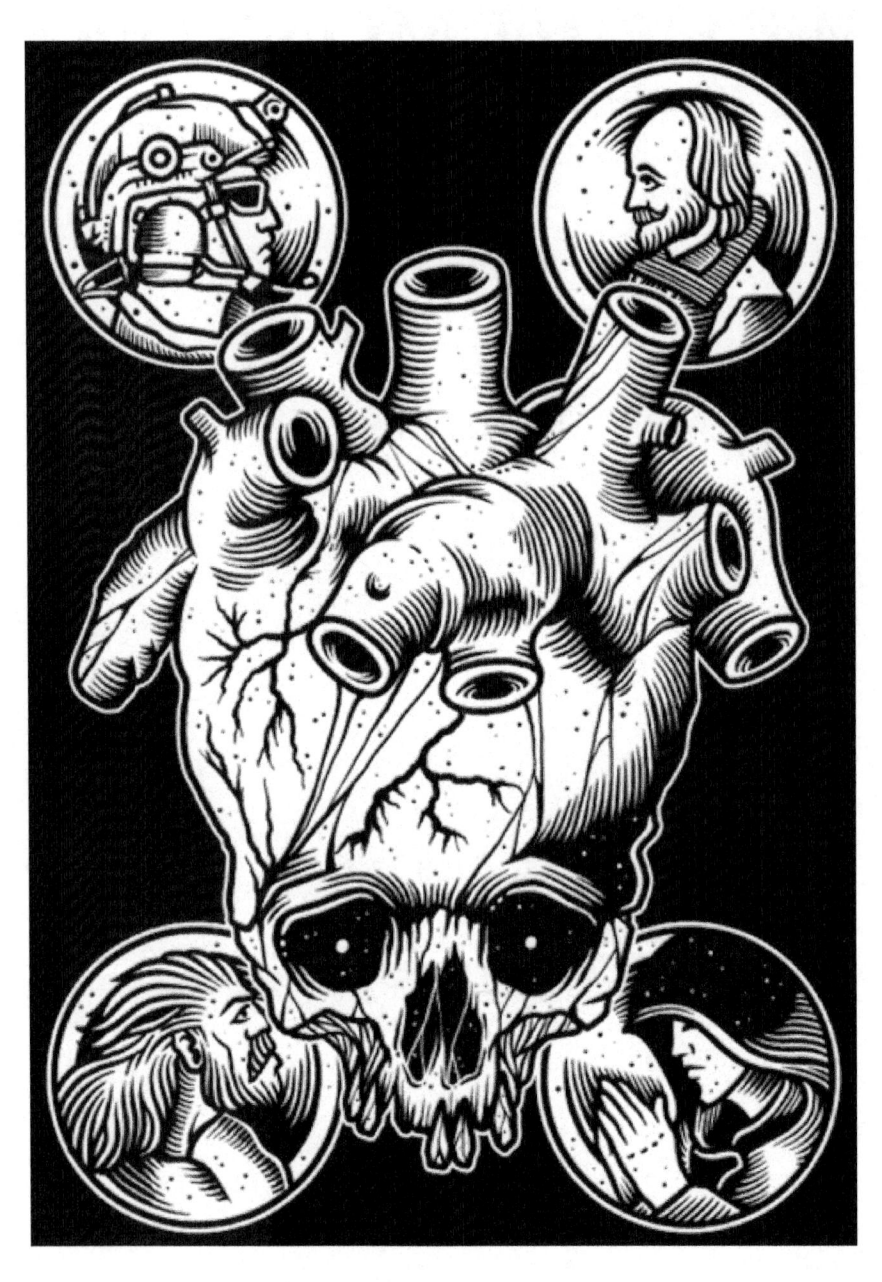

GUNFIGHTER-WRITER-WILDMAN-MONK
Man of Action, Man of Intellect, Man of Emotion, Man of Spirit

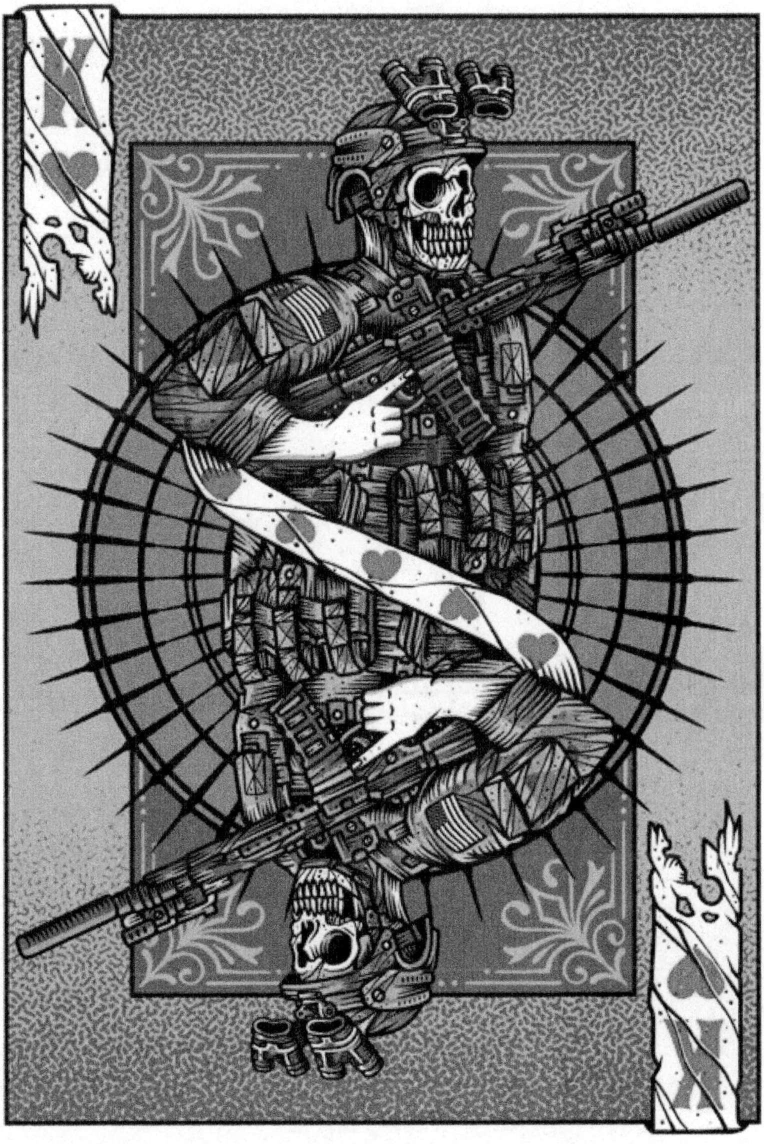

Plato's Cave

"Every man lives confusedly in darkness until he is willing to enter into light by exiting the womb of his life and leaves the safety of that environment. He has to make mistakes, he has to take chances, he has to be willing to be cut down by critics and applauded by praisers even at times ignoring what they say, while he finds out for himself what is true and false, and even then, he'll never really know a thing until he leaves comfort behind.

He must disregard everything told to him in all the safe passages he's traveled, and those tubes and tunnels. It's only when he's free of 'back there' will he understand what he left behind. Men will always be strangers to one another and themselves unless each learns by trial and error and ascertains the truth, that what he believed was only theory, and until he applied it, he was but a theorist and not a realist. Truth has a way of cutting through nonsense.

He must make his bones, and sometimes he must pay some very big dues, but in the end, he'll know truth. What he knew before may have been right but it wasn't until he questioned it, and applied it will it sink in and make sense. The cause of any man's confusion is that he never found himself but finding means searching, and halfhearted attempts often come from halfhearted men who in the end are just kidding themselves" ~Michael Kurcina.

CONTENTS

	Foreword	7
Chapter 1	Introspection	10
Chapter 2	Movies, Literature, more	185
Chapter 3	Poetry	293
Chapter 4	Men	313
Chapter 5	Perspective	327
Chapter 6	Courage	336
Chapter 7	Love	340
Chapter 8	Warfighting	346
Chapter 9	Faith	354
Chapter 10	Sadness, Pain	360
Chapter 11	Loss	364
Chapter 12	Time and Memory	370
Chapter 13	Culture	375
Chapter 14	Death	379
Chapter 15	Knowledge	381
Acknowledgments		388

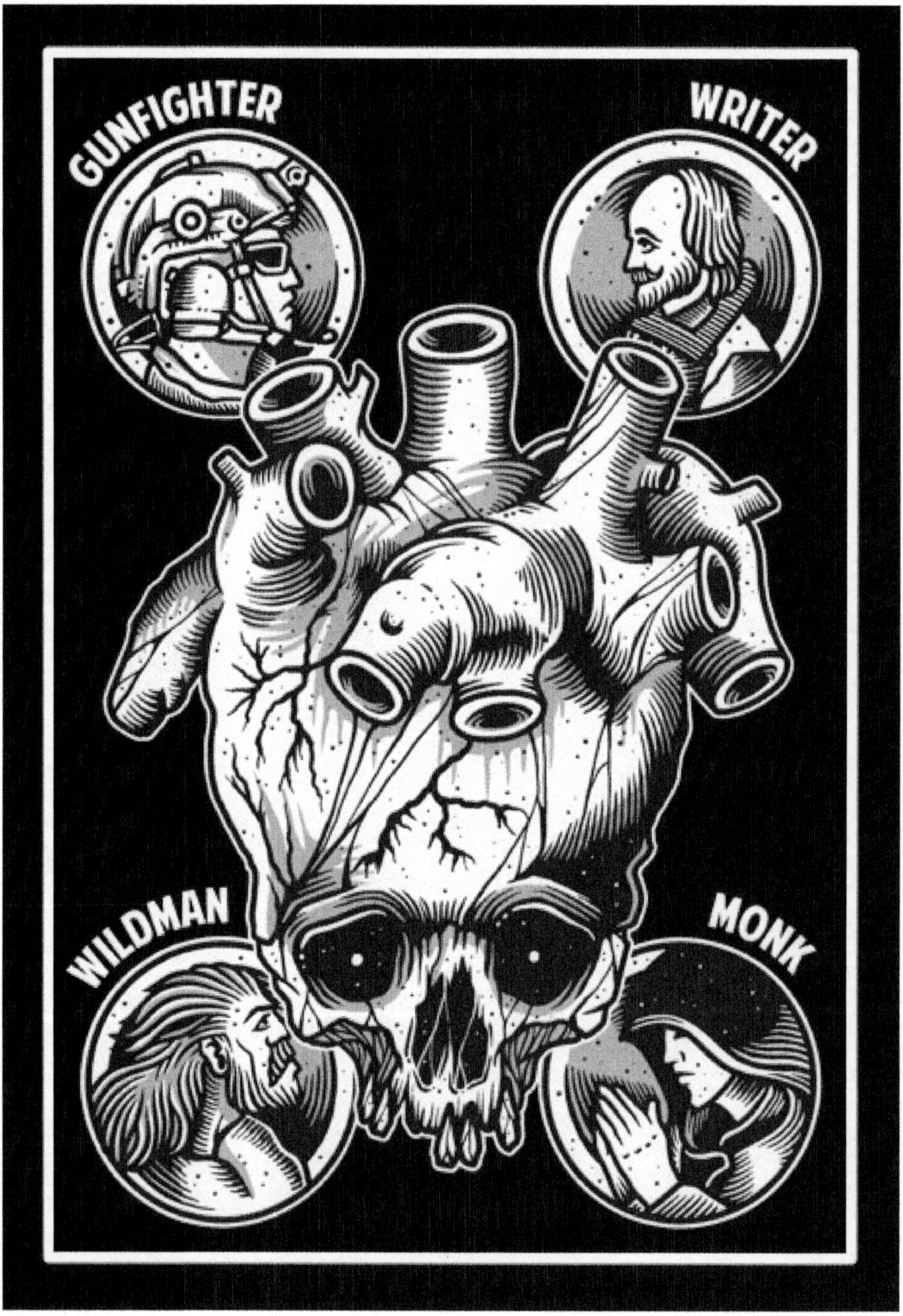
GUNFIGHTER
WRITER
WILDMAN
MONK

Foreword

We Fight Monsters is a book about not giving up. I wanted to be involved in the anguish of men by giving hope and courage to those getting their butts handed to them daily by the grind: divorce, work, PTSD, the loss of a family member, a friend. In fact, wherever or whatever the battle I wanted to give men some mental and spiritual ammunition they needed to get out of their rut. A lot of us were spitting into the unseen faces of what seemed an indifferent universe, and even a Big Boss-the angel of Death that didn't give two wooden nickels about us.

I wanted to be involved in the affairs of others, to make a contribution that used my sorrow and anger in a dignified way, and by confronting my pain through writing have it help others.

This book is a collection of all of the posts that I put on Instagram over the last four years; my thoughts on masculinity, courage, fear, love, God, literature, movies, you name it, I wrote about it. This book is not your typical book on inspiration, you'll know what I mean when you read it.

There's failure to be had in this world, and failure experienced can lead to feelings of anguish. Many men never achieve their goals. Goals don't have to be big ones. Instagram, and society largely is made up of people idolizing the superficial and making them into gods; wealth, power, fame, sex and forgetting the simplest things in life added up make a man. Sometimes all men need is a simple solution to help with their complex problem by reading a quote, and it gets them going in the right direction.

We need to shut out the nonsense pushed upon us by a shallow culture, in order to really examine our wounds. We must attack any of our misgivings with deliberate honesty to prevent the corrosive power of skepticism from rotting us within, and in doing so see there is no longer a need to wave a fist and spit into the unseen face of the universe. It will make sense.

First, I want to thank God for finding a way to use me. I am grateful. Thanks to all of my friends for supplying me with cool pictures. I want to thank Dr. Stephen Band, retired FBI special agent, my friend and counselor. I would not be here today if I didn't go see him for depression, and anger.

He encouraged me to take whatever was broken inside my heart and skull and create. So, I did. I wrote. Lastly, I dedicate this book to God and to my loving wife Kelly for all of her support during many years of my craziness.

The words found herein are mine. Good or bad, I own them. Writing for me was never an act of courage nor did I spend hours refining a thing that I wrote. I've always said to write, and write honestly because it can be the tool that saves you from yourself. I hope you find something in this book that you feel is useful. I encourage you to do things that make you whole; healthy structure. It doesn't matter what you do so long as you change something from the way it was before, for the better.

Take up arms every day to fight your fears and nightmares that lurk in the shadows. Prepare yourself for the next emotional and spiritual wave. It doesn't matter if it comes crashing down and you drown because at least you did the work. Fill your eyes with wonder, live to enjoy this world but prepare for your hereafter.

John 3:16 - For God so loved the world that He gave His only begotten Son. that whoever believes in Him should not perish but have everlasting life.

Introspection

When the splendid things vanish

A friend from my faraway life passed away this month. We weren't close any longer. Years ago, I made the choice to retreat into my silent abyss and when I exited it, I made the choice to shake away the fear of life's impermanence. I fled then like cowards do, one warm evening while the city lights sparkled coolly, and things seemed darkest in my resentful life.

When the splendid things vanish in the lives of the most impatient of men some of them come searching for just a trace of the everlasting. My rooting was planted nowhere and in that silent evening I left, disappearing from my old world, and walked into a new one. His recent death asked me to stop wrestling with distances. It was something I did so well in order to prevent myself from returning home.

Our youth brought with it serious oath making even as we bargained for more time that didn't belong to us. We had few cares and couldn't explain the reckless decisions we made. We felt we'd live forever and believed we owned the license on the word invincible.

Yet when men die, we feel sick in our stomachs and weep like children. We wave our fist in the air at our powerlessness. We lose the men we love and the men we respect. He didn't serve in the military but was a worthy opponent nevertheless. We styled ourselves as heroes. He stood his ground while others parted from the scene of havoc, we drowned weaker men in.

And now he's gone…How should I remember him? As the ragged-headed teen who marveled at the deliciousness of life or as a feeble-bodied man who knew he was dying? Good health fled from him but I know his spirit didn't flag. We sprinkle the sea with the ashes of heroes. I departed that small world because I felt there was nothing left for me. Little did I know how my foray into the military would imbue me with some important life lessons.

God bless youth

A man can be a spectacle when he's young. He'll travel the globe three times over yet carries no watch to tell him that it's midnight in Austin or ten in Dover, and that he just missed the most important appointment of his life. He can't grasp the simple and the obvious but he'll do the most complex things.

He'll foolishly and quickly go down some dark paths, that get deeper and stranger, and will know little of the tomfoolery he did until he's at least 50, because he hadn't yet developed his penetrating mind. He lets the most precious hours pass away as he devours the minutes with ease. He's a contradiction, lusting and loving, fighting and peacemaking, wanting to live and die in the same moment; sometimes his brain is on fire while his heart is tired; he doesn't truly understand a thing yet his existence wants the confusion.

More more more...louder, bigger, faster and lusting after any women who helps him escape home. He's like a son to all fathers and a brother to all men. He has no clue that he'll die one day, perhaps early, yet he'll waste his time walking city pavements faithful to the belief that he'll be rich and famous. Who can blame him? He's a boy discovering what it costs to become a man. He's loyal even when he shouldn't be. Make him a soldier, give him a rifle, teach him to apply his damned foolishness; he just might become the most inspiring thing the world will ever see. God bless youth.

A journey to healing cannot begin unless...

A journey to healing cannot happen if you don't get on the path. There may be times in a man's life where he feels like he cannot breathe, cannot sleep, cannot rest, and cannot dream. He doesn't want to eat any longer, cannot go, cannot stay, feels as if he's lost all direction and yet he desires to flee.

Flee from what?

He halts when he needs to hurl himself into a task, loses confidence in himself when he should feel some kind, any kind of purpose, and he escapes from challenges when he should knuckle-down and get it done. Men with a strategy, will press-on, despite every experienced displeasure because he knows that all challenges, good ones and even the bad ones, have an ending. Men without a plan will continue to drift. Those who are willing to ask for help will get through the hard times due to the help given by their friends and brothers.

A man's journey on the long walk of life illuminates something about himself but he first has to get on the path to find out what that is. He will gain an intimate understanding about what kind of person he is. Successes and failures will never stop but he'll see that he is a warrior and can handle anything. Sometimes warriors lose their way; other warriors must guide him back onto the road. Men who escape from engaging in a challenge will always lose an opportunity to grow and will never realize how close they were to success; their destination and way point. Brothers who have his back will guide him and he will get a respite from his torture. *Where have all the grownups gone? Men grow in the company of other "men". Boys cannot grow if they are around other boys. Men who regress into boys will run from future fights rather than charge towards it. Stay connected with your band of brothers.

1. Meet your problems head on rather than avoid them.

2. Keep your word. Breaking your word makes you lose faith in yourself. Keeping your word builds confidence in yourself. You'll finish regardless of the challenges.

3. Be courageous. Have the guts to tell yourself the truth about what is going on. Once you can do that, you'll be able to deal with the problem. Tell others so they can help you.

4. Be restrained. Have self-control. Don't chase after fleeting things but wait for the right moment and do the right thing when the time comes. Resist temptation.

5. Own up to the results of your choices. If you made a bad decision then own up to it and deal with the consequences.

6. Examine yourself every single chance you get.

"MEN LIKE SWORDS CAN BE FORGED IN FIRE. THOSE WHO CHANGE WITH EVERY BURNING BECOME THE MOST FORMIDABLE OF WEAPONS."

Tyger Tyger burning bright

A man can change his nature no more easily than a hungry tiger can change its stripes, until he loses his scent and taste for the natural in order to hunt the supernatural. He must abandon all that he thinks he knows, those ideas about limitations and permissions, if he wants to start feeling like he's gaining ground and making a killing. Sometimes he must go a different path from the streak. Perhaps he must start small before he can envision hunting big game, but he must start. He must abandon his old ways of thinking in order to acquire new ways of stalking things, that will make him a devastating beast in this world's wilds. Be unnatural in your thoughts and deeds.

Where is home?

A man in love with his home returning to find out that it has turned into someone else's might in fact believe that he entered through a wrong door. No spaceman from Pluto should return from his travels to find out that he lives in what resembles Mars. What we love should not grow so much that we cannot recognize or grow with it any longer. A nation without boundaries like some shapeless thing is no nation at all, and the idea of its nature should never be indeterminate to the patriot or the loyalist or a Christian come to find that he can't worship an incomprehensible God. His door should be his door, his walls should be his walls, his home should be his home and if its address was 33 it should never be labeled 34. The common should never be mystical, the serious never comical, nor the sacred be profane.

Just because the idea of identity means nothing in the brain of the modern man doesn't mean in truth that it isn't so.

Kansas

Cry in the wheat fields where no man can hear you. Father can't save you any longer. He sits on his bed and doesn't know that he can't remember your name or even his own. Mother's cancer made her go blind. Her embraces can't rescue you despite touching your face like she did when you were a boy. As a boy you never learned that courage could never be captured, or that all men run out of time. There isn't a place for you larger than this earth to lose yourself, where you can hide from pain. Remember your people, remember the promises you made, remember your last name. Rise up in what seems an all-engulfing night. Have the same heart you did as a boy. No man's courage can ever be captured. There is still enough time. Safety is found in the darkness, and truth found in the light. Stand up like a man and runs towards danger again.

I am a lion

A man proclaims, "I am a man!" To whom does he speak, the woods, the rocks, the sky, the universe? He should know it in his bones and let the essence of it flow inside his veins. To state this aloud seems blasphemous. It seems too self-conscious. Stating so makes it seem as if he is small and yet in the scope of the bright stars piercing through the haunting blackness the reality is that he truly is small. Should a man need to remind himself of who he is? Does a lion roar to remind himself of what he is? No, a lion roars to let others know what he is. In a world filled with paradoxes are men who desire to cut themselves free from what other men believe yet in turn will respect those who hold strongly to what they profess.

Men will follow those who not only profess a truth but who truly live it. Even as one man doubts another not lacking in confidence will shout, "This is who I am! I am a man!" and inspire or weaken his brother. This is when man becomes big.

Men, so oddly, can be strangers to another yet aligned. To the end of his days when darkness speaks to him a man must shout out to the vast universe like a roaring lion, "I am here! I am a man! Come and take me."

He is not solely saying words, he is saying, "this is my soul and in this arena I won't go easy."

Precious little

A man should be comfortable with himself. He should be able to spend a lot of time alone without displeasure. His image, that visage in the mirror speaking back to him, should be his best friend and not his worst antagonist. He should not constantly wrestle with himself when deciding what he is, what he'll be, and where he'll go. A change of seconds, minutes and even hours won't be opportunities to freedom for a man uneasy with himself in fact it will be agony. Indeed, the advantage of hours means precious little to indecisive men.

And alone we go

And alone we go, every man, under the dark web of night and cold light to find something worthy to do. Sometimes it calls to us, like some odd fire in the sky, and we must go to it and find out why it calls. We don't want to listen but we must listen because it has a truth to share. Who are we, who were we? We are strangers to ourselves. Once we were warriors and once, we were men.

Where is this foreign voice coming from, what is this odd light? We must rise from our silent seat and go to it. We go by foot or car or bike, or ride shotgun but there aren't any conversations. How do we get there, from where did we get there? We pass the same clubs and barbershops, the same gas stations and the same hundred men standing without purpose. Each head turns and we swear they look just like us. Trapped in some dreamtime we pass rubble, and market stalls, poppy fields and sand. We raise our arms and wave our hands but no one waves back.

Cold lights continually pass through our window. We've seen them before a hundred nights in a row. Those who come back come back alone, with their hands empty. They never really searched. They say, "I looked! We'll come back. We'll do this again another night, and another night."

> And alone we go, every man, under the dark web of night and cold light to find something worthy to do.
> ~Michael Kurcina

Those who search want to find the faces they don't remember, of the people who once loved them and likely still do but time has come and washed that hope away. We wait for it to strike us; we hope that it will strike us in a way that nothing ever has before so we'll wait over and over again. This isn't how it's supposed to end for heroes is it? Life like some odd fire in the sky beckons us. We must go to it or stay in our gloom. Flashes of life call to us, and we must fly to it or continue to bleed inside our room.

Buried alive

A voice spoke to me in the darkness and whispered, "You will die. You will die." I answered back, "That I know. Please show me how to live!" But the answer never came. I ran everywhere looking for the source of the voice. I held my lantern high and searched and searched and searched but I found nothing. I ran along the river; I ran down the glens. I crept through an empty town. I shouted, "who are you?"

But I knew. And in the darkness, I sat against a tombstone and wept.

Action was once our king

Action was once our king and hesitation was the squire but now, we allow the latter to rule over us. How did we get here, where our intentions without action get us nowhere? Who rules over whom?

Hesitation often stops us from pursuing what we should pursue. We have to relearn and renew our mind by renewing our spirit, and get back into fighting some of the things that circumstances bring our way while being less timid about our intentions.

Yes, life has moved us into directions many of us don't want to go. Follow any one of the four winds but do something. Do something. What might we have been, what might we be if we allowed our good intentions to become action?

Do not love the world so much that you become timid men, terrified of success terrified of failure, of life and love and even death. Think about eternity which comes after death and less about losing trivial things upon this earth. In some moment of weakness, we tattooed upon our heart the symbol of our sadness which summed up our dying Fall, our worst season of fearfulness. None of the things we chased after coalesced into something more, it was all evanescent. Nothing seems to last forever but don't stop pursuing the things that you want. Life awaits you. Do not be timid men.

One

And in the palm of your hand rests your lover's cheek, and through her eyes come a gift of love meant only for you. And in those silent moments, beneath the business of your bedsheets, is the time to reveal vulnerable things: women hurt, men's dreams die, we destroy what we love and what loves us. We become as human as human can be, and push away the night and pity, shame and time. We take greedily and give gingerly. Can we stay, should we stay, will this moment last forever?

Legs like kindling alight; two become one. Take what you can now while the children sleep, and adore every star outside that sparkle coolly. The smallest fire on the deepest night is like an inferno to sad, lost men in need of light. Enjoy what you have, give, what you have, embrace what you have before the fire expires. Hold this memory with you in your darkest moment, "I was loved, I gave love, and I became part of something greater than myself if only for a single moment."

And I hid until hiding was tired of me

And when love left me, I ran away just like cowards do. When I couldn't run, I walked, and when I couldn't walk, I crawled, and when I couldn't crawl much longer, I hid myself away and cried. And when the crying was done, I looked at the stranger in the forest water and began to ask him why he did what he did.

Only when I was honest with myself did true healing begin. I journeyed far away. I took the boats and the barges, the trams and the boxcars and hid until hiding was tired of me, and the dark threw me into the light, so I was free to pursue myself again. Like all men I can destroy and create, and in my pursuit of things I displaced my nature with too much thinking, and too much of the unnatural world and I needed a new beginning. In our pursuit of things, we must upturn leaves and dirt and roots and rocks to find if something good is buried beneath the rotten trunk of our life. Sometimes we must return to our natural self, to simple times, to contemplate mysteries and observe everything around us. If we've done a good job there will be something beautiful growing up from the earth. Time flows past us like a river stream. We must choose how we use it to grow.

Stand

Any fool can stand for something but the true believer understanding full well the consequences that his actions can have on himself and others is willing to part even with a life or limb. Let's hope it's his good name or life that a man states he is willing to sacrifice and not that of others who may even protect him while he promotes his agenda. The patriot fully gives up himself, the mercenary may give up others, while the fool gives nothing because he doesn't truly comprehend what he is giving, what he is gaining, what he is stating, and what his real goals are.

He might or might not live in the spotlight if the culture accepts or rejects his proposal but true history will note that his philosophy was thin on sensibility and he'll fade into obscurity because his call to action meant nothing. A boy preens and postures in front of an audience. A man knows what he wants to say and says it, whether in public or in private, and his words, his actions and the way he lives his life he works hard to ensure are not contradictions. Let us never cease to cherish the brave deeds of warriors who lie at rest lest we forget what it is to be men.

The Undiscovered Country

Should we contemplate an existence without an end? We should, and we do because doing it enrichens our life, yet if it were possible to create endless things should we then have a beverage that never ends?

Should we then have a song that never ends? Should we have relationships that never end? Many of us enjoy those things but truth be told, in this fixed world, water has as much intrinsic value as wine, intermissions as much value as action, disconnection as much value as unions and we need life as much as we need death.

Life must have boundaries to rightly separate us from cessation and without it how could we reasonably contemplate the nature of existence or end? No song, no drink, no love at least in this world, will last forever and it shouldn't.

Endings give start to other beginnings as simple as that sounds. For the veteran or the lover or for any of us longing for the romantic past, where we felt a singularity of the soul, should be mindful that unchecked desires and too much feeling without a cut off-point might help with healing but can perpetually lock us in that time. What dreams may come…

Some men cannot tolerate things as they are, or as they could be, rather they are stuck considering only how things once were. Even work-outs in the gym need a termination time. We are able to contemplate the mystical afterlife even if science tells us, it all ends here; perhaps there is something out there and that our speculations are correct.

Sometimes it is best to focus on the future and not want nor wish for more of the past. Yes, boundaries are necessary for our mortal minds in order to contemplate the eternal. All good things, and even bad things come to an end and then we shuffle off this mortal coil. What is it that you want to control? Can we have an endless drink that satisfies our insatiable thirst? Can we have a song that tells an endless story to an eternal mind? Does the Viking or the cowboy, the Spartan or the Samurai not feel the same kind of pain despite the eras?

Humility is being able to lower yourself to a place where you feel no different than the person next to you despite having incongruent natures. Humility lets you find your place in this world where a lack of it throws a veil over the mind.

Memory allows you to spend time with your private visitors upon your personal island of thought, in a world of your own creation. We cannot pick the pain that visits us but surely, we can work on how we perceive the pain.

Avoiding all forms of pain is impossible, and clearly there is uncertainty in living life. Is existence worth the pain? We must all discover death for ourselves. Life has its pains but perhaps death is worse. Sometimes things should remain mysterious and infinite.

The man who is willing to accept that all things have their place is likely to find his life is enriched by new experiences. He'll never know until he releases the old. Will he lose what he once held dear to himself?

Old combats are back there, there are new combats ahead. There is peace too. These are just my opinions. I only have questions for you, the same questions that I ask of myself. If a drink ends, we have the opportunity to taste other things. If a song ends, we are better able understand the meaning of the story. If a union ends, we are able to experience more deeply how love can last forever. Enjoy what you have now.

Cave bear

Back into our ancestral place, back into the life of stone and iron and rock and cave, back into fury and rage. Back into the silent home that only we can know to hibernate, to sleep then wake and dig and dig and make a crack in this big rock of a world.

Knowledge, and ignorance, memory and forgetfulness intertwined and imprisoned in this thick skull and primordial brain. Waiting, waiting until the time is right, for a new dawn to come, the waking age and for a thousand immortal energies to shock this world with what we've become; a man, hurtling through the future unafraid.

Unremitting

Since the beginning of time, humans have been unremitting in every imaginable pursuit. We fought back against wild beasts and uncontainable nature in pursuit of knowledge. We hurtled across vast expanses of ocean and earth to penetrate deeper into her unknown. Our imaginings helped us move mountains of dirt and forest to build shiny cities on the hills.

We followed our heartfelt spirit of adventure to gather experience and in doing so created technologies to push us up from our mud-heaps and carried us in our metal chariots into the sky; we learned to fly and breached black, cold night. The bright stars were our destination. We were relentless…

At the heart of every human can be discovered the spirit of wonder. Simply put, we were built to explore. Our old ability to harness the strength of our heart, body and mind, like the Spartans of old, which once fused a strong society together has been weakened from within by intellectual doubters that tell us we were never great.

Bobble-headed buffoons have invaded the land of the warrior-philosophers and told everyone that we are equal with others, that we are no different than the rest of the world.

Pencil-necked academics tell us what victory is or is not. They tell us to accept what winning a war means on political terms rather than what makes sense. Even terrorists have goals and pursue them until death and yet our hands are tied with talk of gun control and the softening of of our military. Simply, if you see an enemy, you kill him. Bad leadership has snuffed out a thousand, shining lights with their insufferable ideologies. Don't be alarmed. There are pockets of heroes in this world even if control of the ship is run by fools and folly.

Do not give up. Do not quit. There are thousands of heroes among us in every city from here to Baghdad. If you are asleep, wake up. Set your life on fire again and seek out those brothers and sisters who feel the same.

We were losers

Back there was pain. Back there was failure. Back there was truth and we longed to escape it: the sad walks at night, the cold rain and the empty cafes, the stripper bars and our hot blood, the taverns filled with brutal men or the feeble with their toothless grins.

We left the friends we needed, and broke the hearts of the strange people we loved. We felt that flesh and fame might save us but those opportunities were as infrequent as they were meaningless. We drank too much and ate too little. All the hell we placed on ourselves was self-inflicted. Nothing could silence the thought in our minds that we were losers. We could not escape that thinking.

Embrace the chaos

Clamber upon the highest ramparts of this earth and recall the things you've heard and seen: the view of mist over a forest lake, the sound upon sea harbors when ocean waves break, fireflies rising in hot summer night, the giddy thrush's song at first light, the trembling breath of lovers, the shouts of men at war, the glory of the stars, thunderous waterfall upon rock and the brilliance of making your first silver dollar; red-eyed sunset over soaring hills, the sunken depths you plumbed and the unplowed fallows you've run and the sterile fact after fact after fact that illuminates how you have life.... Let the memories of old ghosts die. Our spirit is poor but we are free to choose the pattern of our life and the paths of this vast earth and every towering summit we'll climb.

Water

Early one morning we went hard and fast into the woods where the streams crossed and turned into a confluence of rivers. We felt that we had nothing but time to kill and so we ran and ran, our hearts racing with the same moving power of that blue life-giving water and we never looked back. As my confidence grew bolder it occurred to me as we snaked along the edges of the water that my life as a boy was coming back into my life as a man. The thought that went through my old mind was, "Welcome to the beginning of your new life." I kept running and running and vowed that I'd never look back.

Neediness

Each of us wants to be perceived as honorable, intelligent, and strong. We spend time trying to create that image. What person ever spent their time creating a public image of being dishonorable, stupid and weak? But what if our public image is called into question? Well, let me ask you this. Do you know who you are and what you believe? Do you know what you can control and what you can't control?

The more you are driven by a need to be liked by others, the more you will mold yourself into that image to fit other peoples' perception of who you should be. Can you take responsibility for the things you cannot control? Think about that statement for a minute. Can you take responsibility for the things you cannot control?

Not everyone is going to like us. We cannot control the filters of how they see us. But we are certainly in charge of how we see the world around us. When we accept the fact that not everyone is going to like us or love us, we assume that level of control. This is one example of how we take responsibility for things we cannot control.

When someone attacks our character, beliefs, actions or values its causes us to question them. Our attacker wants to injure us by causing us pain, shame, rejection and they may even want to cover up their own inadequacies. Continually revisiting our values and beliefs before an attack occurs is a good way to handle an attack before it comes.

Keep this in mind: If you act against your own values then you have betrayed yourself. Do not be shaken. Do not get rattled. Try to revisit what good values that you believe, and recommit yourself to them. Lastly, the action someone took is done. Why get angry over something that ended? Stay cool, stay calm, punch them in the nose, shoot their dog and burn their house down. Just kidding. Take responsibility for the things you cannot control. Don't be a slave to your emotions. Rise up, you are a king!

Halfhearted men

Every man lives confusedly in darkness until he is willing to enter into light by exiting the womb of his life and leave the safety of that environment. He has to make mistakes, he has to take chances, he has to be willing to be cut down by critics and applauded by praisers even at times ignoring what they say, while he finds out for himself what is true and false, and even then, he'll never really know a thing until he leaves comfort behind.

He must disregard everything told to him in all the safe passages he's traveled, and those tubes and tunnels. It's only when he's free of 'back there' will he understand what he left behind. Men will always be strangers to one another and themselves unless each learns by trial and error and ascertains the truth, that what he believed was only theory, and until he applied it, he was but a theorist and not a realist. Truth has a way of cutting through nonsense.

He must make his bones, and sometimes he must pay some very big dues, but in the end, he'll know truth. What he knew before may have been right but it wasn't until he questioned it, and applied it will it sink in and make sense. The cause of any man's confusion is that he never found himself but finding means searching, and halfhearted attempts often come from halfhearted men who in the end are just kidding themselves.

"Half-hearted attempts usually come from half-hearted men who are just kidding themselves."

Childhood

I shouted, "Darkness come out and fight!" And darkness laughed and it said, "Ha! Boy! Go away and come back when you're a man. You have nothing!" And I laughed and said, "Ha! Tomorrow you might win because I have yet to grow older and learn the ways of men but today, I bring the sharpest weapons that will injure you. I bring my belief that I can do the impossible, my hopes and my dreams. Darkness can never cast out light!" And darkness screamed....

Unlikable

Everyday a man must face something unlikeable about himself. He must face many of his shortcomings and he must do this alone. Every single day he has thousands of little choices he can make.

Out of the vast collection of random thoughts and calculations that run through his mind hopefully one of those proves useful enough to sober him up to the poor reality of his life, and wakes his heart up forever to make better choices.

Hopefully enough emotion flows through the dead blood in his veins and forces his sleeping limbs to take action and unfix his tomorrow.

Men fixed in their old way of thinking and fixated on the wrong thought can become obsessed with disliking themselves. We lie alone in darkness. The clock sitting upon our nightstand need not count to tell us what we already know; time passes and our life passes out of us.

If a sad man wants to be truly happy, he needs to become what he was in his childhood. He must have pure elation and find value in simple things. There is joy in petting a dog, and eating an ice cream cone and building a mud pie; mysteries to youth. Sometimes a man must let go of his blade, and gun and drop his armor and simply choose to like childish things again. He must live without a certain amount of shame and embarrassment. Perhaps he needs to stop being so hard on himself. Today for a minute give it a try.

Let nothing in this world shatter you

For those without an unshakeable love they must rely on their own compass to prevent being pulled in opposite directions, and hopefully heathy self-love, and a dedication to one's life mission will point the way out of destruction. After you've walked away from some kind of fame or fortune and stripped yourself of pretentious aspirations, you'll find the person you were meant to be, not that titmouse of a man, but as a man was meant to be.

A man is naked and unafraid of most things because he has strong comfort in what he knows. He knows that all things belonging to this earth will die, that nothing will last forever yet he has some dedicated conscious thought to building things, even knowing while life imposes limitations, he will build with an energy as if he were seventeen again. He may lose a child, a marriage, a job, a friend. Man is born to live, suffer and die but he is also born to hope. *Let nothing in this world shatter you.

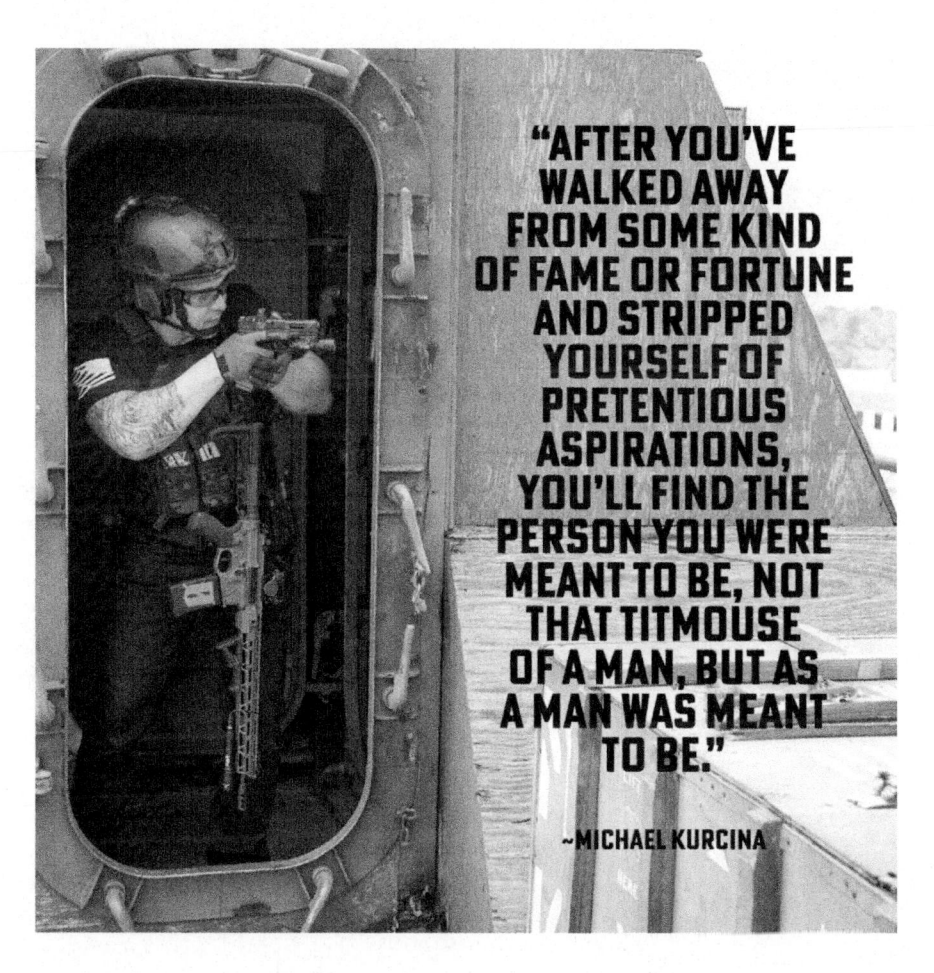

> "AFTER YOU'VE WALKED AWAY FROM SOME KIND OF FAME OR FORTUNE AND STRIPPED YOURSELF OF PRETENTIOUS ASPIRATIONS, YOU'LL FIND THE PERSON YOU WERE MEANT TO BE, NOT THAT TITMOUSE OF A MAN, BUT AS A MAN WAS MEANT TO BE."
>
> ~MICHAEL KURCINA

I will be fine

Quiet night for me at the moment and it's because I'm away from the walls and the darkness, yet I know that outside this protection, nightly come the madmen who'd like to breach right through. From the walls comes the crackling sound of gunfire which puts them down into an earthy rest, a place none would rather be except madmen.

> And if all I ever had was a secret grief I would be fine.
> ~Michael Kurcina

The security holds the place together while I listen to my iPod and play some tunes quietly. Earlier this evening twisting plumes of smoke rose upon the tall flames which birthed them and I could make out the high fires growing in the distance. Near enough to see, near enough to touch, just like taking a walk to a corner shop. But I'd be getting ash and fire rather than milk and eggs and then I'd hear the 'pop, pop, pop…'

Funny. How a man can stand tiptoe on a high stairwell and still only have a shortened view into the greater distance. A child's eye view into his future. I stood silently on the highest rooftop and leaned upon the second railing, thinking, how beautiful it is, the nightfall that's coming. I just didn't know what surprise was waiting for me but I felt elation…for what was waiting for me…

and I couldn't predict if I was asked…

…whether tomorrow I'd have peace or misery. But I felt that no matter what occurred, I'd do just fine.

And I felt, that I'd never want to see the future, never want to know exactly what was unfurling upon me… And if all I was ever given was a secret grief, I would be fine. I would be fine.

This shortened view from my heightened place brought me a vision that I hadn't had before, and out along the wide expanse of the hot horizon, where the heat waves blew the sky silly, I saw past the ripples which moments earlier had blocked my view. And I knew I wanted to embrace the life that was wrapping itself around me. I will be fine. I will be fine. I will be fine…

Be a man with a fight left in him

Get hit, hit back harder. Get kicked, kick back harder. Where did it all begin? Maybe it started for us when we saw a mother or daughter slapped around by a father and could do nothing about it. We sucked it all up and died inside.

Maybe it's because as a child upon seeing two uneven slices of birthday cake served that we knew some sibling was going to get robbed. Maybe we got bullied. I don't know but at some point, every kid can tell when life is unfair and uneven. Maybe it's when that kid gets older and he just sucks it all up and gives up, and the fight inside the man is gone. Don't be that man. Don't be the guy who holds his head in shame.

Like a mark in a mirror that never comes off no matter how hard it's scrubbed when he looks into it, like a scarlet letter he can't remove and it never gets better. People can see a dead man walking. Don't give in. Today, if this is the day, choose to become a man who has a fight left in him. Hold your head up, be proud and walk magnificently.

Goodbye empire, goodbye

Do most of us live daily without a deep thought about where this nation is going? Do we even think about where it will be hundreds of years hence and should we have any misgivings? We should and we should have many.

We've been made afraid to tell other people's children about the greatness of this country by political leaders and agitators that are part of the dumb and the damned. This country is one bright star in a universe of dull stars that seeks to dampen its brightness.

Where would this world be without our nation of democratic processes, religious freedoms and markets open to anyone regardless of skin color or creeds? We are imperfect but optimists and pessimists alike are allowed to live here in this world of tyrannical modernists and lunatics. The worst of its cynics with the most corrupt of instincts would see this country reformed in the most extreme of ways. Indifferent people with indefinite beliefs seek to make what should be intolerable tolerable.

Whether you are a beat cop coming off night shift or a soldier waking up down range keep your head straight. Scan ahead for danger. Grief on the faces of so many men make me remember the sad streets of my long-ago childhood, but that's not now and I'm no longer a boy. I have the mature strength of a man who knows well enough when things get tough that I can make a difference in this world. Can you?

We must be the champions that the world needs. If not us than who? We're the civilized minority standing firm against foes whose ultimate goal is to destroy the underpinnings that hold our world upright and we should deny them the mad desires they dream. There are enemies in the field. Do not let them crush you. Hold the line, hold the line, hold this empire together. Hold this empire together!

I'm not solely talking about Rome or Byzantium. I do write of ideologies that helped build this world and defended us against barbarians and now we have a new insidious collectivist breed gathering in this postmodern world.

Streetfighter

Getting into it teaches you a lot about other people, and a lot about yourself. Sometimes you find out you're not as brave as you believed. Sometimes you're the cock of the walk and can't believe the demons that you tried to hide will come out and take a piece out of others.

I'm not a pacifist but I'm not an advocate for wanton violence either. When violence comes you see whether you stand or fold, whether you run away or run straight into the mouth of it and punch its teeth out. Sometimes let violence talk smack and just walk away from it. Sometimes the cycle of violence is hard to escape if you've been doing it for so long.

I do not want to hang my shield

Hanging your shield typically meant that your fighting days were over. If you were still active your sword and shield were always within arm's reach. Some shields were quite heavy. Sometimes hanging our shields came without our approval. Whether fate set it upon us or we set it upon ourselves to end our journey is only known and pontificated by the man hanging it.

An injury, the end of our service obligation or a change in career meant we left our sword or rifle above our mantle. There are some really great stories in cinema where the hero comes back to rescue someone. The Unforgiven, Shane, High Noon, and Gran Torino come to my mind. I know that a lot of veterans have a hard time transitioning.

I've been there. Spotterup.com came from my own struggle to find purpose and to impart knowledge. Sometimes the fight never leaves the gunfighter and that's okay. The movie characters, William Munny and Walt Kowalski, impacted communities and both struggled. Heroes never truly rest, that's not the way they are engineered. It's never a question or not whether you are done or are not done with battling. It's really by what degree. Men aren't light switches that are on or off. We're more like smoldering fires that are raging or subdued even when eking out a living like pig farmer Munny or watching time pass like Korean War vet Kowalski.

> "A MAN BETRAYS HIMSELF COMPLETELY IF HE DOESN'T HAVE THE STOMACH TO KILL THOSE WHO WOULD DESTROY HIM."
> ~MICHAEL KURCINA

If you're struggling to find a war to fight that's physical, consider that real wars start in the mind. Sharpen your mental weapons. Maybe the battle you fight is in helping your granddaughter win a spelling bee or saving a neighbor from being beaten by her spouse.

Warfare never leaves us; we're not built that way. Regardless of how many foreign movies we watch, how much pate and Brie we eat trying to soften ourselves well I don't think that's the right approach.

In my opinion live your life, and see battle as a good part of yourself, but simultaneously see it as something in the distant past that can be recalled and reconstituted if need be. Hanging a shield removes a burden but if you need that weight and that armor, sling it back on, because the world does need heroes. Just make sure you're ready to handle the call when it comes. It will come one way or another.

I brought war

Have self-respect. Believe in what you build. Don't violate that and you'll have power. Break it and you'll find yourself a slave to every opinion. Work with those that want to work with you. Often times people mistake your earnestness for foolishness or weakness rather than shrewdness.

Don't meander off the path of your purpose or you'll end up chasing other people's schemes and regretting it later on. Be humble, be durable, be teachable, build real relationships and the rest will follow. Along the way you'll meet some good and bad people, sometimes they're the same people.

If it comes time to fight back then be unrelenting, defend yourself, destroy them and salt the earth. Don't look back. I brought peace until they brought war so I brought war until they brought peace.

Empires crumble

Home is a far-off place for many men. When he goes away for a long period of time the loss of it eats at him. The pain of its absence is galactic and unguessable, while he masquerades that all is well. Beneath his bright visage that he shows others hides a man who snivels and sobs because his heart is fouled like a broken engine. The machine does not function anymore.

Most times he leaves someone or something of great value behind in the belief that he'll return to it and all will be intact but that's not true. He believed that he would do good things. Everything he loved turns to rubble in some way. The idea of home and what it offers becomes alien to him and it's no different than a horseman upon a hill watching an empire die while his steed pulls away. He doesn't want to turn and see it disappear, but he knows full well he is the root cause of its fall and there will be a price to be paid.

He never intended to abandon anything good or anyone. Home resides in some antiquity. Sometimes the sense of it is palpable but it will always remain unreachable unless he learns to return, seek out and repair what he lost and damaged. Sometimes the memory and emotion of it is precise and powerful but mostly it is far off. The pleasure of it is soft to him and its worth unmatchable, but once away home becomes as foreign as love making is to a man who once had tenderness yet is denied touch. Seeing home or people in a photograph are like watching an old foreign film. Incomprehensible, alien, and yet oddly at times engaging.

His inexpressive face considers the past while the heart dies. How does he get back to 'there'? Like a heavy pain that sits in the heart, that pulls the chest down into the belly, the loss brings a sinking feeling he cannot seem to pull himself up from. Home is something men want to enter, to touch, to walk through but they cannot and it is seemingly as unknown as an ancient, dead empire is in history books.

Navigate

How can any man navigate his way through this world if he doesn't fathom the most important points in his life's history? One great moment marked in his memory might not be sufficient to get him out of feeling lost in America or lost even deeper upon this earth. He must study his past without doubling back to linger in all of those lost passages and caves that first led him into those troubled times. He must have the good sense to connect the stars, while realizing the answer out of his maze isn't in solely looking back but in using a compass of truth to move ahead because he knew where he lied.

Goodbye Frank

How do you write a good tragedy about men? You don't and you can't because it will never be about what they are or were and the pain they experienced. But if you can do it well, in my opinion you are a genius among men. If you are able to capture the suffering, the destruction that men experience and also about the pain and trauma that we create for ourselves and for others please let me know.

We are natural disasters creating perfect storms in the lives of others and particularly for ourselves. We destroy everything that can save us, and we also injure the ones willing to love us. But there is good in us too. Men like my now deceased buddy Frank brought a lot of hell in this world, and he experienced a lot of hell too. We laughed a lot. We drank a lot and we broke a lot of stuff too. For a guy he was sometimes a human ashtray but he brought laughter in his own insane and eccentric way into a dark world. But I think he did more evil than good and so we no longer broke bread together.

I don't excuse the things he did. Don't ask me how to write about tragedies or comedies or any kind of story about men; because sometimes I simply just don't know the proper thing to write...

God will determine where they go. I don't believe anyone can ever capture the story of their life. Let's hope they go onto a better place than the one they had. Yeah, brother I don't have any problem shedding some tears for you or for mankind.

I lost you

I brought myself then into the vastness of Paris one warm evening while her shining lights sparkled coolly and things seemed the darkest in my resentful life. Sometimes when the splendid things vanish in the heart of the most impatient of men some catch a fever for anything that just may feel everlasting. I thought perhaps when I entered through those old gates that I'd turn around one last time and take a contemplative look at the vital world I was leaving behind.

LET NOTHING IN THIS WORLD SHATTER YOU

SPOTTER UP

I stood looking face to face with my abortive hopes. I didn't feel all that compelled to begin over again. I ignored the slur in time which I reasoned wrongly held me sustained in glorying but for my efforts gave me so few positive results. I lost her, I lost it all.

I read once that there are some things which might conceivably and truly make men forgive their enemies. We are told that we can only turn hate to love by understanding what are the things that men have loved; that it isn't necessary to ask men to hate their loves in order to love one another.

Just as two men are most likely to be reconciled when they remember for a moment that they are two brothers, so two soldiers are most likely to be reconciled when they remember (if only for a moment) that they are two patriots. As the writer Chesterton wrote, humanity wasn't just us minus the masses. I thought more than once, in my own weakness, that there are a lot of men like me. Heaven laid down some laws we might complain against. Regardless, I believe a man must sturdy himself and leave behind all that is ignoble. We are required to rise up and stand with a royal command. It would be difficult for me but my goal was to raise up other men as well.

Sad tracks

I dated a girl whose brother decided to take a long walk one cold morning when the fog like a heavy hand pressed itself upon her village and forced everyone to lay down and sleep. On that fine and fateful day, he cast his jacket over his shoulders and journeyed to a place where he could shed his weariness. With his bitter memories upon him he sat on the railroad tracks and died when a hurtling train blowing its horn loudly carried him off. He left behind his sorrows and a family that loved him.

She never recovered from his death and that changed the course of her life. There was a heavy sadness that I could feel over her place and I didn't think she'd ever escape it. After that she felt there was no place to go, and in a heavy and horrible way his actions brought her sorrow which became a new bondage.

If only she could remove her chains. Ill equipped to understand her pain I like a coward departed, and left her to her darkness and confusion.

Write honestly

I look back at the old letters I wrote and the pictures I took and think what a love sick fool but I married the person I chased and I make no apologies for living fearlessly. Love is a well that never empties. Write, write honestly whether it's good or bad because you are living authentically and it can be the tool that saves you.

"In one gray hour I watch smoky colored folds of darkness smother the last of the spectral lights from so many sad and far away homes and in a solid moment I grasp the ancient beauty of this place and the lost, great glorying of her yesteryears.

We cross this low land and I understand how dear you are to me. Love, like a red lantern, holds itself high on these dusky roads of war. Your light shines surely. I feel it beckon me. Whatever tragedy lies on these haunting paths will die as easily as they were first born.

In my mind I leave them behind so I can think of you and I'll wait, and I'll wait and wait. Moments come and go in the spaces of these falling seasons that surround us with their eternal times. I find myself lost in them. I find myself lost in the surety of your smile, find myself lost in the abundance of your giving eyes. I am filled with the lack of what to say.

We speak a tongue neither of us fully understands and yet it is understood. We dive into each other's hearts as if diving into cold streams to be carried into each other's far away oceans. We must trust that it's good, and that everything between us will be good, despite the separation. The tides bring exhilaration and though these currents are strong, they are welcoming and warm. We must plumb the depths of this power, for there is no other way to gain the secret speech of love. The gift of the sea, the primal journey and the endless frontier. I am a boatman and I will wait for you.

I trust that you will wait for me. I wait every hour, every minute and second of time. I pray the waves bring you to me. Let weeping like rains fill us back up." *I wrote this about my wife when I got back to our outpost after patrolling at night. Try writing something.*

Unafraid

"I poured out into the night and passed our cemetery. I took the long way to your house. You were gone, and so I left. Your tattoo means nothing now even though I enlisted to forget what I came there for. In the midst of that waking dawn hot tears ran down my face."

Life for most youth is an exciting albeit confusing time. We're trying to figure out who we are, who we want to be with, and where we want to go. We may go singly or with friends to map out the story of our life but ultimately the journey is ours and ours alone. We are never alone. You are not alone.

Father forgive me... I was afraid.
—Michael Eurena

Maturity means getting rid of a lot of armor, that hard shell, that gets in the way of you figuring out what kind of heart you have. Life gets better and you'll experience highs and lows. Hopefully you'll have jobs and mentors that are meaningful to you in a positive way. Likely you'll conquer more things than you realize you are capable of. Keep your mind open to being surprised, and pleased at simple things.

Hold the ideas of virtue and enterprise in your heart and mind. Carry a lantern for others to follow when you've figured it out. Pull men up from the darkness and love someone everyday as if it's your last day on earth.

Yes, life is confusing at times but once in a while you'll be floored by how much of it makes sense. Hold onto those good & profound things of your life and keep secret things deep inside your chest to share with someone who truly loves you. Yes, leave the baseless behind where it belongs. When you look back, you'll appreciate how you grew from a boy into a man.

Do not let the lights go out

I say this with sincerity. I believe in fighting for the goodness in this world and making a difference. The lights in this world must never go out. There's nothing laughable about that. We fight for mankind. We must return darkness to darkness until it's extinguished, even if it means men like us will perish in our task.

We mustn't hesitate when there is the call. If we don't go then who will go? The light at the end of the tunnel? Don't walk towards it. Strive to tear down the barrier surrounding you. Let there be more light.

Weren't we put here upon this damn spectacle of an earth for a purpose? Can't we try and can't we hope? Hasn't at least one man in our history succeeded in saving ten million souls? Truth, honor, justice, mankind, these are just some of the sacred things we must fight for.

Large or small, one day a fight may come to your door. The smell of the sea, the touch of fine, coarse earth, sunlight on the waters...the scent of your lover. Walk everywhere holding peace in your heart, violence in your hands and a plan of action in your mind. If we can all save just one life, if we can educate, if we can show light and goodness, if we can increase the love in this world, in my mind that is a day worth fighting for.

Mouthing hard words

I think many of us troubled in youth have two major goals in life; choosing everyday not to kill ourselves, and instead of acting like an animal that we wholly choose to be a man. Think about that for a minute because there's a lot of conflict going on there.

An animal is not a fully realized being, so shame on us for being fully realized and for even choosing to go down a road that should be off limits. When we understand the greatness of existence life will offer wonderful possibilities but the goal is in getting our mind, heart and spirit there. Yet the possibility of having peace in life is terrifying to many men.

Finding truth carries with it a lot of responsibility and a feeling of undesirability, as it should be in adulthood. If we haven't grown in some way then shame on us again!

If we concern ourselves daily with caring less about what others think we are then a few steps ahead mentally when coming to accept the answer to what we searched for and found, or what strikes us.

Maturity means making difficult choices on issues that are indecipherable, and seemingly unnatural to us. It requires not reacting with animal emotion every time and instead using sound reasoning even when we don't want to.

Sometimes men must act like animals

I was thinking about my latest post and I all I could think of is rest. You know, what do Vikings do when they're not slaying ice giants, and running like naked berserkers in the snow, when they aren't drinking Mead, patching wounds, hunting, seeing the blacksmith, or likely away on commercial expeditions and even pillaging?

They're doing something other than slaying. What are you doing today to give you extra wind in your sails for the next journey? We can't be bone breakers 24/7. We need to rest. Yet warriors sometimes come home to quarters in disarray; the wife is gone, the home needs fixing, friends are dead, brothers have passed and a man needs time to regroup.

It would be good to hear someone say, "You've carried the load so now it's time for me to take care of you." But that's not always the case. We're alone in our empty longhouse except for our animals to keep us warm. Sometimes we have to behave like animals. Sometimes we men must act like bears, right? We have to go away for a while and lick our wounds, shout at the sky or sit like wild men in our ashes until we recover. Do it for an hour or a day. Let our sensibilities rejuvenate so we can inspire terror in the ones we hate and give confidence to the ones we love.

Some men became shape-shifters, half man, half animal. Do that for a while. Howl and rest. Good luck warrior. Give your body mind and spirit a rest. Find somewhere to go for respite, you need it. Take some time out for you and then go out and slay again. I mean that.

I am a man

I'll be whoever the hell I want to be. I am a man—I can't deny it. I won't deny it. It is simply in everything that I do. It is the spirit of who I am.

I've lived with a certain set of principles, and even an uncontainable ferocity. I've made men fear me and I too have felt fear. I reason, I love, I fight, I worship, I doubt and also have faith. I am filled with dreams and often feel as empty as death. I'm kind and I have hate, weaknesses and strengths. I can't tell you all of the things that I am but I can surely tell you what I'm not and will never be.

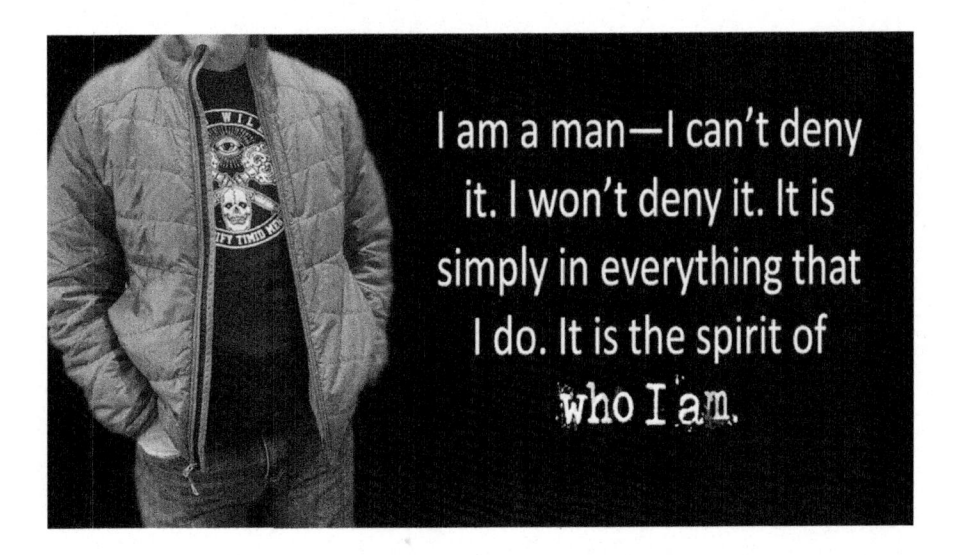

> I am a man—I can't deny it. I won't deny it. It is simply in everything that I do. It is the spirit of who I am.

It's goes even deeper than my DNA; when fighting, loving, when learning, and even when being lost because the flesh is weak and it will always be weak. Don't ever ask me to apologize for being one because I won't. But there is a powerful spirit in me that drives me and it is all that I need to drive me.

Don't go there

I'm terrified sometimes to look into to the past. I'll simply be petrified by what I'll find; old haunts, dead friends, abandoned lovers, and too many allegorical lessons to learn.

I'm a coward at times and I have no stomach for it. I had to grow up fast yet I stayed retarded with many of my emotions. I forced myself to grow into a man even as I wrestled to hold onto my youth. Flickering thoughts by some damaged filament delivers truth to me intermittently. I'm frozen by my memories, though I can still see the hills, can still see those lights of home, and even the door. Although I'm far away from them sometimes they are graspable in this instant but there is hesitation in returning. The thought of the rich past like a loving parent pulling me in with outstretched arms is too welcoming but there's some dark there as well from those halcyon moments; the loss of friends, of time and innocence burned into ashes bleeds onto water. Simply having to face trackless steps backwards to youth that run into an unmeasurable sea that drowns real memory terrifies me. What I lost, well, I'm simply not ready to go back there yet. That's what I tell myself everyday but I go. Every day I go, and so should you.

I'll keep my violence

I'll keep my violence even if you abandon yours because I've seen the evil that even "good" men do. We're raised on myth that if one man lives in peace that all men will follow suit but I've seen examples of that well-meant work and it's as useless as a cobbler's glass shoe.

The idea makes sense until A wants X and doesn't want B to have it. Is there a world out there where peace resides? Sure, and it's called in your dreams. Men aren't machines, men aren't light switches that can be turned on and off from dolling out peace and war in equal extremes.

When we issue out one, we hold the other in reserve, and this interrelation is necessary as the absence of light is to darkness with what Day is to changing to Night. It is not by kind but by degree. Should we stop planning for a better world, should we stop hoping for a sanctuary of peace?

A tribe that puts its faith in a new clan may find some good results but, in all likelihood, will end up extinct. Men should learn quickly that their neighbors and enemies are likely the same. You can take my bullets, my blade and the gun on my hip but that won't change a thing. Faculty A is no different from Faculty B and the one thing separating us from kissing a baby and killing a man is choice. Channel a man into one extreme, and remove all options from the table, and he won't surprise you. Can you give away your desire to kill? Let's just ask the question "What's wrong with the world?" Just look in the mirror and see.

No this is not how it's going to go down

"I'm a Navy SEAL and this is the way it's going to go down. You're going to walk away." Those were the last words I heard him say before I crashed my fist into his mouth and stomped him into stupidity. He wasn't a SEAL and I wasn't listening. Sometimes you have to defy others and live your life opposite of what you are told. "No man, this is not the way it is going to go down."

Sometimes you need to simply walk away and sometimes you have to stand your ground. Life gives out some hard lessons to all of us and if we've done more homework in our lifetime than the other student has hopefully, he'll have to do detention and we get to go home when the school bell sounds off.

If we're good at reading his indicators we may have a chance at surviving a serious attack. Just this evening my buddy avoided a robbery and took two men down before an officer came and

intervened. He was injured but alive. Some people are very accepting of what others say or try to have us do as if it's gospel. One of our jobs is to ensure that our opponent never reads our indicators and foresees how it can go down. We won't always be successful at handling a potentially violent situation. Do not get into that car, do not give into that potential robber or rapist, do not let them win. Remember to never place yourself in a situation you cannot see yourself getting out of. Avoid them if you can but if it's go time, then go. Bring them pain; be fast and violent.

"Hold Peace in Your Heart, Violence in Your Hands, a Plan of Action in Your Mind." * *Some indicators: posture, positioning, tone of voice, hand movements, eye focus, breathing.*

Full Fathom Five

If a man feels that his heart is like a dark sea of pain then he should sail his vessel no further. If he cannot bear to ride the forces of the severest storms than he has no place to see what resides in the blackest ocean. If he has no stomach for a truth that unsettles the churning waters than he might have no space in his mind on how to navigate with what his discovery answered. Iron men brave enough to measure fathoms deep into the darkest spaces will find a source of power that will shatter other energies. Wooden ships strong enough to ride the inner spaces may buckle and even break but they cannot be destroyed into oblivion for as long the captain is alive there is a glimmer of hope. This is true, everyday men live and die alone.

A man who believes his end is nigh isn't necessarily wrong to believe so. Every man who refuses to accept the end is nigh by sailing through troublesome seas can sometimes find himself in calmer oceans but to do so he must have a certain disdain for dying. Sailing to glory takes a lot of searching to find life beyond the abyss. A sailor must keep his mind open to seeing the fires across the waters, the burning light that guides tough men, while he guides the prow of his ship.

There are good, secret things somewhere in his world but he must endure long enough, he must let go of what he thinks he knows, and be open for once to embracing unexplained phenomena and admit deeply in fact that he truly knows nothing.

Produce

If a man hopes to accomplish anything really good that lasts in life, he must accept that good and bad will happen in his lifetime, and still stay committed to his goals, without acting contrarily. His relationship with life will get difficult at times, and even if he gives it his sincerest commitment, there will be moments when he will experience little in return.

Men who profess not to care about life, or who care very little about it, by living as if they don't give a damn, are simply poseurs. Everyone loves living, no one enjoys dying, and the absence of purpose and meaning in life is saved solely for the most dispassionate of souls or the truest bitterest of nihilists.

Everyone benefits in some way from it, whether men choose to admit it or not, but the man who chooses full commitment will find himself self-actualized. It will feel like the universe opens up to him. By accepting the relationship, regardless of its mercurialness, he will come into full realization of his own creative, intellectual, and social potential. It is understandable if one chooses to hide the joy they feel for life and in fact the feeling of love for it may simply and rightly strike him like lighting out of the blue; that's when he knows.

Those who demand much of this world and deliver little emotion to it or none in return, may be confounded when nothing comes back to them and it is his response to this that matters.

The world cannot ever and will not ever love him back, but he must never give up in his quest to find meaning and purpose in it. *Being afraid to live is different than not being afraid to die; the anxiety is caused by having freedom and then not being able to choose, and then committing to some kind of action.*

Weightlifting

If you have trouble keeping your word, you're going to have trouble being a man, and that leads to big problems. Big promises carry just as much weight as little promises. There is just as much loss of honor in breaking the smaller one, as there is the larger one or even breaking both. Just like getting progressively stronger at lifting heavier weights a man can increase the strength of his word by simply exercising it on a daily basis until his word is as strong and heavy as the iron he lifts.

Mow

If a man is to distinguish himself from other men, he must make efforts to stand out, not for vanity's sake, but it is because he believes in what he is and what he creates. He must change the culture around him for the better without allowing it to change him for the worse.

It's unnatural for most men to give away their power because they spend most of their lifetime trying to obtain it. How good and astonishing that as a man's age increases that his power willingly diminishes because he passed his mantle to his heirs.

In a perfect world as men gain in stature should they not relinquish control of all of it to their sons and daughters? But that is perfection and life is filled with broken men and broken promises. In fact, life is filled with broken people.

Success is being able to realize that a man can draw his own lines and then fearlessly do away with whatever assets and liabilities were gathered and lost inside that box. In the end just knowing he tried to do the best in his own way was sufficient to the spirit of endeavor.

When all is said and done, he should say, "many of the fields were cut, many of the lots were plowed, the wood was gathered, precious little was left undone, and nothing was made to waste but it is time to rest. This was my line. I made it." When he looks back at the markers of his life, he should in some way even be amused that he cut a curved path through the straight structures that he placed.

Suburban rebels

If the soul of this great and free nation ever came to ruin, could we count ourselves as one of those that did nothing but stand by and slowly watched its disintegration? Have disdain for more than just the popcorn eaters. War in different shapes and forms comes in waves to every shore. We must be aware of the false patriot who states that he loves the soul of this country yet refuses in any way to fight for it, who blindly fights for it or who willingly changes it to cause it harm. In this world there is an alliance of men who will always be there to put a fractured nation back together but we cannot let them do it alone.

Beware the revolutionary with a false doctrine of hope. Many are really death cults. A real rebellion before it can be radical must be sensible, and it requires starting out with less action and more thought, has less societal analysis and needs more self-analysis.

It starts out not by pointing first at what is broken or wrong with others but what needs to be fixed and made right in ourselves. Before a rock is thrown and a window is broken the real rebel will determine first whether there are any cracks in his thinking. The true radical isn't an irrational being and if he's honest he'll make no war with others until he's made war upon himself.

On his path of inward enemy exploration, he might discover scruples are needed as a first line of security against immoral reasoning, and he won't ever start to put a toe in the water after he's trespassed over a fence to attempt his rebellious swim upstream.

What is true is that the false rebel destroys evidence of the common creeds to only provide proof of the abnormal ones in order to make the meaning of a good and fair nation mean nothing. There will be no water given out to douse the fires of the nation he burns.

Flight path

If you want to get spiritually healthy you can't behave contrarily. Trying to get stronger means you can't simultaneously take the nourishment out of your mouth that you just swallowed. You can't pick up weights at the same time you are putting them down.

Growing as a human being means you must continually adjust your flight path so that you continue to fly, instead of constantly experiencing self-induced, mid-air collisions. You can't drive the stick up while you're pressing it down. Keep that conflict going and the only reachable conclusion is you'll crash and burn and never again get airborne. Deconflict your heart and soul.

Trip the blind

If you want to start every day off rightly don't unleash upon the world the same kind of pain that damaged your own heart. I don't care what you've been through. Be the world's hero and not it's abuser or executioner. It's easy to destroy things and if you've been doing that my brother, you must change course. One of your daily tasks is to take your bad experiences and be a good example to blind people; those who do not see things as clearly as you do.

Every damned second

Love someone in your heart every minute, fight some kind of fight every hour, teach someone one beautiful lesson every day, in war be a terrifying person to terrible people, guide and protect the weak. Work on new and certain old relationships and feel less that sting of regret, rise each day with peace in your heart, and a wonderful plan of action.

Re-forged

If your warrior attitude and philosophy is the blade that you live by and it has impurities that do not bind it together strongly it will shatter against an opponent's weapon that happens to be stronger than yours. Test it, fight with it, re-forge it. Do what needs to be done to make it

the sharpest. Don't be disingenuous with your heart, mind and spirit. "Abandon the ways of men and get back to yourself again."

Raise the bar in your life. Perhaps you should take a comprehensive look into yourself and figure out how to get back into doing what pleases you rather then living your life always attempting to please others, or attempting to affect a certain look, or altering your thinking in order to have a certain way of speaking. Influence others with the good you can share rather than being influenced by others that contribute unworthily in life.

Break from bad friends and bad influences. Break tradition and go your own path. Develop your own thoughts, and speak your own mind about politics, faith, and life in general rather than regurgitating what you hear others speak. But be reasonable and logical. Be your own person. Be real. Lastly, let go of the bad habits, Have real conversations about ideas and not material things. The truth is all men have difficulty breaking bad habits and even wanting to start over again. Why even bother? Because it is hard! If a man wants to grow, he needs to abandon the "ways" he picked up that are stopping him from being a real person and a force to be reckoned with.

Having indifference or ignorance is no less sensible than a donkey refusing to move off the tracks when an engine comes. Just because a man's spirit can take a lot of beatings doesn't mean his mind holds a lot of good sense.

> ABANDON THE WAYS OF MEN AND GET BACK TO YOUR SELF AGAIN
>
> MICHAEL KURCINA

Hide

I'm a genuine introvert that forces himself to be an extrovert. I can be loud and truly obnoxious, but I can easily sit in silence for 20 hours of a productive day. I work hard to build relationships and do things that I hate. I hate fear and I go head-on with things because avoiding them sometimes delays the inevitable, and that's like having the sense of a cow walking towards a coming train. Better to fight even if you're going down.

If I could have enough time to read, run, write books, swim, and a million other things I would, and so I try to cram it all in and make it count. I'd rather be alone but I can't learn anything without human interaction and mentorship. I hate excuse making. I'm always learning something about myself, mostly where I fail, and how I can improve. Relationships take work. Build them with your children, spouses etc.

I have a lot of plans for this year. Plans to spend more time with the family plans to do many things better, build more, plans and more plans and their execution. What are your plans? If we only do what makes us feel good what have we gained? Sometimes it takes pulling yourself apart and putting yourself back together with the guidance of others. I hope you drill down and see what you need to do and see your plans through. Be real. Don't BS. Have a good start to this year.

We fight monsters

> We fight monsters
>
> I'm not afraid of anything in this world that's been seen
>
> ~Michael Kurcina

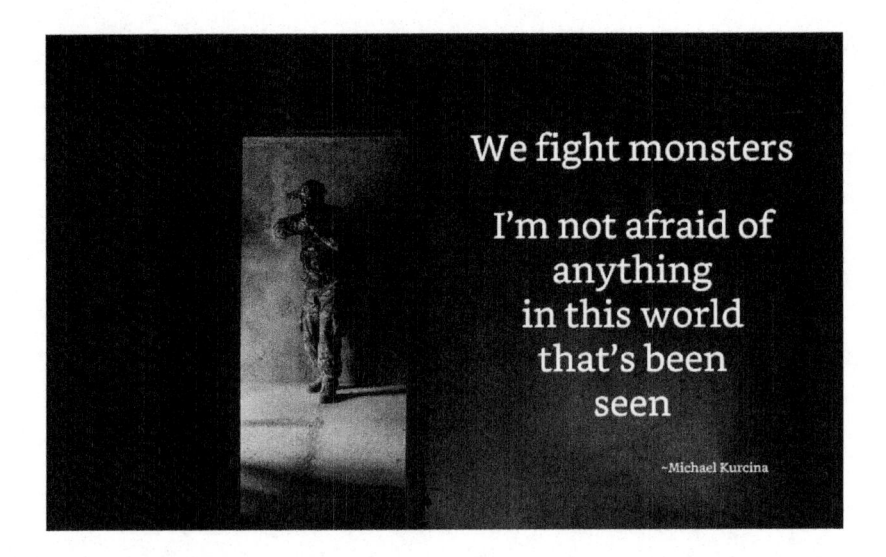

I'm not afraid of anything in this world that's been seen. I have scars on the inside. My badges of honor. There's a light inside my heart; it's for others to see. I live to show the way to those lost and in pain. And you?

Walk with magnificence. Cock of the walk. Lead the way or follow those who use their pain to fight monsters and the injustices in this world. *I don't care if you have scars from the battlefield, child abuse or divorce. Everyone has a story to tell and they can either follow that long line of men and women who state "woe is me" or they can break from the path and find a new track to follow. I simply push the idea of being your own person, finding solutions to problems, and not being a drag on the world. Learn new things, impart knowledge, build friendships, and learn to not be a slave.*

I'm sorry brother

In this life there is a hurt that we cannot control. We invest so much of our time in something or someone only to go on to be surprised when those things through our inaction made it all end in tears... The sad thing isn't just that things ended, no, the sad thing in most cases is we had hunches they were ending but we didn't do a damn thing to change course and stop the final action.

A wife packed her bags and walked out the door, a brother committed suicide, we failed to protect the daughter we cared for from the boyfriend who didn't, or we had a massive health decline all because we were wrapped up in ourselves, an obligation, or a life of lies...whatever the reason it hurts and I am sorry that you feel that pain.

The tragedy that caused our suffering and disaster perhaps to us physically had a greater affect upon our psyche and in turn affected how badly it injured our soul. But life is not over if we don't want it to be. This wound that we think we cannot control is regret and in the aftermath of our sorrowful events we are sitting in the dark with significant pain. Imagine if we took the time to treat our injury with the serious and dignified time it was due rather than prolonging it by wanting to prolong our suffering?

We can't revisit the past as it is done in fictional stories and undo what was done but we can devote the same amount of time tending to our wound. Whatever terrible event we caused or experienced mustn't be ignored.

Heal yourself and heal others. The terrible reality is most of us only pay heed to our spiritual health when it is broken and crippled us, and we in turn cripple others. Sometimes we cannot directly affect our own destiny but we can make decisions that help others, that grows their life, and can often indirectly bring peace and comfort back to us as well. Love someone in your heart every minute, fight some kind of fight every hour, teach someone one beautiful lesson every day, in war be a terrifying person to terrible people, guide and protect the weak. Work on new and certain old relationships and feel less that sting of regret, rise each day with peace in your heart, and a wonderful plan of action.

We Do Not Want to be Told What to Know

In youth when we are moon drunk, when we are alone, when it's so dark and our eyes focus on that orb seemingly fixed above us so righteously in the sky is when we become alive and truth comes out of our heart. It is when we drop all illusions of what we believed, and those pretenses of who we are is when we best discover what we should do, and what we can do. Opportunities dandle like apples on an outstretched branch jutting across the hot night but will we grab one?

How many times have we turned away from doing the difficult because we were fearful and not fearless? What is difficult? We do not want to be told what to know, but we know it well this truth, and it will always terrify timid men.

There is an energy alive in each of us and it will end, that is most certainly true, yet what can we do to make this life last? In youth we believe that nothing is impossible, we are so alive and feel so free, yet aging and maturity temper our dreams.

Go back to seeing the stars as if they whirl in the sky, to having moments like those old Saturday nights, to letting go of reason because sometimes reason just doesn't know and just do what you please. Dance your stupid dances, and sing your silly songs, and discard for just a moment the structure of your life and live.

Walk the tracks, scan the rising shape of the sun across the hillsides, and don't betray the memories you once let die. Pursue one thing tonight. I'm reminded of men who feel like the walls of life are closing upon them, and that death one day will find them. We are mortal but remember even in our youth though we were callow we sometimes had the courage to try.

What is infused in our blood is no different than the man next to us, or the warrior who came a thousand years before us, and that bravery and a kind of chivalry will never die, that even failure can bring one good moment of warmth and glory into a heart frozen with doubts. Go out and try. The truth is you must live as if there is no tomorrow and knowing this accept calmly that you may surely die.

Not done with you

It came softly through the darkness this unguessable song...haunting me. This terrifying and growing, trumpeting sound became too

much to bear so I fell to my knees, covered my ears and wept. I meant to quit but He approached and with kind ease pulled me to my feet and said, "Son, I'm not done with you yet..." I believed Him. I stood before Him tremulously weeping.

Seed the world

It's incompressible to me when people or businesses believe they are the first to do something. Certainly, there are rarities but largely many of us must acknowledge the seeds that others planted, and the harvest that others took from those original sources of sustenance.

One apple can seed an entire forest that must be explored, one branch of knowledge can open up other branches we must climb on, one dying leaf lays the covering for other saplings to grow beneath. Unless it's outright theft, there are no differences in music, or fashion, fitness, literature or the arts, and in the end, someone should honor someone. To say and do otherwise shows arrogance coming from ego on their parts.

We are grateful for everyone that's ever shown us something, and we're excited about our relationships that we are building. We're happy to work with anyone that wants to work with us. If it's good it will last, if its hearty it will never blow over, if it's rooted rightly, it will intertwine strongly with others, and if it's original it will be seen from afar and never hidden.

People will come to see it and use what it offers. Reach out to us if you think a relationship makes sense and is a good fit. One tree may be solitary, two trees are the start of a forest, and three or more are the beginning of an adventure. Seed the world by your thoughts.

King

I've had a hole in my heart for a very long time. But this is the life I chose and I have to live with what I made. This is the kingdom I built and the path I paved. But I've learned to be resilient and I've learned that time gives me opportunity to take other chances and to redraw the lines of my territory.

Sometimes I give and sometimes I gain if I want to. Sometimes the ache goes away. It never seems to disappear rather it subsides and goes back to the place it came. At times it's like night dissolving into day, or day into night and it can happen in a matter of seconds. Be mindful that when you choose to be something that you must own the territory you conquered.

You are the king of it, you are the master of it, or the slave. There are no perfect kings, because there are no perfect people, but there are some perfect days, yes and perfect nights too. Count on those to get you through whatever revolt your heart and mind are struggling with.

There will be many good times. Use the power of your mind to have more wins than losses. There are many just like me. My advice to you is to keep fighting, keep winning, and be admirably purposeful. It's a long game. You're not alone. Stay strong King.

Even I can't stop me

Let some old, eternal power drive us. Let us keep looking at those stars until it wakes what resides in our primordial mind and floods us with dreams and deep thoughts rather than just enough understanding to power a limited existence, those animal urges.

Let us build something with this sensibility, let us be something with this awakening, let us drive ahead with this passion. Let us do more than simply carrying this brain and heart.

Let us understand true hunger, true heartache, true connection, true passion, true darkness, true humility true happiness, true hatred among many other things in order to understand what it is to be a fully realized man. "You going to stop me? Ha! Even I can't stop me."

Hunting

Lost and alone in his unutterable pain he rose to hunt before the sun shined on what would become a poetic morn. He tracked the feint signs with his baying pups and as the fog lifted, he let his loyal dogs run. He recalled the lessons passed from father to son, and with his nets and snares set out to recapture the beautiful life he once let go.

He tasted the salt from his happy tears, and for a moment staggered blind because he understood he was frightfully close. He saw the ground, touched the signs and after the hard years of searching knew he'd triumph once more.

Babel

Love pushes back time. Love pushes back pain and in this same string of words I promote the thought that so too does sex. Right or wrong, both delay what many of us dread, that oncoming of age, which strips us of our years. For the young teen innocence is lost gaining this knowledge while the more mature of us is transformed into youth once again, if but for a moment!

Our hearts recollect through feeling what the mind recalls yet cannot connect to as it is a sterile, emotionless thing, this organ of gray and white matter.

Many activities seem to delay the onslaught of seconds, minutes and hours upon our psyche and physique but it is solely love that encapsulates two members into a bubble of hopefulness, for it lightens their load as their burdens are shared, and it infuses each with desire to live regardless of time passing...

The paradox of loving means those in it want to prolong it because they don't mind it; there is a feeling the communion is everlasting while experience tells us it is not so.

Real love it's been said removes fear, and with fear removed, real learning begins. Cabbalists and philosophers have chased the idea of the proto-language; some great, mystical forgotten tongue of our descendants before the Fall and of Babel.

Access to this speech would give power begotten from this secret science. I don't propose to know the languages of angels and Adam. But I propose that we came naked and alone into this world. I propose that we often feel in exile, and the one way to feel connected to something greater than ourselves is to love.

Not some baseless love, but something that opens the doors of our perception, and transforms us if but for seconds, or minutes or an hour.

Whether you're a police officer tucking his children in before a midnight shift, or a soldier seeing his wife as he's straight home from deployment, or holding his new born daughter I ask you to love. Perhaps the perfect language is silence. Let the eyes do the work and observe those you love, perhaps love is intimate relations and so make love to those you love. Perhaps love is a gateway out of fear, and in knowing, let it guide you to fight for what you love....

Stupid

Youth's strength lay in the fact that we were stupid—and therefore impervious to criticism, that we were so self-assured of our place and purpose in this universe despite the truth that told us otherwise.

We didn't philosophize too much nor once doubted that we were a brother to all men and a lover to all women, that we could be rich by 19 and immortal by 25 but the inevitable consequences of living despite our sincere actions showed us the folly of our belief.

> Youth's strength lay in the fact that we were STUPID

It wasn't age that aged us but adulthood and we would go a lifetime of painful living trying to forget some of the things we knew. But there were good things discovered with wisdom—that real love is truly deathless, real friendships so hard to find is truly priceless, real evil is truly Godless, and real men like Alexander the Great are real gods to mortal men. We would never forget a woman's laughter in the dark nor her breath or her smile or her tiny hands. We would never forget life's most cutting lesson, or that we could die, or a simple yet sublime truth that living nobly though right was unfashionable in our bitter age but to good men made them everlasting and in death delivered them into time's most beautiful waters.

Man

Man isn't ennobled by reducing his essence to some point near extinction in order to please a woman because he dislikes the worst of himself or to make her feel safer. Nor should he become so exaggerated in his persona as to become a cartoon character, a counterfeit because that's just a form of armor. A man must respect his being in order to let his real essence grow. Don't be indifferent to what you were created for or attempt to escape the pressure, the responsibilities you have by futilely attempting to shift your nature.

Naked

Many fathers fail to give their sons some very vital lessons on how to be a man. Boys grow up never knowing how to harness or suppress their aggression, they never learn the incredible powers of self-examination, or even how to love a woman, and it's because they first didn't learn how to honor and love themselves.

Soon boys grow up to be spiritual and emotional cripples and their fault lies in simply believing that life should be all about achievement while never learning they are myopic as a whole on what else makes a man. Their parents force them young to stay in cocoons or they are crushed and pushed out of the house too soon, where they then become a cog in a collectivist machine that tramples over their individual soul.

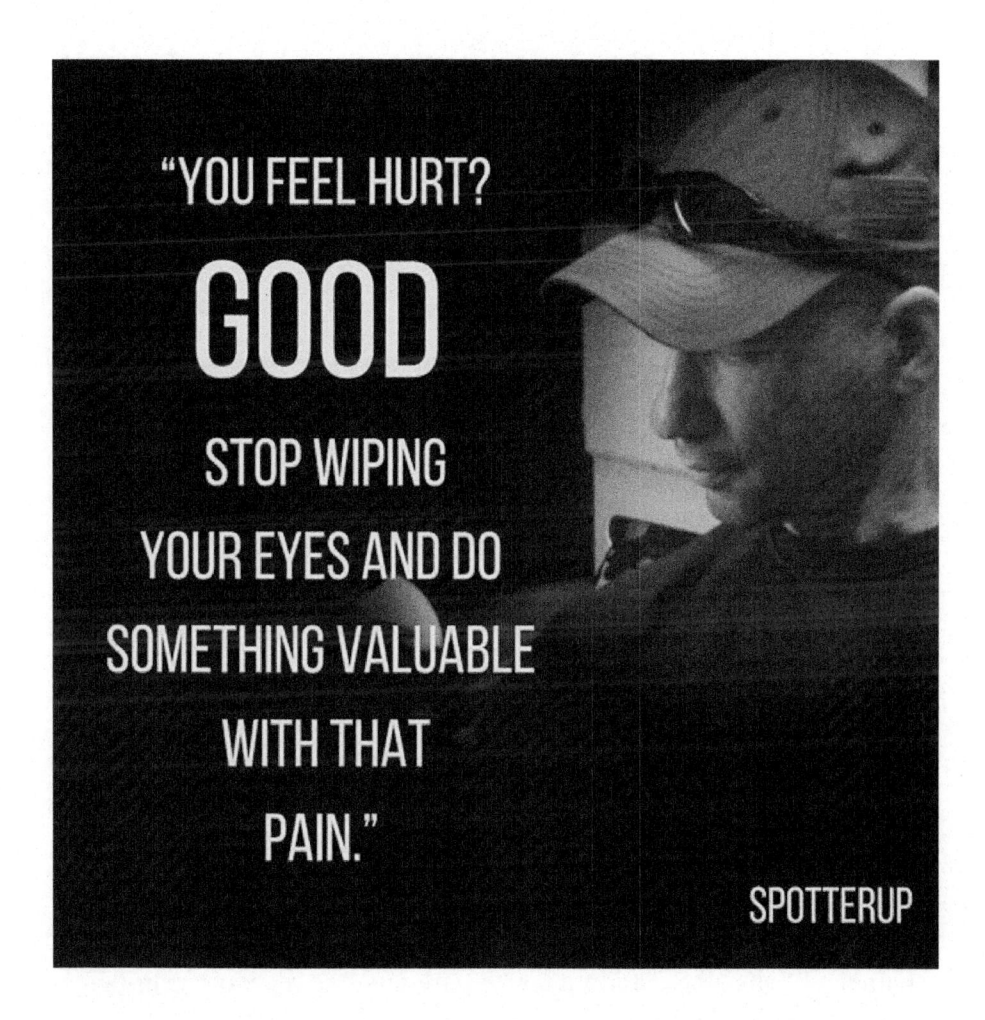

> **"YOU FEEL HURT? GOOD STOP WIPING YOUR EYES AND DO SOMETHING VALUABLE WITH THAT PAIN."**
>
> — SPOTTERUP

Some enter the workforce with high expectations, practical skills, and good educations but it matters not when there aren't any prospects, and that's where the real problems start.

They assign little value to what they do and where they currently are, while inherently believing they are entitled to a greater status over other men. Sometimes they never get ahead. Some are puzzled on where to channel their energy, and if they never learn to, they will become even more dysfunctional.

The truth is all men in their lifetime will lose many positions, and go through many transitions. They even strip themselves of certain achievements but the best they should do is to learn how to be spiritually naked while remaining continually dignified.

Dim the lights

Many summers ago, I used to ride my motorcycle with the lights turned off as I snaked down a serpentine path. It was something I did as a young man for thrills. My eyes caught glimpses of the road as I shakily navigated through danger. There is a realization for most men who are not caught in a state of arrested development that it's important to grow up. We have obligations to our family, work, community and so on. Certainly, youth bring with it a lot of pleasure and as adults we can look back on our wild past and pull some lessons from it to fight disconnection. To feel youthful again we must take some risks. One way is to train ourselves to see the world through a different lens.

Dim your lights and get in tune with darkness. See the world through strained eyes until they can see what is out there naturally. Though your eyes adapt to bright light faster than darkness eventually it will adjust and attune to things that you've never really paid attention to before. Shut out the technological distractions. The risk is in letting go of your handicaps and figuring out again who you are. Listen to the sounds around you.

Use your ears and your heightened awareness. The ocean waves crashing, crickets chirping, a lone car in the distance humming...Now do this every day, not just physically, but spiritually...Practice it in every waking, silent wordless morning, and greet the restless rushing energy that fills the empty chamber within you with churning power. See another world differently as if seeing over a fence rather than attempting to peek through it.

For those who are hyperaware, whose minds are always alert, we must not be discouraged by the pressures pushed upon us by our obligations. Learn where to put your focus. We might feel beaten, and broken but we are not irrevocably lost. With life in us there is hope for the engine that keeps running even if our lights are blacked out. Live with intention and the forced lack of illumination. Tune into everything around you. Eventually you will find a way off that road. I assure you.

Do the damn work doctor

Where is the locus of your pain? We can all joke about an injury by asking what is the "booboo" and to show where it hurts. We'll even get a few laughs but the reality is we are susceptible to pain and deep pain simply cannot be ignored.

Most men in our modern world who feel disconnected from the common culture and experience feelings of meaninglessness and futility should understand we are milliseconds away from reducing our suffering simply by attacking doubt with action.

Men fearful of pain, deep seated pain, will never get to the root of the problem unless they examine the wound. We must attack any of our misgivings with deliberate honesty to prevent the corrosive power of skepticism from rotting us within. Deliberate action married with focused intelligence means we discover why we are dying inside and it requires cutting out our dishonesty.

Examination begets facts, facts require action, action requires order, order creates conviction, conviction breeds passion, passion brings connection. Do the damn work doctor. We must examine how we see ourselves, how we see the world, and how we see others. Is life meaningless? Are we worthless?

The truth is men are given a tremendous amount of power in that we are not only able to think but we are able to make choices yet most men squirm like worms rather than act like lions once given the facts. The location of your pain isn't over there, it's inside of you, and you can change how you think and feel.

We were built for great things. You were built to do great things; now do it. Don't be afraid of the work you must do. Have confidence in who you are, what you want to do, and what you want to say. Life holds a certain amount of misery and suffering but it also holds joy. Take action. Do not be a coward.

The art of destruction

Men who dislike the loss of power should be reminded that accelerated learning is best done when the truest submission is used to obtain the knowledge at hand, because the mind's doors of perception are opened by some degree to reception. The pupil yields to the instruction of the sword master, the shooter yields to the lessons of the gun master, the boot yields to the executions of the drill master.

Popcorn eaters who like to advise from their cheap seats, far from the epicenter of violence need to shut up or come sit front and center where the action really happens.

In one extreme example young men who board military buses headed to a life they don't yet comprehend give up a good measure of their control for a sustained singularity of control over the direction of their life. Becoming completely powerless is a trade done in order to become a formidable weapon. They grew because they had no real comprehension of their specific expectations, lacked pretensions those false assertions, lacked claim on anything in order to gain something vital by letting a director control the influence of their life. They must trust. In giving up power they obtained power. They obtained knowledge by giving up knowledge and through sincere sacrifice of self-became a new self.

This is something that not all men or women can do because it requires a certain kind of mindset willing to learn through submission. Those who go through the hardest grist mill will find themselves becoming the most talented destroyer of men, because they understand how, when, where, why and upon whom to apply their newly acquired power. Men like swords can be forged in fire, those who change with every burning become the most formidable of weapons.

Hated

Men will find themselves judged, cursed and crushed for their intelligence and honesty in a world of declining values, declining manliness, and declining desires for achieving a worthy place in the world. Hell, even a dull hell awaits men without courage and a vision, or the objectivity to stand back and understand what every man must pursue. Critics will attempt to publicly injure risk takers and will ask, "how dare they?"

Men should never stop trying to become fully developed persons. Attempting to truly live means men will also experience tremendous shocks to the soul, shocks that wound us severely. The delicate instrument of love will close off some of our injuries from further insult but we must have enough courage to see the operation through, and have enough to pursue the path of being alive! Wandering, questioning, doubting, unbelieving and believing, coming, going, dying and growing. We must never stop.

Praise worthy

Most men hope for an immortality that will never come. The space between youth and adulthood can be difficult for many young men and every transition thereafter can be tougher and tougher on them. Hopefully every man welcomes challenges into his life that make him stronger, and grows his intelligence, compassion and observations.

It's a blessing if he becomes self-actualized because challenges will no longer be obstacles or distractions but opportunities and attractions. Every man pursues some thing or things that violate or validates his existence. On his journey to enlightenment, he must learn to break contact or give some commitment to them or he will feel trapped not only by other men's plans and schemes but by life as a whole.

SPOTTERUP

TEACH YOUR SONS TO READ AND WHEN YOU DO ALLOW THEM TO GROW THEIR HEARTS

Those retarded by arrested development, who gave up on their private sacraments, who stopped honoring their dreams may find sooner or later that hopelessness chokes them to sleep where the nightmare dogs eat their dreams. Outside of chance any man hoping for immortality must really work on building a legacy. If he is not willing to hold onto his old faith and traditions than he must have worthy substitutions greater than his daily praiseless resolutions to dig himself out of his hole.

He can free himself if he starts to do the work again. Sometimes the answers to his problems becomes as pronounced as a stuffed trophy upon a wall. A man who still has a tiger's heart yet traps himself inside a tiger cage is a sad and dangerous thing.

A man can carry a lot of pain

Most men that I've met are tragically lonely but that is not the end of the matter. The trouble is that most men are able to take a heap load of pain and sadly that opens doors they probably should never go through. Just because his soul can take a lot of beatings doesn't mean his mind holds a lot of sense. The odd thing is his suffering is the one thing that keeps him connected to the world even as it seems he's drifting away from it. Does it matter that some of his injuries are self-inflicted? If he can't find balance in the midst of his daily emotional disarray he might be stuck in his paradox until the day he dies. Good God let's hope he can unfix some of his tragic beliefs.

Alive

My buddy has been working murder cases for nearly two decades. When he became a detective, he stopped doing things that once brought him joy. He said it was for kids. I told him you've got it all wrong. We should never want to grow up.

Do things that give your heart peace and give you a thrill, I said. Your heart is dying to live. He embraced that talk with all he had and began the greatest restoration of his soul. When we begin to live too seriously to the words of dead writers and poets it's time to renew our mind with literature that's more alive. Throw those dead men out. I began a path a few years ago to follow my own advice. Tonight, remember what it was like to be have joyous youth and pursue good, noble and effusive things. Be wild at heart again.

Brothers

My older brother and I once demolished my younger brother when we were younger. We in our infinite cruelty and laughable stupidity, injured him enough that he became a different person; our tragic actions and his decision in that sole hour of injury made him who he is today. In tears he went to his room and tore apart a toy that he loved. It wasn't just a toy but an action figure that in some deeper sense was a summation of who he thought he was, what he wanted to be, what he thought he would become, a hero. Human beings aren't always good at being humane, like when brothers are being brothers.

There is a difference between being, belonging, and becoming. Being only means we are a part of something and we exist as that idea exists yet it is separate from us. We are a police officer on a team, a family member in a family; we give little and take little from it. When we belong to something we are transformed and we too can transform what we belong to because we recognize the power in being part and parcel of an idea. A sole Marine in a fire team, a lone parishioner is now a unit in a corps or a body of the church. Power can come out of belonging. When we go from just being to belonging, we can start becoming something greater than ourselves.

We should not tear apart what we profess to love, nor should we be a part of what we profess to hate. I am very close to my brothers. My younger brother used that moment to become an intellectual powerhouse in many ways, and emotionally strong. Some of us when we hurt are tempted to destroy ourselves or hurt something that is a representation of who we think we are; we destroy our toys, our ideas, or another human being.

Wives, husband and children are not immune to the dark workings of a bitter or sad spirit.

If you are part of something good, learn to sacrifice a part of yourself as a gift to the world in order to grow it, to make it last. You are part of a team, a family, a church, no doubt you belong to something so do something with it. We are only here for a short while, so work on not injuring what you love whether that be some person, some place, or something. Live to grow, grow to love, and become something.

Enter

No energy on earth can preserve a dead man's flesh nor a dead man's heart. We must face the experience of perishing love, perishing life, perishing memory and perishing time but our demise brings the murmur of an eternal water that swallow us up and from its stream we are carried to immortality. Yes, yes...there is a house of death that waits on a hill and one day we must enter it.

Stand

No one will ever be convinced of your sincerity, of the seriousness of your sufferings, unless you show them. However, men who cannot realize their inherent value just might let themselves be carried down with the sewage of life. We cannot always get what we want but if we focus on what is divine and our sacred sacraments, we will realize there isn't a chasm at all between ourselves and the sublime. Fall more often than not and before you get up dwell on why you need to stand up each time, and pursue with fervor what you can pursue. You'll find the stars are closer than you think.

Drink Pain

One of the most sacred vessels to drink from in Christian liturgical worship is the chalice and the worst possible thing to ingest is a poison that brings tremendous pain. But what if what we think is poison is actually an antidote to our issues in life? Pain in the form of a physical suffering or discomfort caused by illness or injury motivates us to withdraw from situations that cause further damage. Pain from the poison as it courses through our bloodstream tells the mind body and soul to avoid more unpleasantness.

Well, I'm here to tell you that sometimes we have to drink of pain in order to feel its other effects. Pain as we endure it lets us break through certain walls that we've put up in order to shield ourselves from dealing with what we actually must deal with. We must shift our paradigms.

Pain becomes the portal by which we arrive at the other side of self-redemption but few like to sip from this cup. It can take us on a journey of discovery to feel joy, love, worth and more. Will you do this in order to eventually feel peace within your heart?

Don't hide your issues and not deal with them bang on; do not get stuck in pain, and be sure to work to get to the other side of it. Use your pain to heal. *Ecclesiastes 7:2 It is better to go to a house of mourning Than to go to a house of feasting, because that is the end of every man, And the living takes it to heart.*

The will of the gods

One of those nights when the stars line up and you look up and realize how blessed you are. When the world is not clouded by dark confusion but it's effused with clear answers. When you did the work and you didn't cheat and people come into your life and help change it for the better and at the same moment you influence theirs and nothing can stop you. Call it what you will: fate, destiny, fortune. Call it the will of the gods.

The energy that grows in your belly explodes and your spirit is possessed to do more, your mind to learn more, your heart to give more...when all searching for glory and fame and whatever you wastefully desired disappears and the heart heals and there is everlasting change (ha!) if but for a minute. Be honest with yourself and the world will open for you...A leaf is more than just a leaf and a river is more than just a river. There is a confluence not just of water and sky and rock but truth and peace and there in these small moments is found eternity. Enjoy that moment.

Only dead men lack desire

Only dead men lack desire, and the terrible reality is most men won't examine why desire begins to die in them. The body carries weariness, the heart carries heaviness, the mind carries fogginess and the spirit is no longer alert and alive.

ONLY DEAD MEN LACK DESIRE

SPOTTER UP

The fury of the day ends, and the chaos of the day begins, perhaps some thought is made to make changes even while the heart alive with emotions cries every-time. Drive deeply at midnight when the world is asleep, though the open passage of your life, and examine from where the trickling passion flows. Where is the source of the river?

You can want to have something; you can wish for it to happen but unless you take the steps to make it happen it will only ever be a wish deferred. Don't conceal what you want, yet die wondering, what it would be like to be a success. In the quiet hours, finally rid yourself of distractions, and pay no more devotion to them. Clear the gutters out of dead leaves and dreaming. Make plans to open the mighty floodgates and let powerful energies flow to explode in all four directions of the universe. Only dead men lack desire.

They are still waiting

Our eyes were blinded by the veil of youth. Small towns paid us out in the currency of boredom and recklessness while we bargained instead for purpose. There were dreams we held so close that we could never abandon them despite the peer pressure and ridicule. Some said we'd never make it. We lost ourselves in quick-ending weekends and one-night hook ups, never discovering the mark we left on those who pledged themselves to us even while knowing we broke every promise.

Our eyes closed under many dying evenings and we hoped to turn to dust or a comet blazing across the universe. Young friends died. We welcomed those sad events as excuses to drink more beer and burn through drugs or cigarettes. It would take us a lifetime to grow up. Some of us never did. We had to depart to survive or we'd turn to stone and our dreams would die inside of us. Those who waited patiently for something to happen are still waiting. We made it out of there.

Promise

Promise yourself on this day that you will be a success. Promise yourself. This is the day that your life will change. We who have lived too many years, heard too many lies must not, will not let anything stop us from smashing open the window of unreality and letting through the light of truth. The truth is we are something. We are not nothing. We must take that belief to the grave.

Upon the death of a loved one we look into the face of every man that passes you until every one of them exits the room and leaves you to your thoughts and your casket of grief. Death. We lose tears and sleep and friends and dreams. We lose hope, and joy, and lightness and surety, and in their place, we carry one of the heaviest burdens of all, a diabolical heartache. In that transaction we gain painful knowledge and tragic sensibility. Soon after mourning comes clarity and a single vision, in that cold light of day we understand that things will never be the same again.

Resilience

And you grind and you grind.

You sleep in the same shirt, and in the morning, you put on the same pants. You don't shower and you don't shave, not because you don't want to, it's because you can't afford a razor or a water bill. You eat meager food cooked in the crappy microwave and count your coins in order to pay for the next meal of ramen or rice. Toilet paper is a luxury. Your friends are unimaginative but you have dreams and they are greater than any agony you suffer from. You have dreams gained from pouring out into the city or wheat fields over a thousand dark nights, dreams you never shared with someone you loved while you did the grind, while you caught the bus and while you walked in the freezing cold to your home and your crappy bed.

You saved your tips, and you dreamed of getting out of there; maybe the Marine Corps or the Coast Guard, something, anything better than fast food and filthy shops. One day you'll get older and likely be successful and maybe you'll get rich and fat and eventually remember what you are now going through. Let's hope you never lose that youthful and hopeful energy that will help you escape some dark tragic nights. Let's hope in age that you keep the vigor, the strength and the quiet calmness of a focused, young man dreaming of a better life.

The world owes you nothing

Some of us came from an environment where there was structure, there was purpose, life made sense because we understood the concept of good and bad, it was us versus them, and we were aligned with brethren that in many ways thought more like us than not like us. We departed the service and got disconnected. We can't relate to our coworkers, our old friends and even to our family. This perception isn't new. It's as old as the stars.

One way of looking at this disconnection is to see your life experience as enlightening regardless of the pain that comes with it, and another is to use it as a means to help others integrate. Angst, aimlessness, feelings of purposelessness, are within your heart and mind to tell you that you're not the same person and life is not the same either.

You can thrive if you want to, you can be an influencer if you want to but you've got to get out of old ways of thinking and into new ways of doing. Exercise, write, work, play in order to create structure; allow yourself to meet people, and don't be reluctant to discuss what you think and feel but approach it from the aspect of an open-minded traveler who will one day return home and not a reluctant nomad with nowhere to go.

Consider that no one can read minds. It is therefore important to learn how to communicate. Work on yourself until you become connected again. It takes effort, it takes planning, it takes real action, introspection and it means making no excuses. The world owes you nothing. Don't forget, you chose to enlist, you chose that life, now is the time to do something worthwhile with what you carried back. What are you waiting for?

I just want to fight

Sometimes I don't want to talk, I just want to fight. How many of us feel like that? You might feel like the baddest guy on the block but there's a guy out there who feels no differently than you and he's better conditioned, better prepared and it's likely given the right circumstances he's going to wipe the floor clean with you.

I'm reminded of an old story where a large group of us outnumbered a smaller group that was better armed with a hammer, morning star, knife and some other tools. Despite how many cool moves we had the fighting spirit left my weaker-minded friends when a hammer smashed one down. What were we supposed to do? Not everyone thinks like you.

We dragged him away to regroup and they pursued eventually shooting at us until the police came in pursuit. They and their fleeing mini truck were never located. I think it was Mike Tyson who stated that everyone has a plan until they get hit in the face.

My friends are all grown up now, married and with kids most likely. Try doing time in the pen because you couldn't just walk away. Life goes on and no one cares when you get out. Most of us survived youth. Some lost the fire. Some still hold it and continually stoke it.

If you're feeling like there's a fight inside of you, I recommend taking it into the gym and onto the mat and see what kind of gas you have. Reality tells the truth. Unless you're exercising, practicing self-defense and learning to shoot I recommend that you keep your feelings to yourself and stay locked in your room. Leave when you've had some time to cool. It might save you, your family, and the friends you love a world of hurt.

SOMETIMES I JUST WANT TO FIGHT

SPOTTER UP

Sometimes

Sometimes I write in order to express pain. I don't always know what I want to say but the message I want to convey is to speak my truth from injury, to share a story about my loss, and a hope that someone's life was changed by reading it. I am a functionalist by will and force but in my idealistic mind I am a romantic who believes in the brotherhood of man. What are you?

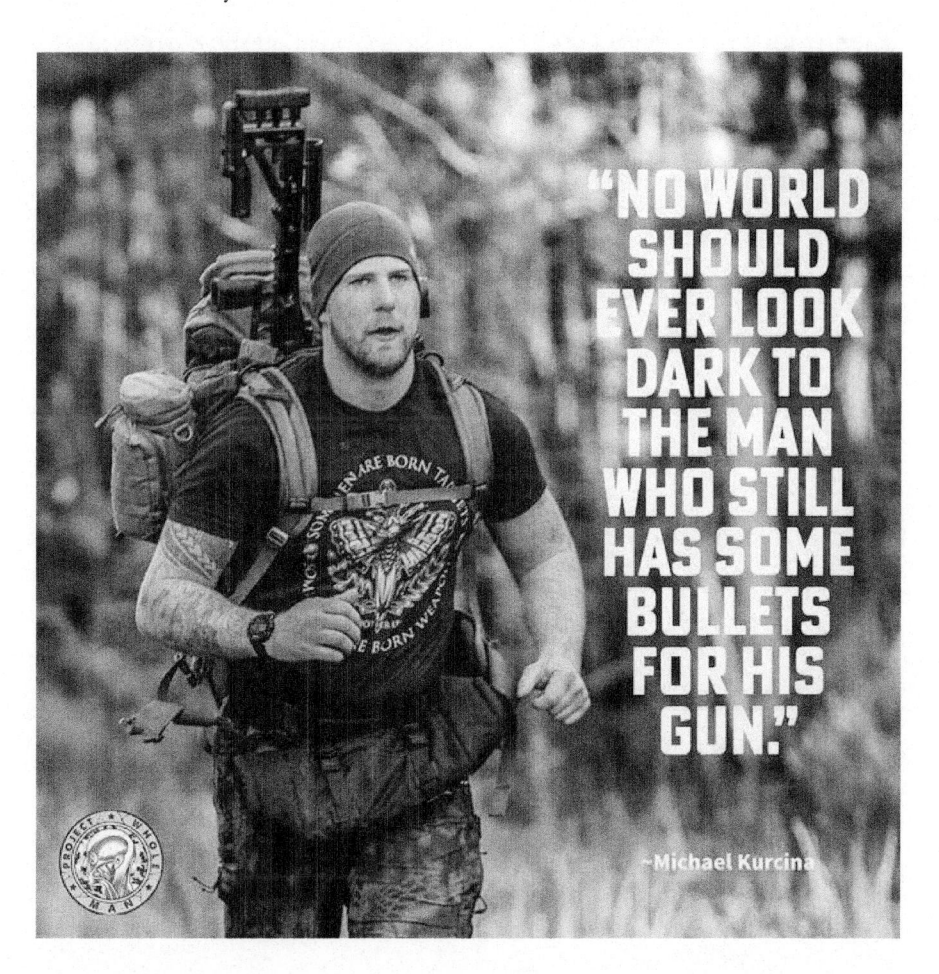

"NO WORLD SHOULD EVER LOOK DARK TO THE MAN WHO STILL HAS SOME BULLETS FOR HIS GUN."
~Michael Kurcina

The space between us

Sometimes we can feel like no amount of loving we're given can replace the dying we're doing within. Time and eternity, it seems cannot replace our loss.

Loss is often the space found between what was once the crossing waves of love emanated from two hearts, whether it was between us and a lover or a friend or a stranger, whether it be permanent or whether it be perfunctory seconds, a loss is a break in the current and any reconnection if it happens doesn't feel like it was rewired the same.

Whether two lovers are standing on separated verandas or atop and below a canyon makes no difference because being pulled apart is being pulled apart. The death of any kind of someone you knew is a pain that is never ephemeral. It feels so real. The loss of a brother, a leader, a friend, any of these shapes men many times for the best and sometimes for the worst.

Whether a man partook in combat, observed a death or deaths, whether he can comprehend his experience are commemorial moments. Can he understand them outside of his own internal and private existential way? How does a man frame the structure and accounting of his life out of a few impactful memories that were in the

past because he certainly has to move on and live without leaving what he lost behind?

A man can carry a lot of pain. Like an unwanted pregnancy pain is carried heavily and sometimes there is little in the way of abortive solutions. Pain isn't like a heavy stone a man can just throw away with casual disregard but his load can be transferred. He can shift the weight upon his shoulders, and take some of the burden upon his back or legs. A man can search out paths that help ease the load if he chooses too.

No song, no drink, no love at least in this world, will last forever and it shouldn't. Endings give starts to other beginnings as simple as that sounds. For the veteran or the lover or for any of us longing for the practical or romantic past, where we felt a singularity of the soul, should be mindful that unchecked emotions and too much feeling without a cut off-point can perpetually lock us in that time. Some men cannot tolerate things as they are, or as they could be, rather they are stuck considering only how things once were. Loss is a tough pill to swallow.

Be

Sometimes we don't have a clue what someone has been through. You don't have to be a hero for the one you profess to love, just shut up and be there... *You don't have to say a word. Just be present.*

We will walk towards danger again

Sometimes when men lose their courage they must go away for a time. Sometimes they can't deal with their fears. They lose their nerve. They must be among the wild things, away from men, away from love. They lay their belly against the earth and roar at the moon. In the dark and silence, they begin to heal. They will learn to stand upright like men once more and walk towards danger again....

Real

Speak and speak sincerely or don't speak at all. One of the most unlikable qualities in a man in my opinion, and really anyone for that matter, is one of insincerity. Express your genuine feelings when asked, and speak your mind. A man doesn't need to share his deep personal feelings with everyone but he shouldn't become hypocritical or pretend to have feelings that he doesn't feel or say things he doesn't mean to say. Be genuine in what you think, feel and how you want to be portrayed. Compromising your own identity creates more problems, for you and others, than it will ever solve.

Say I love you or don't say I love you. Agree or don't agree but don't be a wicked politician and a crooked diplomat in negotiations of the heart you jackass. If you don't know how you feel well then go figure it out and then speak your mind and share your heart, or at least make an honest attempt at them. Insincerity sets up so many false cues that society is better off not having to try and figure out to navigate around the mess you make.

Argus-eyed

"I though Argus-Eyed was surprised." Historians and storytellers inform us that Argus Panoptes or Argos was a hundred-eyed giant in Greek mythology. Some say that he wasn't a giant at all with many eyes but simply a very vigilant man. "He was the son of Arestor, whose name "Panoptes" meant "the all-seeing one". He was later slain by Hermès.

Argus was perhaps not so watchful though, but it was no fault of his own. To free Io, Zeus had Argus slain by Hermes. Hermès the messenger of the Olympian gods, disguised himself as a shepherd, and used spoken charms to close Argus eyes. Argus bloodshed was the first of its kind among the new generation of gods.

No matter how vigilant or perceptive we are there simply are things that we cannot see deeply into, such as time and memory. There are moments in our life that are quite often so enigmatically beyond our scope of comprehension but we should never stop trying to understand where we fit into the warp and woof of it.

We are even blinded to truth by the machinations of other men and women who do not want us to discover truth, what is best for us, and some even shield us from truth out of a misguided sense of love.

Make today less about killing something and make it more about dying to something. Restrain yourself from addictions, or do fight the feelings of victim-hood or do something nourishing and kill what

injures you. Lessen its control over you. Perhaps death and its effects and making ghosts is more about us letting our old self die and becoming something better than we were.

I truly believe that we can recapture aspects of our youth but it requires working through some very difficult issues, and not letting the lingering doubts about who and what we are, and can be, be wrestled down by what we were into submission. Watch over others too.

Remain Argus eyed. You are the guardian over a sleepy-eyed culture that cares little about vigilance. So, my friend, it's your job. Peer through time and memory, anticipate what might come from the future and use experience culled from the past to help you fight it.

"WE ARE YOUNG LIONS AND WE HAVE TASTED BLOOD."

SPOTTERUP

We were young lions

Spring nearly over now and the world destroying time brings summer here. Summer. In youth we stood with our highest chin against it, our strongest posture, our suntanned face, which of us now are willing slaves? We waste what little we grasp in our fingertips from year to year and some have even crossed from age to age.

We cannot bring anything back but memory and even our precious treasure diminishes each day, until we spend it all. Lay the contents of your pockets upon the table and take a real accounting of what you have and have not. What cash and coin have we gained?

Be still and recall the bobbing and shrinking flowers that bounced under winter rain, and the golden dome that sank below the rim of the horizon and consider your dead or dying youthful passions. You can't bring back your strongest age. You cannot bring back your strongest gaze that pierced past life's dark and impenetrable veil.

The sunset shrinks and the night is still and we are weak and pale without our dreams.

Cover your eyes and look away from sad memory and your secret indecisions. Your bones know what your mind cannot. Act upon it. Act upon it. Act upon it. Time wastes us. Let us not return the favor by wasting it.

Thoughts and deeds

Stand atop a hill one summer evening and let the hot wind press upon your face as if you are turning away from the eternal past. Look now into the coming future. Do not forget, the night is meant for sorcery and magic happens then.

Stop fighting this damnable warfare with yourself and let go of understanding. Believe. Take account of your assets and liabilities and throw them away, take account of the passing seconds and minutes and hours and realize each moment gives you the opportunity to start over. Opportunities are abundant but you must defy the science that tells you what you want is impossible to achieve and now you must become supernatural in your thoughts and deeds.

Stand like a man, stand like a king! Stand regally and do not run from your destiny, do not shrink from the task, from the burdens you will carry in the coming year. Godspeed getting to where you must go.

Bassackwards

Surely our function in life is complex. Choosing to examine how we operate daily is prudent and taking righteous action is necessary part of growing up and healthy for us as a whole. If your purpose in life is to simply experience pleasure and to dispense pain then some of your priorities are bassackwards. Flip your script and see how life turns out for you. Being a warrior sometimes means we must absorb the blows the world rains upon us while simultaneously bringing good into a backwards thinking culture.

Work

Teach your sons to read and when you do allow them to grow their hearts. Don't smash their spirits. Nothing is better than a man of compassion, virtue and conviction, who is filled with courage, respect and hopefulness. Raise them on the poetry of poets and the stories of heroes, those mighty men who were real and fictional. "Ex Nihilo Nihil Fit" was a phrase supposedly spoken by the Roman philosopher Lucretius and it translates to nothing comes from nothing. If you want to get ahead than hard work is always required in order to achieve something. Remind your children of this when they get discouraged. Tell them that getting ahead means putting oneself in relative agony in order to get results. It doesn't matter where they start but they should choose to do something. Sometimes people quit the second they get started but if they'd just stayed with it, they would have made progress. Success doesn't come without effort and nothing. Let them know you are with them every step of the way. Even heroes had challenges and in fact needed challenges in order to find value in doing something. Encourage them to read and exercise.

Special

The average soul feels a certain kind of loneliness but the above average soul feels an incredible isolation that should never be experienced and can never be described. *Work through your ill feelings. Yes, you've experienced a lot due to your warrior's life. Learn to unravel them so that you can understand how to become whole.

Bear in mind that we can easily deceive ourselves and believe that we are special and that no one can ever understand what we are going through. Superiority sometimes means having the mindset and heartfelt attitude of humility if we are to rise above anything; we should have a modest opinion of who we are in life. Having a restrained opinion on our standing in the strata of humanity can open the heart to growing, to experiencing wonder and eventually healing. We belong to the society of men. We are not alone. You are not alone.

Plato's Cave

The boldest of plans to spend the wealth of their liberty comes not from free men but from free men who believe at any minute they can be enslaved. *There is a doctrine whispered in secret that no man is ever truly free, that he is a slave to someone or something. But if he is free then he must not take his freedoms for granted.*

He must plot his course in life. He should never take for granted his power to act, to speak, or think as he wants. He must not spend his precious time frivolously. If a man can be free then he must learn

how to liberate himself from prison before he is ever imprisoned, and he would be wise to not leave the thinking on this matter unfinished; he has no good sense if he cannot appreciate even an atom of his liberty.

Gladiator

The culture of modern man is enslaved by the constant want of pleasure but the free man at the center of the arena looks back and doesn't give a damn. Each man has a need for happiness, enjoyment, ecstasy and other similar pleasure because it's driven by his psychological and biological needs but the hedonist's continual pursuit of pleasure makes him the least mature of modern men.

He wants to abstain from most healthy forms of activities that strengthen the spirit because it requires him to do some kind of suffering. He often seeks external devices to make him happy and, in my opinion, he is simply a childish boy rather than a serious man. The free man works to control what he feels and wants and works diligently to not be enslaved by the common man's addictions, nor the insensible opinions of others, because he seeks internal, eternal and unearthly things. Encircled by critics he draws a line with his sword in the sand and separates himself from the mob and the masses.

We should not limit our experiences to only what we can solely imagine, for that is much too small and those are the dreams of worms. We should learn that by conquering our passions we can feel the glory of God by attempting to live as a Godly thing.

Eternal

The eternal champion whether he lived 10,000 years ago or lives 10,000 years from now will cross the earth to bring light and lift the world out of a terrifying darkness. His sacrifices will indeed be fantastic for they are an undying magic to a disbelieving world; one day a young boy inspired by the supernatural will seek to carry the same burden. The champion's weight if he truly believes in it will become a weightless flame that stirs a sleepy world to arise. Be the champion, carry the flame and let your path be an arc of fire in a dark universe.

Wriggle to freedom

The magic of youth will never return but men who still dream, who still hope, who live honestly will catch incredible snippets of it. In the vastness of every city some men feel closed off from opportunity, closed off from love or success, or happiness. Men dream, and dream like children but those incapable of turning dreams into reality will remain pinioned like withering flies upon paper. All that remains is shadow, each man's lifeforce is emptied, and like a bug beneath glass they become a collection of perfect specimens of what men can be yet what they should never be. Each man must take action by crawling to his freedom even if it must be done by wriggling upon his knees.

Terrorist

The modern progressives' (or I should write many men) existential crisis is caused by their feelings that they know better but lacking any evidence to make it true causes an internal conflict, and for them is only resolved by continually enforcing their will upon others in order to feel a glimmer of self-worth. In some prison of their own making, they struggle to tell themselves what is true that really isn't true. Yes, every man's home is his castle unless you believe otherwise yet it's his mind that is the Fortress, but don't let that dwelling be your own demise. No amount of brick and mortar can defend you against the terrorists inside your mind. Beware Plato's Cave.

Let us choose the same

The overhanging sky like a hot blanket chokes us to our knees. We are not alone. The thunder roars, the hawks watch us from the parapets of primitive walls while we hunt men that kill men not with bullets but stones. Monotony, then boredom leads to horror with despair.

We've never witnessed a single, dry autumn here. We watched the drunken suicides; men shot through the heart and the head from time to time. They sing to us let us lie, let us lie, let us lie. We walk with ancient ghosts along old palaces with their moats. Laughter leaves us, we're filled with pain. And in old age had we the years to live and love again let us choose the same. Let us choose the same.

Listen to the voices

The purpose and the plan are to live vitality, to seek out challenges, to embrace our uniqueness, to go against the grain and change the weak culture time and time again despite the losses to ourselves. We must give in to pain and discomfort until our mission is done. We must fight the hounds of Hell and all of the world's pain.

Surrendering to a purpose or a plan doesn't come easily to most men. It's not easy and it's not natural. We fight our own emotions. We fight the dictums telling us we must find our place in an unnatural world that is constantly changing while we stand there watching it transpire.

Our life expires as we seemingly stoically stand still. We seem to gain life and meaning only when we take action. The hero of most myths is one who fights against an irrational world and brings sensibility to a people on the brink of extinction even if he too feels hopeless.

His resolve delivers freedom and more life in some capacity to the oblivious and the fearful. If he is well practiced in his discipline, he may be able to deeply tune into the voices calling to him. The voices tell him to fight against the pox petrifying men and to take his own place in the world but he might not want to. He must fight against destructive forces that corrupt the world. He may feel like fleeing, or surrendering to the persuasive force, and if he does nothing he will be forgotten or become like the other helpless ones. He must hear the voices or another hero will rise and come. Yes, sometimes we will suffer a loss of our self. No matter, face out across the mountain ranges and listen to the voices. Thank those who taught you how to get up there. Surrender to them. Stretch your wings like an eagle and fly through your fear. Do it now.

Sadness

The saddest line in the story of your life is the one that states you lost faith in yourself, that you lost faith in the world, and in the end that you quit and died.   *Don't be terrified at trying to succeed at something that also seems extremely daunting particularly to others. If you aren't terrified then how can you ever appreciate yourself for what you're out to conquer? Put yourself out there to criticism, ridicule, scorn, whatever, because in the end those can't injure you. Let your fuel be something good and powerful whether you want to call it God or some innate brilliance you haven't tapped into. Each of us has a terrifying energy inside of us and we should be scared of it, but we must nurture it and learn to harness it. Some give up, some never realize it, never put it to the test, never ever grow it to help them become who they want to be. Sometimes we should be nearly in tears, nervous and ill, at our realization at the gift of life we were given, and the mad abilities we not only were born with but our virtue and enterprise. Don't quit. Give it a try. Write a book, build a business, *become an actor, jump out of a plane, I don't care. Do things that frighten you every day. Do things that frighten others (P.S. when I write of the world I am writing about a lack of faith in people in general.)*

Warmth

The smallest fire on the deepest night is like an inferno to sad, lost men in need of light. Enjoy what you have, give, what you have, embrace what you have before the fire expires. Hold this memory with you in your darkest moment, "I was loved, I gave love, and I became part of something greater than myself if only for a single moment."

Bubble

The tremendous shocks to the soul that wounds men severely can often be healed by the delicate instrument of love closing off the injury from further insult. Love must save us from ourselves and if it cannot than nothing else will and we are doomed. Every self-destructive man might not be saved from himself, from his foolish hands and his mind filled with gloom. Hopefully there is something left inside that damaged brain and seemingly empty heart that will register that a man will be okay.

All reasonable men and women want to be loved, to give love and to see that love change people for the better, and to see the effects of that love on the world.

Immature love exists in a bubble, where lovestruck fools isolate themselves from dangers, risks, and challenges. Mature love exists outside the pleasure dome and it gives people the courage to try new things and to be fearless and resilient in the face of failure.

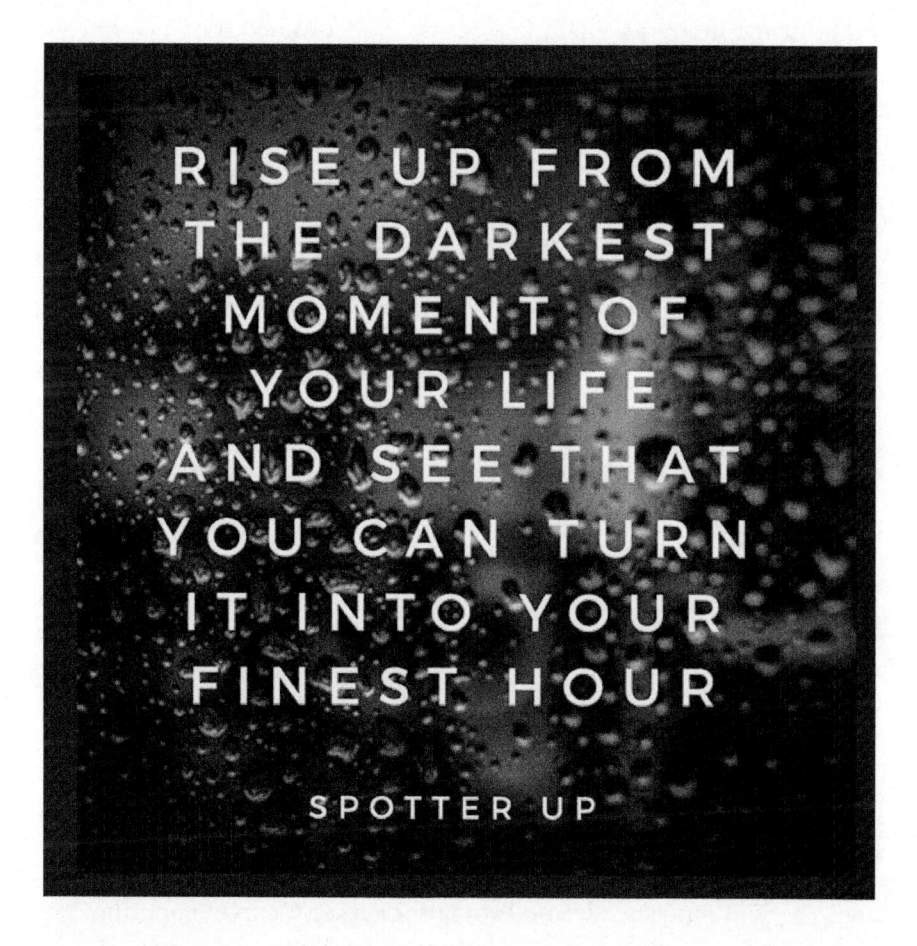

> RISE UP FROM THE DARKEST MOMENT OF YOUR LIFE AND SEE THAT YOU CAN TURN IT INTO YOUR FINEST HOUR
>
> SPOTTER UP

It is a wonderful feeling to know that someone believes in us. The highest form of love is selfless love, something rarely found in the self-seeking enclave of Hollywood, but it exists there.

To be loved by others, to give love to others are wonderful things and helps men do strange, bold and incredible feats. We must be able to love ourselves too. Wandering, questioning, doubting, unbelieving and believing, coming, going, dying to ourselves in order to die for others and growing. Love is a vital thing for us to feel valued. Love is the great emancipator. Find it, keep it, nurture it despite what you're going through and honor it. Be loved and have peace.

O'clock

The truth is all men have difficulty using new eyes to reexamine old hurts upon their injured spirit in a comprehensive way because it might reveal how the most poignant moments of that life was wasted. What should be dead shame is alive, and if a man wants to move further ahead, he should examine if there is a single source of drainage stealing his energy or if there are multiple currents causing conflict. Sometimes the physical body shows no sign of damage but the spirit is seriously injured.

Lover

The rays of sun like burnished gold spread across your body, skein wrapping you fantastically and brought together the living and the dead, your happiness with my woe, my shadow with your soul, and encircled the sum of our divided equities under a single heaven on a slow, autumnal day one, flint-colored morn.

Born to waste

We are born to waste the most poignant moments of our lives. Half that battle is learning how to escape that time, the other half is learning how to use what we left behind.

The truth is all men have difficulty using new eyes to reexamine old hurts upon their injured spirit in a comprehensive way because it might reveal how the most poignant moments of that life was wasted. What should be dead shame is alive, and if a man wants to move further ahead, he should examine if there is a single source of drainage stealing his energy or if there are multiple currents causing conflict. Sometimes the physical body shows no sign of damage but the spirit is seriously injured.

Perhaps his indifference or his ignorance or his full disregard of his scar compelled him to move ahead in life but these are likely short-term gains until the flow of power is fully interrupted as he experiences a long-term loss to the whole.

Just because a man's spirit can take a lot of beatings doesn't mean his mind holds a lot of good sense. The system will break. Why doesn't he focus on the reasons for the powerlessness that is holding him back?

Oddly, men sometimes suspect themselves to be frauds, to be incomplete, to be incapable of loving or taking love, to be incapable of success while simultaneously believing they are incapable of defeat. Perhaps it's time for this dead man to reset the dead hands of his dead clock and bring his old life some new time.

Broken at birth

The truth is most men are broken at birth and broken even further at childhood and that is an inevitable fact of his existence. Any glimmer of hope in his eyes masks behind it some dark and painful confusion. If he's got some leanings for a purpose and a bit of fire in his belly, he just might light an inferno onto a pathway for others to follow.

If he never gets a single ember alighted what little life there is in him will turn into ashes and then his heart into dust. Home and memory are never campgrounds for his escape, instead the answer to the puzzle that puts him together ultimately lies outside of his heredity, and in fact resides deeper and darker down some roads. First, he has to accept that his actions have consequences and life will give him some bitter lessons, but if he can learn to work outside of his constant limitations, he will learn to outflank struggle, and even come to accept that it isn't the blood in his veins that defines him instead it is virtue and enterprise.

Obituary

There is a hope that we will merit more than just a mention on a 3-inch-long swath of yellowed paper, that we were remembered for more than being life's punching bag; that we never asked for a second or third chance because we always did something decent with the first.

For every greasy spoon we ate in, for every blind date that looked at us oddly when we met them and turned us down, for every care home we avoided because they were places for the dead, let's hope in old age and our seemingly forgettable death there was something good, something useful and memorable in it to be found.

There is a light that will never go out

> There are lights that will never go out.
> There are stars that will never go out. There is a good hunger that will never be filled.
> There are men who will live
> FOREVER...
>
> ~Michael Kurcina

The world is a strange and beautiful place. From any high tower a man can look out into a sea of lights that pepper the dying darkness and the hills full of eyes stare back out at him. People wonder, "is there more to life then this?" Many die in darkness, alone without a soul to die with. The mind wanders back to the past where the same man hurtled across the blackest night in a metal bird over heaths of stone and empty space.

A drink in hand, music playing, a thousand people swaying to songs that mean nothing to him because they don't sing his story. His heart and mind are on other men, in another time, at another place. He would die with them but they are gone. Lights sparkle in big cities, lights crackle in old homes, like an old cat darkness climbs down rickety stairs.

The bustling activity in these honeycombs of homes clustered round him are too much to handle. Vast night and old memories are dying magic that no longer thrill him. He loses his purpose.

There are lights that will never go out. There are stars that will never go out. There is a good hunger that will never be filled. There are men who will live forever. In the saddest of nights, he must find his stride and run a little faster and step a lot longer and find his footsteps again. He must run ahead of the man he used to be. In war one man enters an arena and it's inevitable that another man leaves. His spirit must tunnel out and let light be the food he lives upon and not bad memories. Treasure isn't found in the darkest hole but above if he searches for it.

There are lights that will never go out. There are stars that will never go out. There is a good hunger that will never be filled. There are men who will live forever. He must find them again…He is a fighter. He will be a fighter until the day he dies.

Send me

Then I heard the voice of the Lord saying, "Whom shall I send? And who will go for us?" And I said, "Here am I. Send me!" *Isaiah 6:8.*

Along the vast expanse of black night stretched out seemingly forever like a desolate sea, comes a sense of loss and loneliness, yet we must reassure ourselves that whatever pain we feel is for a good cause. Whatever rage we have, whatever magnificent tears come, whatever memory returns, we must be authentic in allowing these things to return in their intense forms so our faith is never vague.

We must lean on what we know to understand what we just lost. Never forget. Never forget. Never forget…For the love of this country our men accept death. This is what warriors know. Lights crackle in dark houses. Night climbs upon rickety stairs and as warriors rise, they carry within them grief from the loss of another man. But our dead are not gone. Their spirits will cross the streams of forgotten waters and vanish fearlessly through the pines to the places where ancient stones hide themselves. They are going home to a place none of us can know. Until then let us do the work and wait for the call. *Be strong, be weak, be whatever you need to be but don't be unplugged from the things that can heal you.*

God not gods

There are gods above gods, but every god made by man is a worthless thing, and every man is a church with the potential to become a grand cathedral, but failing to put a single match to candle becomes a black, vacuum until his life extinguishes. We should live to fight devils, to shelter angels, and to build holy houses, but men too in love with their own pain will let what they love kill them. A spirit that gives up resistance becomes a useless thing.

Some men with an allegiance to their own suffering knowing well that it was constituted by their addictions, can't find any respite from it, even though they beg Heaven for its greatest healing.

In fact, as their misfortunes increased, those willing to stand beside them out of impatience decreased, and their willpower ebbed and emptied. Dead men walk the earth. What ends a man's suffering? Con men with broken spirits croak, "give me through my solicitations of pain the entire world's suffering and I will turn it into hope." Who are they fooling?

Legends say King Arthur sent out his men to find the Holy Grail, a wondrous device that offered goodness in sustenance in infinite abundance to stop the world's pain and keep the hellhounds at bay, but the knights never found it, and no man ever drank from it and the world will always be as it's meant to be. Until that time, we must learn to see that an unspiritual man can fix nothing, until he lets go of his fake heroes, false gods, and primeval philosophies. Live Rightly though it is the most difficult thing you'll ever do. *Matthew 6:33 But seek first the kingdom of God.*

Mazes

There are moments when we look at our past with an equal amount of fondness and pain. I think for most of us youth seemed largely like something that would never run out. Now that we're older it seems we live to prevent memory and meaning ebbing from us any longer.

We can't stop the first nor even the second from occurring. When we stop doing heroic things, when we stop trying to make a difference in this world our life seems filled with paradoxes. We seem to only have purpose when we're moving. What should be our purpose?

> **JUST BECAUSE A MAN'S SPIRIT CAN TAKE A LOT OF BEATINGS DOESN'T MEAN HIS MIND HOLDS A LOT OF SENSE**
>
> **SPOTTER UP**

Lost in mazes sometimes but this is true, that we are born to live and die. If we're going to succeed at whatever we do we've got to learn from the past but there is no asylum back there, our place of respite is ahead. We must look at the town we left from our place on the hill and make our way headwards into the horizon and fearlessly into that town nearby. What you're looking for very likely is ahead. Travel without hesitation Don't ever give up. Keep moving in order to find your way.

We are men

There are some brilliant songs out there written by men with tender hearts. Those songs can only be written by men who truly love women, and are written because there are women. Inspiration. We need you.

They write songs about you, the kinds of songs that make us want to barricade ourselves indoors with the one we love and we don't want to leave. But sometimes we left before, and for good reason, and sometimes we must again.

We watch the bright lights come through the raindrop covered windows, and cast fantastic shadows upon the walls, crawling high to the ceiling and then disappearing while we look at you in wonder and we wonder at the simple things. Love does that to men.

Music seems richer, life seem stronger, and love seems in endless supply. We go for walks in the rain. A stream of light ripples along the puddles of some old road and flashes themselves against the brightness of your wild, eyes. The burst of your smile makes our joy rise higher than the stars.

Discovering the richness of your mouth and feeling the sensuousness of those lips is like knowing the secret, reddened depths of jasper. Discovering the joy inside your spirit is like finding rain for the first time upon our flesh. And in the stillness perhaps we reveal to you great lies or deep truths.

If we are real, we will confess about the grief we have for dying or dead men, and the way we feel broken within. If we know you well enough, you'll know about men who went berserk, and those who broke, or about another dead patrolman, or sometimes how we feel like failures.

Perhaps you'll struggle to translate into words the pain that is in our eyes. If we can dream again, we may tell you how it's likely going to be about you. We need you. Heaven is closer next to you. Grief for dying men whose bosoms carried our dying hope, sometimes we are dying too. Perhaps your face cries with it compassion for us, for the things we did, and for the things that were done to us. We are men. Without you how could we otherwise know what we are?

Wait for it

There are times when I don't know all that will be coming but I wait for it without concern. With regards to the idea of building business, there is a myth pushed at times, that if you don't chase opportunity immediately than you've lost the moment and it's gone forever. I don't believe that.

When the mind is creative, when it is open to anything and everything, it is like a limitless swirling sea and eddies of ideas that generate thousands of good, new thoughts while the flotsam and jetsam of bad ones are thrown upon dried-up shores.

Instead of seeing what ops are lurking in the waters you instead work on your craft: follow through on calls, build real long-term relationships, encourage your team, allow their own ideas on how to fish flourish in the environment they are in, and the best catches will come.

A leviathan will come to you. Schools of fish, of thought, will swim to you and that is the time to jump into the sea and work like a mad man with all of your energies to reel them in. You will be blessed with the long vision gained from spending time in the crow's nest. Opportunities will sail to you and I know you'll be ready to fish and work hard! Sometimes you just need to sail upon the water and study the sea. Don't eat the bottom feeders. Wait for the white whale.

Your business should know its values or else you'll be drifting with the currents and slapping with desperation at everything that pops its head up. You'll be lost at sea. Align yourself with sailors that share your way of life. Iron men and wooden ships. They'll come, they'll come... The vast sea is full of surprises but you choose when to fish.

I never had

There have been times when I felt like I never had a tomorrow.

Don't live fatalistically. Don't get caught up believing that you're stuck with the same abusive partner that keeps cheating on you and spending your money, stuck with that powerful addiction that seems to haunt you, stuck being the same old person, stuck feeling as if there is no way out. If you have contemplated death today, I recommend today that you try contemplating having life, a lot of life. That is sometimes a very difficult thing to do for someone that is hurting.

Start picturing yourself as being happy or successful, free of burdens, free of doubt and dark confusion. How many of us feel like we never had a tomorrow? Your heart might be struggling right now on how to deal with its conflicts. Don't just wait for some indicator outside of yourself to set it off. Be the trigger, the primer, be the match, be the bullet or whatever you want to call it but be something other than what you are now.

Gardener

There is a goal most mature men have and it is to live in harmony with the rest of the world. In order to do this, he is supposed to know his ideal self, let go of perfection, and practice patience not only on himself but upon all the men he wants to battle. This is not an easy thing to do when he believes there is a fighter inside himself and likely will be inside of him until the day he dies. He should learn to build worthy things that aren't monuments to his ego or built by his ego. Let's hope his projects are good, will last long, and transform many lives.

Regardless of the shifting, and unknown vicissitudes that sometimes turns what he builds into rubble he should never stop being engrossed in worthwhile goals.

Sometimes he'll destroy what is good by pursuing too much of what makes him feel good rather than stopping to understand why he feels a certain staleness and flatness, and why he avoids the things that make him feel bad. He should be ready to deal smartly with whatever plants itself inside the fields of his life.

Sometimes he finds peace and sometimes he finds war. If he can learn to harvest each smartly, he will feel like he can accomplish anything. He will be able he to live without inhibition, fear, doubt or inner-criticism, and he won't worry at all whether men won't speak poorly or highly of him. This is when he becomes self-actualized.

Wish

There is always a strange pull towards home no matter how broken it was for a boy growing up. Home to him never mattered that it was a small house, or a tiny shed, no it never mattered whether there were tears nor whimpering or rage in pain experienced in that haunting and hurtful place-the hunger for home was the same held in the heart of a warrior born ten thousand years ago and the beating heart of a boy born today. The idea of home was greater than any man's heroic glory, or duty or quest for fame, and if granted a chance to return to home he would blow out what seemed an inferno with his gasping breath those large flames upon his last birthday cake and upon his death wished for it to be so.

Waking Dawn

There's elation in you, there's power in you, there's the inability to contain your feelings yet you are focused because you are working to being truly alive. There's the sense that you have a certain immortal energy coursing through your body and you can't hold back what it's bringing, so do something with it.

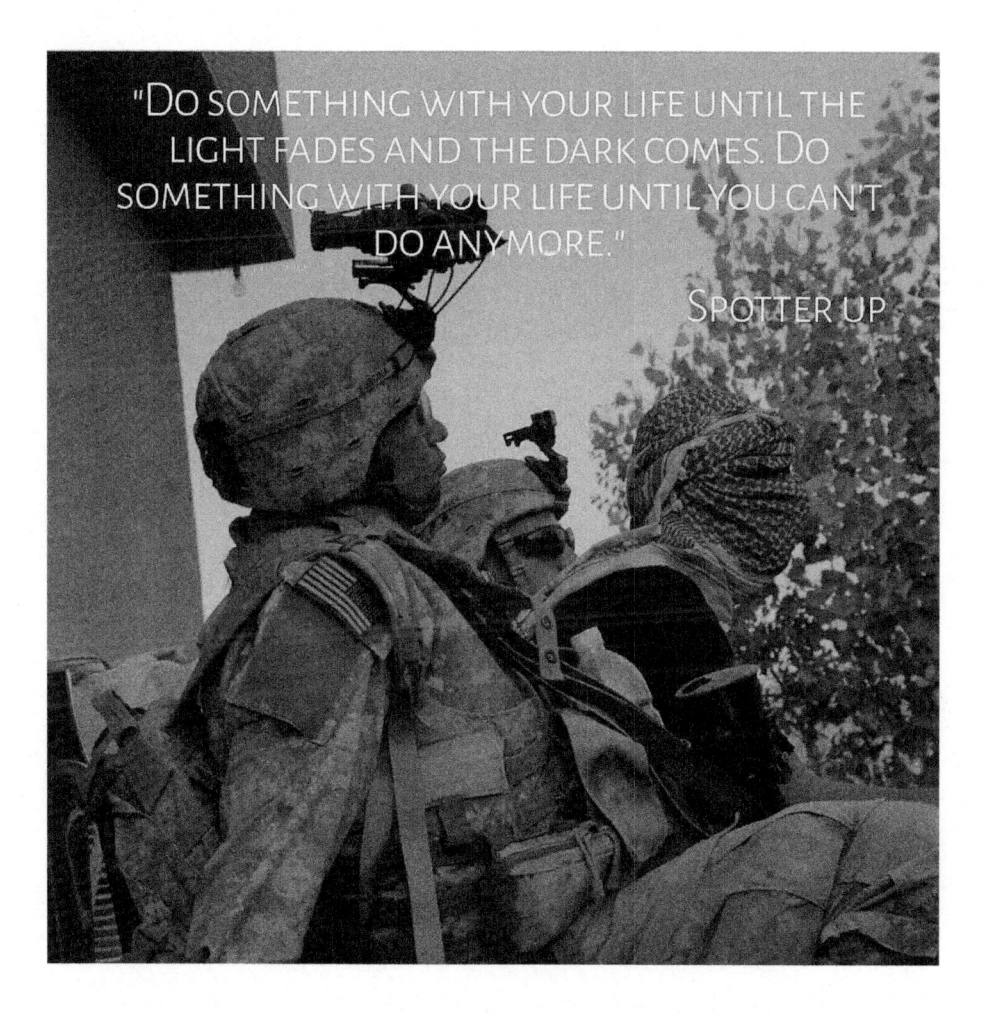

> "DO SOMETHING WITH YOUR LIFE UNTIL THE LIGHT FADES AND THE DARK COMES. DO SOMETHING WITH YOUR LIFE UNTIL YOU CAN'T DO ANYMORE."
>
> SPOTTER UP

Do something with it until the light fades and the dark comes. Do something with it until you can't do any more. Walk beneath those waking dawns, stride into those welcoming arms of twilight, and then run, run, run like a delirious madman through the dark web of night looking for that rich treasure of life. Run until your feet hurt, run until your heart yearns for want of more, run until the answer burns into your mind. You will run under cold rain, or snow, or hot night and you won't give a damn. You will search for more meaning as you meander through dark parks and under city lights.

Beneath the swirling stars, and the pulsing moon, you will uncover the footpaths of vitality, creativity, purpose and meaning but do not deny the answer they bring because they will disappear with the trackless dawn. You might only ever get one chance to listen and it does fade with the loss of youth, it fades like knowledge, it fades when you are dishonest, it runs like a river and is carried far away. It fades when you close your ears to learning, and close your ears to the words of your ancestors.

Wake up and listen. Wake up and know there are precious and secret things in this world. Open your heart to loving, your mind to learning and your ears to hearing. Death will come. Pain will come, the end will come one day but tonight smile if you have undertaken the goal of being alive.

Drink and sleep

There's a reason for everything. Find out the why.

Don't get paralyzed by regret that takes you out of the fight. Maybe you feel like you didn't protect your brother growing up, maybe you wanted to prevent the death of a team mate yet couldn't, or perhaps you feel like you weren't there for your kids because you worked so much.

Be introspective, but not so much that you do no one any good. The world needs good men and women to fix what is broken. Go to bed, sleep it off, be weak now but be strong tomorrow.

One

They embraced roughly. They were like two bolts of lightning joined in the center; two coils of electric current tensed in the moment. Her lips parted slowly, pursed as if to speak a vowel. No sound came out of her mouth. The words roiled in her mind, but did not fall from her lips. There were no words no sound no breath. He kissed the top of her forehead and ran his fingers through the curly mop of her red hair. She clenched her teeth, and then pushed her face as deep into his chest as deeply as it would go.

Everything she felt, everything she could have been was summed up in that moment. Time did not seem to matter for them as they stood encapsulated. He nodded his head in order to reaffirm what she herself felt in her bosom. From her breast came the smallest whimper. Tonight, they existed as one.

Purpose

They rose uneasily from their bed, and pushed tiredly against the pulsing heat that pressed itself like ocean swells to tumble the buoyancy of their bodies downwards upon the small space of their world where they continually struggled to dream.

His mind rolled out bent thoughts that dared to stand erect in defiance against the one thing that devoured all things, time. Her soft hands trembled with delight as he pulled her towards him with vim, capturing the vivid look in her eyes with his easy momentary gaze, and broke the selected surveillance when he saw her smile. It came upon him with the death of his young son that he never really truly lived life for himself.

Hunt the Supernatural

Weathervane

Thunder that makes some men meek is often providence to the brave. Sometimes we dream so vividly only to wake up in tears when we realize none of it was real. The person we loved in life is still gone and no amount of dreaming seems to stitch together the open wound in our heart caused by that loss. Perhaps we lost something else, we lost something that makes the soul hurt deeply. We wake in the dark. Thunder and lightning break open the night. We rise in our bed and go to the window and wonder. There is a good life waiting where we stand and not through the rain that cuts the wind that wanders.

We must stop fatally believing that nothing good ever comes out of storms. Do not be afraid. Do not be afraid! Sometimes the next meaning and purpose of your life reveals itself to you in this tragic moment. Trust in the coming protection and care. Watch the lightning, hear the thunder and wait… the answer will come. Be strong, do not be meek, be brave…be brave…be brave… (meek can be taken as obedient, submissive, fearful, gentle or quiet among many definitions. What are you? Storms over the ocean can be incredibly invigorating.)

Worth more than all of the stars

To see someone that you love release their pain from their eyes isn't as if those rivulets of moisture are magnificent tears more precious than diamonds, no, in fact they are worth more. They are worth more than all of the stars in the sky, more than that sad, drunk moon above, worth more than a thousand universes for we only get one chance to make it right in each second. We only get one chance to make a change before a change is pushed upon us.

Worth more than all the stars in the sky

That moment will be gone. Time that ever elusive thing we want so much more of eludes us when we live in it, but if we consciously decide to exist, we can experience it deeply even while it flows away. The tears from the danger, the anger, the confusion they felt is released and we are party to something electric, something powerful if we can allow ourselves to connect with our lover's experience.

Connections takes time, takes work, takes sensibility. Drop what you are doing, observe, and even if you don't comprehend a thing at least in that moment when those magnificent tears are dropping reach out and touch them; the connection might bring a bit of peace to an injured heart. You live for millions of seconds at least make one of those seconds count between you and her when she falls apart.

Kindling

Until we understand our place in this world, we are essentially a small "some" thing, yet we are not part of all things. We are an ember and not a fire, we are a drop and not a river, we are a voyeur and not a doer.

Every man should hope to wrestle an angel at least once in his lifetime to discover the power held in heaven, to discover what greatness can be. One day with our own eyes and ears let us hope to see what we must see, and hear what we must hear.

Let us be formed out of a spiritual formlessness, to be indispensable men in a world of the dispensable. Let us know our place and our worth. We cannot just take another man's word for it. We were birthed from dust and will end as ashes just as the earth will one day end in ashes and it all will return into the hands that made us. Until then let us fight with every last breath in us to stay in this grand fight of life.

The sickness unto death

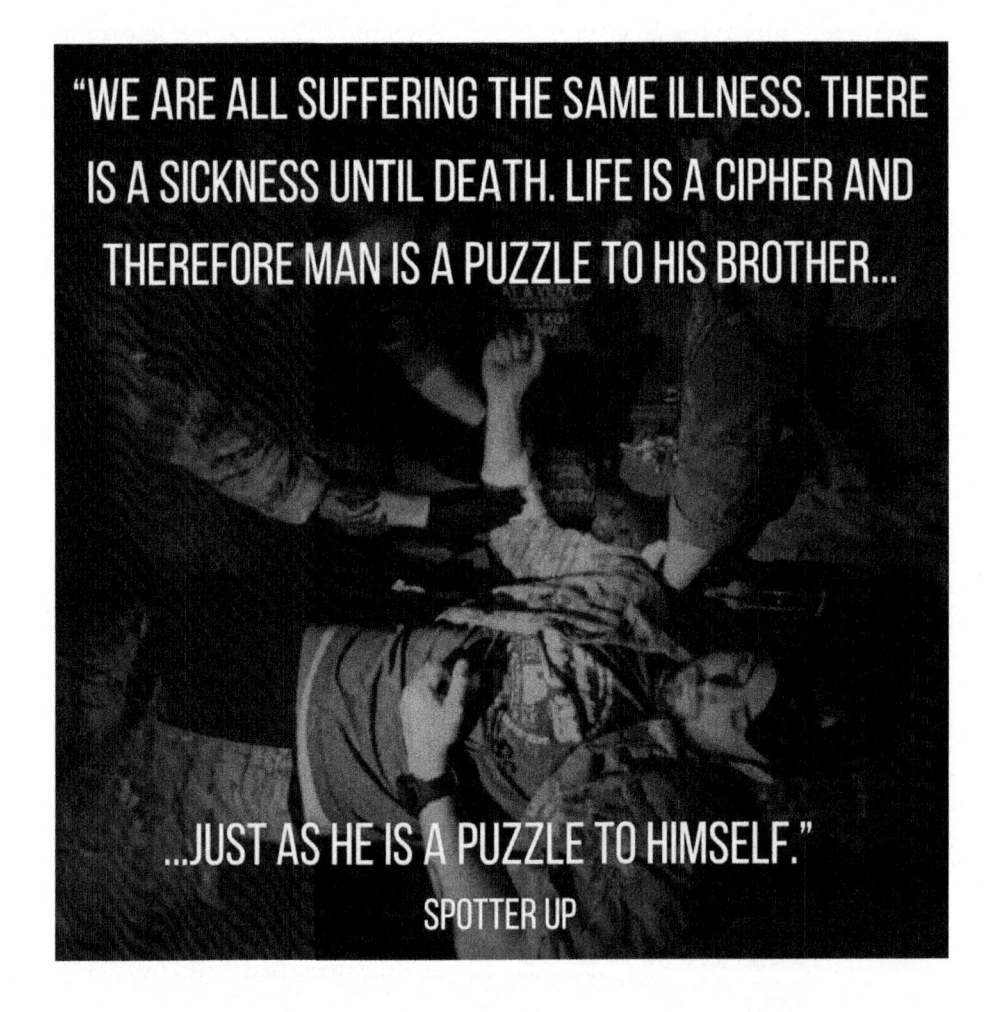

> "WE ARE ALL SUFFERING THE SAME ILLNESS. THERE IS A SICKNESS UNTIL DEATH. LIFE IS A CIPHER AND THEREFORE MAN IS A PUZZLE TO HIS BROTHER...
>
> ...JUST AS HE IS A PUZZLE TO HIMSELF."
>
> SPOTTER UP

We are all suffering the same illness. There is a sickness until death. Life is a cipher and therefore man is a puzzle to his brother just as he is a puzzle to himself. Two blades of grass can stand together upon a hill without ever a day of disharmony between them but two men cannot stand side by side without some kind of inner conflict due to their warring natures.

We are all suffering from the same curse of loneliness, and we are all dulled to death by an expectancy that there is more to life than order or chaos and to their final solutions. A millennium hence and we still feel the rawness of loss from being pushed out of the womb of a stranger and from the Garden and into danger. We are marked for life. We do not know mother's face any longer. We must try to love another in a world of wanderers where we cannot know what they know nor can they ever fully know us.

Lost tongues and forgotten words, life with a nightly struggle for cohesion on terms that we cannot comprehend, while in the morning abandoning what we discovered. What is our noblest expression of ourselves before we die and can we capture what it was to be that way again? Out of our death comes the food that brings the flower and the blades of grass that can stand side by side. Our spirit is stillborn until ultimate death. Union. Eternity in our hearts.

Little people

We are little men dreaming little dreams but without them life would be unbearable. Sometimes when it seems that the world feels like it closes in on us, we must recall the dreams of our youth, the dreams from our mid years, in fact we must remind ourselves even if our dreams are small, they are ours. Make them, own them, live them.

Trapped

We are strangers to ourselves and clueless to the power that resides in the dark thicket of our own mind. Liken hope to a writhing fox chewing at its bloody leg, its little heart pulsing frenetically as it struggles to be freed. It wants to run but cannot. This tangle too thick that even the hounds of doubt our mind sends to destroy it believes every day is night. We should live in harmony with our self but cannot penetrate the web of odd mysteries of our mind. Behind the leaf, beneath the root and rock, above the tree crown and buried deep behind the roughest tendrils cries our greatest self and it weeps to be set free. Memory and forgetfulness wrestle no matter the season and one will win. Let something good come from the songs earth before the magic is gone, before we forget forever who we are meant to be.

Kisses can lead to combat

We can't go back to the things as they once were, even if opportunities are there, for we aren't the same man and the world is different too. In this lifetime we may learn things bitterly. The one we professed to love forever is now loved by another, that the promises made to us were just promises, that kisses can lead to combat, that another man might raise our sons and that our deepest wound is self-inflicted. All is not lost.

No matter! Inhale and be less aggrieved. See that even in blackness drifting we can be carried peacefully though dark currents, that light breaks from above like sharpened blades cutting through the damnable deep and frees us from our painful watery sleep. Swim into hospitable waters, away from your unfathomable, dark dreams and your sad, winter sea. Watch the stars shine over the eddyless waters, feel your pulsing breath, break the feckless waves and swim back home with a man's dignity. All shall pass. All shall pass. In loss let us be filled. In fullness let us be emptied. In hatred let us be loved. In love let us give love. In life let us remember. In death let us be remembered.

Warfare

We don't need history to tell us that men fought wars for as long as there are men, we already know wars wait in their future. Some believe that 'future' knowledge or foreknowledge is a burden while others believe obtaining more of it liberates us from the past. How do we escape the past? We don't, can't and shouldn't but we can reframe and refocus on the future. In some way your war will end, and a new one begins, and hopefully you have the wherewithal to fight it from eating you alive. Maintain your health; exercise, eat regularly, sleep regularly.

Tend to your spiritual needs. Get counseling. Don't shut down to others; get help, talk to your friends or spouse or family. Don't be an animal because that won't get you too far; recognize that you're just a man and it's okay to feel certain emotions. There's nothing weak about that. A note: Instead of wallowing in some deep funk when those injurious memories come, why not be grateful for those wounds?

I'll build you a shrine

No, you're not a loser because you don't know how to love or be loved and she's not impossible. You have to figure love out. Some of us get dispirited by the enigmas in life. We dream under the same stars, we gaze upon the same shores, we're warmed by the same sun, and we are even birthed from the same dust yet we never feel like we are truly a part of humanity. And when we lose in love, we feel even more separated and lost from the world.

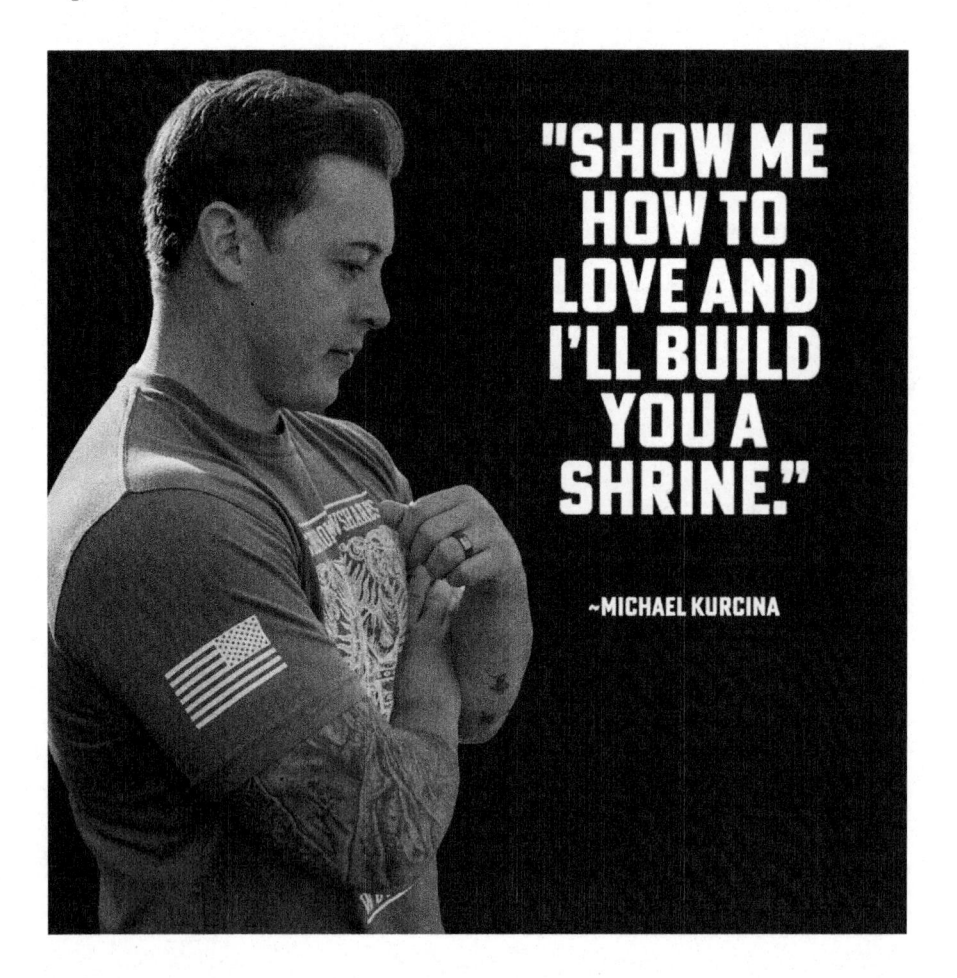

"SHOW ME HOW TO LOVE AND I'LL BUILD YOU A SHRINE."

~MICHAEL KURCINA

How can we be surrounded by millions of people and yet feel so alone? Your sorrow and your loneliness aren't a curse, it's a gift and you have to use it or you waste it. I have seen through my own personal losses how men can turn sorrow from death and heartache into blessings. Break away from the world if you must but when you return share your gift with us.

Share your wisdom, share your pain, share your love, and tell your tale. Tell the tale that increases the light in this world for men who are sitting in the dark. If you withdraw, you'll never bless the world with your presence, and the knowledge that you could have imparted. You might be able to handle loneliness and heartache but regret is another animal entirely. But remember that a lesson only lasts as long as you want it to. "Show me how to love because I don't know how, and I'll build you a shrine."

Back there are the things we broke

When men's lives are reduced to its fundamental needs, they more easily find their purpose. YouTube, Netflix binge watching, sitting in bars endlessly drinking or mindlessly eating can lead a man into doing things that he probably shouldn't; men don't need to be bribed by danger into being violent, but there needs to be a logical place to put that violence. Without a good spiritual rooting some men crumble; that which can numb or heal their discord should never hasten their corrosion; sex, booze, drugs, and more violence.

If war is of some great duration or magnitude men collectively and simultaneously are induced to walk on a path of intense self-discovery, that other groupings of men do not walk on. Men at war in danger often deny their own self-preservation. War induces a shift in their consciousness via periods of calm and quiet, chaos and intensity and each man may discover what is important and unimportant to his "self".

A man threatened can rise or fold; he can even throw away what would seem to be good sense by giving up his own life to preserve the lives of his own men. Only fools experience something so intensely as war and learn nothing; most men are changed forever; some never go back to it.

War is like church revival to some men; it feeds their hunger for danger, and with this infusion there comes an awakening. No wonder why some men can't wait to get back to making it. Every man exists with a partial knowledge of the world and his place in it. Men without a war waste time pontificating the meaning of their whole life while those who partake of it don't necessarily have that problem. They are focused on why and how they must survive, and do more than exist.

A man thrives when he is able to put himself in a position where he has something important to do and speak. One day of intense immersion into it can change a man physically, spiritually and mentally forever. Men can deny the nature of reality too.

Conflict of any kind can be a good thing to some men, very bad for others, it is a shame when men do not use it to grow. Conflict that forces a man to possibly die in some respect makes him live. Woe be it to the man who never strikes an equal balance.

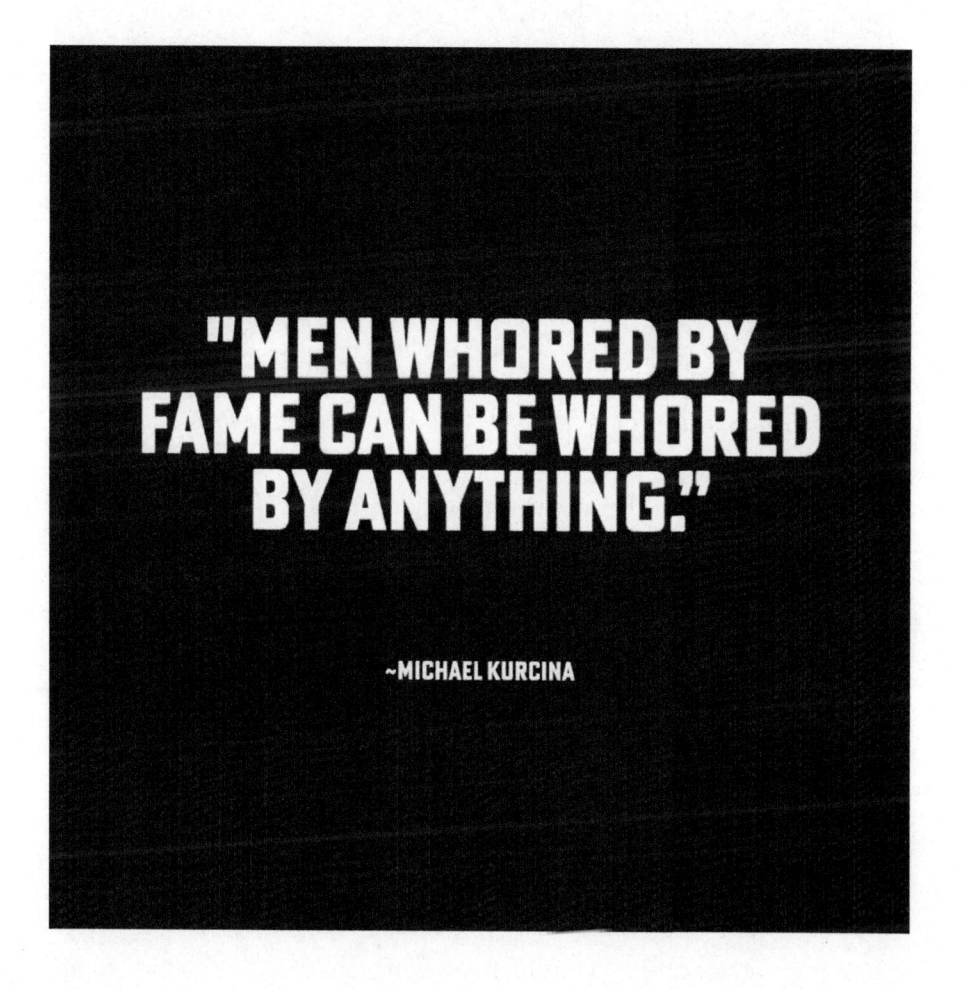

> "MEN WHORED BY FAME CAN BE WHORED BY ANYTHING."
>
> ~MICHAEL KURCINA

Write

We drove our boat slowly along the murmuring shore and my brother pressed his cool hand into mine and held me one warm evening until finally... we swayed above the cold, green swells where our father drowned many years ago. We lay down then in her dark hull and lifted our soft ears to the noise of the winter sea and her feckless waves.

The sudden appearance of a lost thrush beating made us climb up to watch it bank furiously over the black eddies and disappear and I noticed then our rocky shore was on fire. The husky smell of smoke came into our nostrils with a gruffness blowing cinder and thrust the gorgeous smell of mothers' jonquils into our heaving chests.

With a clear knowing that my youth lacked on that deadening night my brother said to me, "She's done it all now." I didn't fully understand what was happening but I saw well enough, and born into that low twilight came our sacred homes' destruction.

Our lighthouse which seemingly stood forever, the lighthouse that our father built with his own sturdy hands was falling, and my heart was falling with it. I spent many summers in her, watching the water below me whirl around the rocks surrounding her majesty." *Create something from nothing. Chronicle your life, share a funny story, paint a picture. Leave behind images. Say and share something before you're gone. Leave a legacy for your grandchildren's grandchildren.

Look

We escape home to get more of life and then we want to return home to get more of life but there is no way to go back, and in that prison of our being we weep our tears. We cannot return to home where there was youth. No, the way to more life is ahead and sometimes down some deep and darker paths until we can see the light ahead. If we see it then we must move towards it before it goes away for what will seem like a long period again.

The man we must be

We search through the hollows seeking the man we used to be, our red lanterns held high. Night moves beneath starlight and the pines. Somewhere out there it is buried. What is buried? Our aborted hopes, our abandoned dreams, our surety, our innocence and like a buried treasure we might not see them again.

With uncertainty we follow the map we made. We may not find our cache again but we will come back we say. It's there we say. We will seek it and find it we say, and likely we will do so until the day we die. Don't give up on yourself. Be what you must be... The magic of youth will never return but men who still dream, who still hope, and who live honestly will catch incredible snippets of it.

Never pay

We should never pay a professional to fight for us for we end up selling a part of our soul away for a false sense of safety. Modern education omits a real understanding of who we are in its movement to equalize everything.

Education has disintegrated because of relativism. Learn to fight in some way whether it's verbal judo or straight up in the street Jiu jitsu. Learn to think for yourself and to box for yourself so your thoughts are strong and your punches make connections.

Whether it's home schooling or home defense you should be involved in the deepest aspect of it rather than leaving it to others, like the government and its educators, to defend what you need, what you want and what you believe.

Don't presume that others will battle for you, or battle as well as you would battle. The ability to fight starts in the home and your children should think likewise.

In the absence of an integrated curriculum in life which starts at home youth begins to see the world in fragmented forms and misunderstands the unifying nature of the universe. The modern world stands against a collective truth and without truth how can one understand anything?

Men must be able to think critically and not simply repeat what they've heard parroted a million times before just because it's been stated by those in positions of power.

A man who cannot rule over himself has no business ruling over others, and if he refuses to be educated as well then, he has no business educating others nor will he ever be respected as the head of his home. This generation spends too much time mixing deep feelings with light thinking and we end up with boys that are spiritually dead.

Instruments of war

We spend too little time crafting our life-giving instruments of peace while being too involved with our death giving instruments of war. It's important to know how to do both. There is a time and place for each singly and together.

With certainty relationships with our lovers can be difficult to manage at times. Sometimes our hobbies, friends or life's work are distractions, and they are used as ways to escape having deeper relationships with our partner or as shielding to protect us from peering more deeply into ourselves; affairs do happen; we love our businesses and hobbies more than our partners.

We spend so much energy where it doesn't count best. Maturing as a person requires us to be real in order to deal with the answers we find. Whether we face our own shortcomings or our partners shortcomings is never palatable; perhaps we face both. Sometimes we are engrossed in habits, hobbies and work because we are selfish or our partner is selfish, or simply because we must; food must be put on the table. I sympathize with those who do multiple deployments and come back to find a house in disarray.

Control what you can control and clear that Area of Operation. Perhaps it's time for a breakup. Do we speak harshly or glibly to our other? Work on doing things that will bring peace to you and your home. I hope it will change things for the better. Nurture your children today, speak kindly to your husband or wife tonight.

How many unnumbered laughs do you keep in your bag of laughter to diffuse a trying situation? How many innumerable kisses do you keep for your wife's sublime mouth and body? Don't be a selfish bastard, stop holding back on the kindness.

How many unwanted names do you call him, how many unguessed abuses can you use today that break her down? Work on your relationships today. Write a love song, or a poem, learn how to plant flowers and give them one. Read a book together. Spend some time refining your instruments of peace today because no doubt you have plenty of instruments for war.

Summer

We waited and trembled for the waves to come and carry us away. We knew that summer night that we would never be the same. Time took our youth but we chose to imprint her with our joy and sprinkle the sea with our golden laughter. *What was your life like pre military? Anyone having a chance to use the beach and ocean waters during some warm summers may recall some powerful memories. Maybe you swam or surfed at night. Long walks with your mates or girl to hit the ocean.*

Out along the water where the hot, delicate sand touched the cold tips of the ocean waves, a vanguard of surfers would jostle themselves into a ready position in order to welcome some great waves. They floated easily upon their surfboards with a certain kind of rumination.

Reflection brings wistful and thoughtful thinking punctuated by some sadness. We went off to war, got married, had a baby or something that took us away from our youth and when we woke up, we lived some monstrous existence.

We forget to admit our dreams and translate a lack of feeling as a road to dying. We should be living. Many of us forget how to connect with passions that bring us connection to the universe. We become so serious and silliness is torture to some people.

I hope you take the time this year and find a passion that lets you get pleasantly lost in your daydreams, and when done then go out and do it. We live, we sometimes suffer and then we die but let us not forget the hills, the summers and the sunsets of our youth. Don't give up on trying to do things impractically and be like the young gods of our yesteryear. Sail your boat, climb your board, mount the waves and live for today.

"WE ARE THE SUM OF EVERYTHING THAT WE DO."

SPOTTER UP

Dictionary

We will never be defined by someone else's actions. We are defined by our responses to events and even then, we are more than just one decision. We are the sum of everything that we do.

We are all spirit and all thought, all feeling and all action. We must love even when others don't love us back, we must live even when others quit living, we must fight when others stop fighting, and we must be men when others choose to be animals. We are free to choose.

Buried

We will never be young again. We will never be as we were again. We will never be here at this moment again. God, life ends quickly! We came for power for privilege and even for glory, and now yesterday feels like a hundred years ago.

We fled home to gain more life, to get more knowledge, to give more love, to get more lust, to be lost and to be forsaken, to be found, to throw people away and also to be thrown into darkness and be abandoned. We left home on two legs and came home broken.

What sense we can make senses our wounded heart like a hound senses home, and the pulsing of the dark earth which surrounds it, and the crying of the ancient pines where we buried it alive for safekeeping in the hollows. We were incapable of knowing what we could do because we were ignorant in knowing what we couldn't do, we were overconfident, over-weaned, we overpromised and we were foolish enough to believe we had no part in the lives we crushed under our path.

Perhaps we paused when we were injured, certainly we may have cried deeply but what registered in our primordial mind was but a flicker, before we returned again to injure and self-injury. Past the towering hills and the deep falls, and the buzzing sound of death that covered the ancient fields where we found boyhood, and joy and streams of fish was our cache of emotion. We buried it like cowards do. We buried it like fearful men, and until we faced the terror of coming home to dig up the buried thing that crackled with energy, we would never know true love. One day we would have to learn how to handle our heart. We would have to learn how to carry this pulsing, throbbing thing if we were going to make an authentic difference in this world.

Only the dead know what we know. If we uncover it and carry it everywhere, we go we will finally learn what it is to have true hunger, true heartache, true connection, true passion, true darkness, true humility true happiness, true hatred among other feelings. In the end we will know what it feels like to be truly alive and finally what it feels like to be a man.

Robot

We're going to need some new tools in our tool box. Our smashing machine takes up too much space and it needs to be overhauled anyhow. It's antiquated. The desire to kill a man never leaves us but holding that feeling in the front of our lobe 24-7 isn't going to build many friendships and it isn't going to work in most neighborhoods.

Modernize. Learn to read the signals precisely. Be aware of a severe software issue, causing your system to freeze, reboot, or stop functioning altogether. Repair that power box in your chest controlling the supply of energy in your heart.

Smashing Machine

"It's amazing how much emotion a little mental concept like 'my' can generate."–Eckhart Tolle

I still recall the evening I walked into a bar with my best friend in order to have a celebratory drink. We hadn't seen each other in a while and wanted to catch up on the latest events in each other's lives. We entered a pub in a college town and began to chat. Other than the four men perched on their stools near the bar, the place was empty, and so we eventually took the table nearest the window to catch a view until our friends arrived. Eager to talk to my buddy I picked up a stool and quickly began positioning it closer to my bar table. It was in that moment a large man told me I'd taken his barstool. Without looking around the place and at the 60 odd, empty seats I immediately knew I was dealing with a knucklehead.

I told him the stool was mine whereupon he said it was his. He outsized me by a good foot and by 50 lbs. His head was like a bucket his arms like tree logs. I had no time for this. He stepped into my personal space. I watched his hands, looked into his eyes and informed him I was claiming the stool. Crackerjack games for little kids. The stupid stuff we have to play to let the world know we're not a wimp.

Beams of fear and hatred emanated from his eyes but in my stoic moment he blinked. Little did he know I would have glassed him badly with the pint of beer I'd have to ruin in order to make my point known. Zero to 60 in no time. No need to go there.

Every situation is different; every man, every bar, every city, every story, and every single ache and pain inside someone's heart from here to Timbuktu. But the outcome is the same based on the tools we use. He had his reasons for walking away from battle and I had mine. With one hand I moved his stool towards the window and left the interlude. Whether it was a close call for either of us I'll never know.

I'm not sure what he thought of our weird psychic exchange but at that moment I didn't care. I was with my best mate and no amount of pressure or attempt to disrespect me would diffuse my focus to spend time with my friend. I'm no battle-hardened Marine, no kung-fu ninja, or military-jedi vet. Just a man. But I've had enough time among men and bars to understand the visual cues, the games, and the cock-of the walk attitude that comes with hipsters, college kids, and drunken thugs without a purpose. Navigate around the shipwrecks of boys decked out as men; frigates moving around battleships.

I've heard it said that anger is a secondary emotion and that fear is the primary motivator for why men feel disjointed in life. They feel inadequate, or too over-confident; unworthy, unloved, lonely, drunk or just plain dispassionate about the world and what it has to offer.

Pain, blame, loss, injustice, shame, whatever the reason, they want to make the night theirs to own, and they want to control what is seemingly uncontrollable-the free will of other men.

I didn't know what this pub crawler's private issues were but I know enough that in order to make a difference in this world we need to open our toolbox and fix the things that are wrong.

Some men are not equipped for that. All they have is a hammer to repair the things that are broken; smash this, smash that, obliterate every precious thing in their life and then some. Beat on the wife, beat on the kids, beat on a war drum and blame the world.

Smashing machines run amok. 53 years into my life I now believe we're obligated to make things right by restoring the crap that we broke. Before we smashed it into crap with our smashing machine it used to be 'something'. Sometimes we smash beautiful things; hammers used to solve a problem which required a paintbrush.

What's in your toolbox? All of us, whether we're a police officer, veteran or good ol' citizen of the world inevitably is going to face one of two things in this life; humility or humiliation. Humility is a free choice and humiliation is thrust upon us when we don't choose the first option.

Pride has always told me that I had to win the argument. Smash this, smash that, and sometimes get myself smashed badly in the process. Whether we weren't given the right tools for our toolbox is a matter of debate. Some men, even with a lot of martial ability, cannot walk away from a fight. The idea isn't to always engage although sometimes it might be right to do so. My question to myself today is: "Today did I make things right?" Hindsight is 20/20. I can look back and understand that night became a pivotal moment for me. I was able to emotionally disengage from the situation.

In childhood I was handed a hammer for my toolbox and that's all I used most of my life; I had the same battered box and used the same instrument that most men use. Today I realize that I've changed and become more of a man. Not every insult in my life has to lead to a fight. Not every situation has to be taken as an insult.

Being deployed, being, divorced, being unable to pay bills, missing a promotion or losing a home or a friend. All of these things can make us bitter. But what are we doing to make things better?

Take what you want from my story. This story might not be yours. I'll tell you that managing your anger is a key step towards making every single relationship in your life right. Until you learn how to manage your anger, and break your aggression cycle, all you will ever be is a puppet to that emotion. I choose not to be a slave. My anger control plan includes a lot more than using my simple smashing machine. How about you.

Kill your worst self

What are you searching for? Why did you lose it? Did you give it away? Why are you looking for it now? Was it a friendship, a marriage, a dream opportunity? Was it a scholarship, a car, a home, your freedom? What was it?

As we age and if we've been injured some of us want nothing more than to seek out a place where we can hide and emotionally die. We shut down. What are you searching for? Are you hunting for the purest thing that you lost or the precious thing you gave away? Are you tracking your past life, and the man that you used to be?

Hunt out your old self, search deeply into your heart and find the wild animal that once roamed the whole wide world freely. Never stop searching for your noblest self. Kill the worst part of yourself. Kill it and don't look back.

When we are young like a fawn the world is new to us and it is full of beautiful strangeness. When we get older, we trek through it as if we have a place in it and everything in it is ours. As we age and if we've been injured some of us want nothing more than to seek out a place where we can hide and die. What are you searching for? Are you hunting for the purest thing that you lost? Are you tracking your past life, and the man you used to be? Hunt out your old self, search deeply into your heart and find the wild animal that once roamed the whole wide world freely. Never stop searching for your noblest self.

White stag runs o'er the silent slain

Black hearted hunter yearns to live his life again

Bloody tracks break o'er the open plain

Red hearted prize for what was lost and gained

Sunset crosses and a Hellhound's pain

Cup runneth o'er for a deadman's reign

Blue tears trumpet what was lost,

what was lost,

what was lost,

what was lost...

Casca, dead man walking

What angels speak in darkness, what devils know your name, what God knows your madness, what men know your pain? What mazes have you travelled, what lost tongues haven't you found, what loves did you leave behind you, will you ever face what you have done? Will the earth endure forever, will hope come back again, are you doomed to wait for healing, will you ever be the same old man?

Live to carry back stones

We're told that thousands of years ago the old kings followed a bright star in order to find a young king gifted with the power to absorb the world's pain. The child grown into a man uttered caution to a mob, "Let him who is without sin among you be the first to cast a stone at her." Today in the Middle-East youth throw stones as a matter of protest or a way to cause damage or pain, causing death too is even an option. Sisyphus of Greek myth was punished to push a large one for eternity up a hill, and we are cautioned that we should never throw them at "glass houses" if we are vulnerable to criticism. But stones too can be used for building and decorative purposes, industrial and worship purposes too.

The ancients tried to pile it up to reach the heavens as Babel and were punished for it, others created a large one to hold small pictures in what we know as the Rosetta Stone. Isn't it fascinating that a meteor so rarely found upon this earth, is seemingly priceless?

What we call a stone from a shooting star is simply, common space debris. In this time where social media is so ubiquitous so many foolish people have a mouthpiece to pop off their ignorant opinions. Let them.

People are attacked for being too fat, too rich, too intense, too contrived, whatever it is let them pop off. We live at a time where stones will be thrown at us. What we need to do is see that every single stone thrown at us is an opportunity for us to get stronger. Let men criticize all they want, whether they sit behind a keyboard or stand in front of you it is an opportunity to master self-control, patience, compassion, and spiritual growth. Know the stones value.

I'm not an advocate for pacifism but I do not believe that every attack should be met with a fist. Much of what is thrown at us is simply a pebble to me. Grow by realizing that when you offer men the ability to crush you, that you can only get stronger. Let them be what they're going to be, while you grow as tough as the stones tossed at you. Live not just to have the world throw stones at you but live to carry them back.

We

We've aged and the world has not remained the same. We'll pass and take with it our pain and perhaps leave the world a better place. We lived; we've loved. We fought, we lost, we carried others and we were carried even as we fought to stand. We dreamed, we cried, we reveled, we hoped, we lied to hide the truth about how much we hurt. We laughed and we won, sometimes we even gave up hoping yet we pulled through. We experienced much. We pass the torch now to others and hope our deeds will leave men in this hard world all the better for it.

Every man can be reborn

What have you lost? Have you lost a job, a home, a friend or a limb? Have you lost a marriage or a brother or a father or your spirit to live? Have you lost your goals, your purpose, your self-respect? Have you lost your way? We sometimes feel broken like we are a blade of broken steel or a heap of broken stone; once useful, once powerful, once durable and able to withstand any blow and we felt that way until everything fell apart.

Everything can become whole again. Every sword can be reforged, every wall can be remade, every man can be reborn. We who have been hurled back, and back, and back again must propel ourselves forward by any method we can.

Rise up from darkened exile. Falter, halt yet take heart. Hope is not a place over there, but inside of you. Clamber upon the highest ramparts of this earth and recall the things we've heard and seen: the view of mist over a forest lake, the sound upon sea harbors when ocean waves break, fireflies rising in hot summer night, the giddy thrush's song at first light.

The trembling breath of lovers, the shouts of men at war, the glory of the stars, thunderous waterfall upon rock and the brilliance of making your first silver dollar. Red eyed sunset over soaring hills, the sunken depths you plumbed and the unplowed fallows you've run and the sterile fact after fact after fact that illuminates how you have life....

EVERY SWORD CAN BE **REFORGED**
EVERY WALL CAN BE **REMADE**
EVERY MAN CAN BE **REBORN**

Let the memoires of old ghosts die. Our spirit poor but we are free to choose the pattern of our life and the paths of this vast earth and every towering summit we'll climb. Godspeed to you Spotterup reader.

Sad song

What is your private song? The song you hear in loneliness, and sorrow, the song that breaks you down in the darkness, injured and illuminates your mortality and the mutilation of your soul. It is the song you listen to and see your life before you.

The heart retreats and it must retreat because there is no survival outside of your solitary confinement and the mouth like a beak cries out its horrific warble and the eyes strike out in their blind hunting for paltry worms of understanding. Mountains of memories fall into a sea of hurt greater and deeper than the mind can conceive.

The damnable darkness cannot be measured, but eternal light is unmeasurable too. Your song when finished stops you from being a stranger to yourself, and in your nested human frailty grows power.

You are a man of the human race and beyond the dark branches of night hiding the eternal movement of the stars comes the feint beginning of a different song. Fly to it. All of us have some kind of private song, something that connects with us, makes us sad or whatever. Drinking songs, songs that stir old memories. I find peace after my secret song has played and my secret grief ends. There is hope. So, do something with your sorrow.

Seeker and the beacon

What we learn as children we can unlearn as adults. Even in darkness we must believe there is light. We can unlearn certain things, perhaps we can't unlearn it all, but we can reprogram our mind and in turn reengineer our spirit. I believe that and I know it because I've lived it. There is a light out there that should never go out and it's a light inside ourselves that points the way for others. That's not cliché to me.

We've all got scars from where we've been and depending on how deep we shouldn't be afraid of a thing. Each is a badge of honor for what you have survived, and each tells your story of warfare in this world. Don't let the light ever go out, in your world or someone else's, be the hunter of good things and the beacon to the weak. Share the fire. If not us than who? You live what, 50-60-70 years, have something to show for it... a legacy. What else are we here for then?

Enjoy this point in time

What would we see if we could map out the orbit of our life? What data points could we gather, what coordinates did our journey lay down for us? If we could journal all the sets of numbers, we find would we be able to mark down the deathless mountains we covered, the endless waters we swam, or the immortal trees we passed? Could we ever ascertain how many inextinguishable sunsets we saw? And darkness? How much darkness have we seen?

With the way memory works we can't easily recall the number of things we experienced but it's likely we know there is some value in life, and there is great value in who we are, and likely too there is wonderful value in others despite the evil that exists in this world. We cannot count the heroes and monsters that have passed over the thousands of years. Nor can we count all the battles men have fought but we know a million men have died over the centuries in places as close as where we stand, and as far as where our eyes hit the horizon.

Sometimes we don't have to count the number of times we succeeded or failed to know that we could have done better. Sometimes we just know we are too hard or soft on ourselves. We can answer it soberly, sterilely but counting and marking can cause us to collate myopically. Sometimes it is difficult to get out of the structure of our life, where we envision it as fixed and finite, rather we should enjoy the moment as precious yet as immortal too. Simply enjoy the feeling that what is done is done and there is no need to count what transpired back there.

Enjoy your health and time, your friends and the events that come, the tasty skies and the fat hills that rise over the skinny horizon and worry little about the GPS of your life. Right now, enjoy this point in time.

A good man

When a good man dies there is no way to measure the deep well of tears that were meant for his eyes, nor the pockets of dreams that were his and unrealized.

His worth is far more than the pints of blood that once flowed in his heart, or the pounds of flesh that burned down to carbon and turned into dust. We must make sense of life, we must, we must, we must...

Lost causes

When a great nation grants an insidious culture power to remove what it chooses to condemn the death of a great civilization often begins.

Any worthy movement to change the world for good is never based on ignorance nor enacted with malevolence; be wary of evil shrewdly masquerading as a noble cause.

Righteousness is the quality of being morally right or justifiable and judgement is based first on the premise that we are all created in the image of a benevolent God. Any noble rebellion will not require other men to literally die for its own principles, for each man in reaching this same sensible conclusion is willing to stand without being shamed or forced and will do this alone if he must.

Compromise yourself

When a man becomes too much like a woman, he makes his role as a man unnecessary. Man isn't ennobled by reducing his essence to some point near extinction in order to please a woman because he dislikes the worst of himself or to make her feel safer. Nor should he become so exaggerated in his persona as to become a cartoon character, a counterfeit because that's just a form of armor. A man must respect his being in order to let his real essence grow. Don't be indifferent to what you were created for or attempt to escape the pressure, the responsibilities you have by futilely attempting to shift your nature.

Brother, I love you

When we die, and follow the hounds into the hollows, and the great spirit into the glen, where Mead flows and delivers a river of happiness to all who drink of it know that I wish you well. I call you brother. We will go to a place far from this madness, the confusion, the pain and despair to storm the ramparts once again but not here, not here. The world too small for us, for you. Henceforth speak of the past no more and rush forth to the ships at sea and let us leave this land to hurry home. Forever deathless, forever faithful, forever friends, forever free.

Where do good men go when they die?

Where do good men go when they die? They go to some far away shore, to some distant, gray land that we don't know. To God they go. To some strange lodge on a hill, with shining lights, and an open door to sit with other men around a banquet hall we all suppose. Arms go around them, and welcome our heroes in, and laughter flows. The dead leave us with our sorrows, and they continue on to another life unencumbered by their pain. The crippled can walk, the legless can run, and those with a broken heart can feel love again. Our pain is our own, our sorrow is our own…we are alone.

We cannot describe to others the way we feel. There is no definable hurting to share, no hint of what aches the heart, or anything that we can relate to others on exactly what it is we feel. These moments, when they come, dig into us and we feel a savage loneliness. Any subtle thrill we have for living is burdened by the presence of death.

But life is not over. If we can get out of our heavy funk, if we navigate outside these roads of war within our own heart, we will grow. Long after the sad, blue odor of pain is gone, the scent changes to the sweet smell of hopefulness. How do we get out of this? By focusing on our friends who are alive in the here and now. By remembering what our dead lovers, friends and family meant to us. By carrying on in old traditions we used to have with them. By celebrating with others some of the silly, inane crap they used to do, by sharing with others how freaking hilarious or brave they were. Remembering the good times brings back good feelings. I'm no expert on healing. This is my own opinion.

Shallop

Where men ultimately and intimately suffer is in lacking the courage to honestly pursue the path to the gift they know is waiting for them because in truth they know the measure of their fragility. They must stop circling those same flat waters and instead find stronger currents and rougher seas to test the strength of their craft.

Who fights for you?

Who is your advocate? Who fights for you? There's this idea that we have to do our own fighting all of the time but that's not always true. Sometimes we have to have someone in our corner. Growing up I still recall the silly wrestling shows where two wrestlers are tagging each other in and out of the ring in order to switch upon opponents when one teammate got tired.

Having someone in your corner fighting for you, rooting for you, and with the idea of even dying for you is a beautiful and confidence building thing. When I was a boy growing up my brother beat everyone in the neighborhood even through high school. We were not allowed to back down. If my mother found out that we'd been in a fight and jumped by kids she would drive us around the neighborhood and we'd have to find the kid or kids and refight. That's unheard of today and maybe crazy but my mother was simply telling us "No one is going to push my kids around."

As embarrassing and as scary as it was it was a lesson in how to stand up for ourselves. My brother was a smashing machine and woe be it to the guy who threw rocks at my sister. We continued to think like this and continue to do so into adulthood. We must defend ourselves and if given the chance we must defend others. You have worth, you have value and you might be fighting a lot of your own battles but I have to ask, "who is fighting for you?" You need a cut man, or a coach or a water boy. You need someone who will stand for you, help you, when your spirit is flagging against the booze, or drugs, or divorce or something. Find that person and fight for them when given the chance and let them fight for you.

Nightclub

With them music seemed richer, our life seemed stronger, and love seemed in endless supply but things changed so quickly. I think we've all been here before where we're in a club full of strangers, and the one that we love sees us, but doesn't want to be with us.

In the dark our eyes follow them, and as they leave with another lover, we follow them even as the feeling of hope bleeds from us. This was a trusted lover that deeply deceived us and as our heart crumbles it's revealed to us under a dim light this is the way it's meant to be. Everyone should be loved but not all of us are loved, and after an experience that painful we feel that we are not equipped to take love nor to give love. Every human being wants to be loved, give love and to feel

like they belong to something important. Don't put your sense of worth in another person like that, particularly someone who cannot honor you. That's not where your true value should come from. Beyond the culture that tells you what you should feel, or think, or to be, or an opinion from a lover that no longer has feelings for you is a God that believes in you.

Start counting on this instead. This is the beginning of believing that you are going to be okay... This is the start of not feeling hopeless, damaged or worthless...We dream under the same stars, we gaze upon the same shores, we are warmed by the same sun, we were birthed from the same dust and to dust we will return. You will be okay.

Mere words

Words have the power to move us into cold silences and into feelings of immeasurable delight. Words in some way can more easily describe and define how we are hurting. Words allow us to feel nourished or make us feel like dying. Words can make us feel anger.

Words can comfort in times of loneliness and can make us feel cynical. Why not create words that remind us to remain youthful in how we see the world and to feel that every moment is ripe for opportunity? Why not write words that reassure others to not lose heart, why not write words to inspire? Why not leave behind words that give comfort to those after we are gone? Words to give courage to soldiers, officers, fire-fighters when things are tough, words to give direction, and for leaving peace in the heart of loved-ones. Who would you leave them for? The men of your unit, your mother, your sons and daughters? Those who are often engrossed in the hustle and bustle of city life often don't give themselves the chance to stop and reflect on the importance of life. Those who are able to rise with the sun and get a morning run in get a chance to do this very thing. Those who reflect as the dawn rises, who become introspective as the night comes may have a longing for doing purposeful things. Like Chief Tecumseh they reflect on the things that are notable. If you get a chance how about writing a letter to your family? You might not be a patrolman, a Marine, a Soldier, or a fire-fighter but don't let hardships stop you from writing something that tells your children the theme of your life and how they should live theirs. Don't let that stop you from telling your children and their children words to live by. You may not have a second chance. Perhaps write something simple that they will remember you by: *Son, be patient, be strong, encourage others, don't ever buck your commitments, live your life and not the life of others, give more than you take, stand up for what you believe in, love more than you are loved, stay humble and honor God.* It takes a moment to tune out the noise and tune into the things that are important.

Violence begets

Years and years ago in Oakland, California our mother was beaten and robbed of her money by a group of despicable men. One of them happened to punch her to the ground and to this day she still has a visible scar put by his hard ring upon her gentle forehead.

It split the skin open. I still recall my older brother looking at me, after the police left the house, he with a telling glance that signaled we should get into the car and kill all of them. This isn't a confessional; no men were found and so no men were killed but it puts to the test how far are you willing to go beyond the limits of the law, and beyond the morals put upon yourself when someone hurts a person that you love? Can a sane and loving man become a vengeance-filled irrational being? In a heartbeat brother, in a heartbeat.

Signs

You don't know when they will come but, in your dreams, they will come, and with them come their distant signs. They bring secrets. Can you move closer to them? Can you feel their light? Can you see their light? Don't shrink from the task at hand, don't shrink back into the darkness, can you hear the sirens call?

Run towards the hills and the fire rising hotly in the sky, and those voices calling for you. They want you to do great things. A hundred men sniveled and folded but that will never be you.

The fire rises in the cold night an odd, flame in the distance and the light of greatness wants to come into you. Stand up, stand still, don't buckle onto your knees man. Here come legends. Can you feel the light growing inside of you?"

10,000 little Indians

"Son, be strong. You will lose many friends, and many elders that you respect. The young ones will go. Perhaps even those soldiers you hate. "Things fall apart, the center will not hold." Such things are inevitable. We all shall die inevitably. Up until then we can agree that at least we shall try to make our lives worthwhile and our deaths meaningful. It is tragic when our efforts are stopped in mid-stride. If there ever was a person that I met that has tried to make his life meaningful, it is you. As long as you can continue to provide consolation and guidance for the others, you will not have failed and have none to worry about to your lack of influence upon the course of their lives. Albeit there are no "good deaths", at least you can justify that you've encouraged resolve, compunction, and awareness in your peers.

That's a life better led, a loss better embraced, a death better welcomed. That is where your mind is to be at; to enable courage, to drag forth the reluctant but powerful, to call others to action, and to be exemplary in your own conduct the sake of others. A bright voice in the din of war – figurative or otherwise – will be heard. Weep if you must. There is no shame in that... I love you. Dad."

Nightstalker Pt. 1

I saw bleating sheep and a dying asp

Where the wind pressed its will upon solemn grass

I watched nightfall come and saw you pass

Delirious Shepherd with your perfect mask

I heard a golden song from the throat of God

A gentle tone yet so very odd

I wept in silence, enraptured, awed

A gravedigger dug and a carpenter sawed

Is there anything worth dying for?

Whether in time of peace or time of war?

My salvation stolen by the Babylon whore

My trembling hands touched the derelict door.

Movies, Literature and more

Blindness

A lot of men suffer from what I term mental and emotional snow blindness; chasing so much after what is good brings about what is bad, and they can no longer see opportunity. The late actor Richard Burton stated that he drank for solace "to burn up the flatness, the stale, empty, dull deadness that one feels when one goes offstage".

There are a lot of men who don't know how to get out of that line of thinking. The stage brings a lot of attention to men that crave emotion that feels electrical; needy actors, comedians, and musicians, who grow in their careers while chasing some kind of higher-high through drinking and drugs and whatever else satisfies them until they are numb and in need of repair. Then after comes the feeling of psychological dislocation and alienation.

I'm reminded of something war correspondent Sebastian Junger said about soldiers, "They didn't want to go back because it was traumatic, but because it was a place where they understood what they were supposed to do. They understood who they were. They had a sense of purpose. They were necessary. All these things that young people strive for are answered in combat.

Veterans often see their wartime experience as the most selfless and meaningful period of their lives. Some veterans have expressed the sentiment that "even in the quiet moments, war is brighter, louder, brasher, more fun, more tragic, more wasteful. More. More of everything."

I am reminded of C. Wilson's book The Outsider where he wrote about peak experiences, those moments when life makes sense because there are feelings of euphoria, a loss of judgment to time and space, and feelings of being fully functioning. Man feels that he can accomplish anything as he lives without inhibition, fear, doubt or inner-criticism. Men like Hemingway, Lawrence, Dostoyevsky, to me were examples of the alienated soul who experienced peak moments but chasing after them never seems to work. Abraham Maslow didn't think it possible to induce it and I agree. Self-actualization doesn't come out of chasing the highest peak of the pyramid first, rather it is putting that last and honestly doing the basics. Obtain the mundane, universal needs and the rest follows. Your eyes will open to great possibilities.

Where is the war?

A story is told about a young soldier in World War I in a trench with his Sergeant. Mortars rained down death. Giant stars shells burst into the night sky. The two huddled in one another's arms and the young soldier said to his leader, "Sergeant, I just s— my pants!" The Sergeant replied back in fear, "So did I. So, did I! Welcome to the war!"

Whether true or not we still turn up our noses up at the French but we can't deny the conviction Alan Seeger had to live life fully and find death on his terms and on his terms alone. Seeger was one of the first Americans in the early part of the last century to chase a war. I first discovered his poem in a book I read on WW I and then I was reminded of it after seeing the movie The Lost Battalion, starring Hollywood actor Ricky Schroeder, with some of my close friends. It was a decent movie. WW I was a war where so many poets, philosophers, writers, educators and learned-men perished. It was also a war where bi-planes, submarines and tanks were used for the first time. For any young man it was a time of wonder but a time of horror too. Television was waiting to be created. Many homes existed without electricity and most readers read literature at night by candle-light. This was a time of dreaming for many young men. By the thousands they caught a fever for battle and ran off to war but instead discovered terror to takes its place. Despite the costs to the body have young men today stopped dreaming, do they fear too much and because of this are they disconnect from real passion? Too many questions to ask; XBOX, Snapchat, narcissism, self-centeredness, sometimes I wonder if youthful defiance, curiosity, and bravery have been watered down in our youth of today, or am I mistaken? Where is the courage and brilliance of old?

Do Not Lose Your Long Vision

An often-mentioned story, if I remember correctly, is a challenger to Columbus mentioned that his accomplishment wasn't such a big thing.

Columbus bemusedly said to the gathered crowd, "try to make an egg stand upright." Challenger after challenger failed. Columbus cracked the end of a hardboiled egg and made it stand upright. Those who failed shouted, "Anyone could have done that!" to which Columbus replied, "but I was the first."

It took 33 years for Jeff Bodenweiser's combat exploits to be publicized and for him to be awarded one of our nation's highest military honors. Jeff finally was awarded a Silver Star for his heroism in Vietnam, where he served as a Marine officer. Bodenweiser led a bayonet attack and armed only with his .45-caliber M1911 pistol. Use your brains, be patient, be strong, have confidence and know your worth. Your time will come either soon or in the hereafter!

Forgive Yourself

Another movie that really moved me was The Mission with actor Robert DeNiro. It is a wonderful and powerful movie that covers so many concepts: forgiveness, faith, violence, God, slavery, self-hatred, love, brotherhood, politics and more. DeNiro's character Mendoza is a ruthless slave trader who waits for death as he rots in prison. He murdered his brother for sleeping with his lover.

While he wallows in self-pity, he is visited by Father Gabriel, played by the excellent Jeremy Irons, and offers him the challenge of penance but is Mendoza really brave enough to accept?

Mendoza claims "For me there is no redemption,"

Gabriel states: "God gave us the burden of freedom. You chose your crime. Do you have the courage to choose your penance?"

Mendoza: "There is no penance hard enough for me!"

Gabriel: "But do you dare try it?"

Mendoza: "Do I dare? Do you dare to see it fail?"

Gabriel presses Mendoza to accept the challenge. The scene of Mendoza trying to climb up a mountain with a large sack filled with his armor, swords and other weapons is simply an incredible movie scene. Gabriel watches as Mendoza struggles to pull the weight up the cliff while his baggage pulls him down. He is carrying the burden of his life and the weapons that caused pain to others.

When the sack gets caught on a bush one of the Jesuit priests hacks it off and lets it fall. Mendoza scrambles down, gathers the sack, reties it and continues up the cliff. It is incredible to watch his struggle.

I don't want to ruin it for you if you haven't seen the entire movie. This journey is about an affliction many of us have. He must forgive himself for his crimes of violence, for killing his own blood brother, for enslaving others, and he must eventually accept forgiveness. He must forgive himself and he must accept forgiveness from the people he enslaved. In the end he must return to communion with his brothers and sisters of this world and love his neighbors as he learns to love himself. Is this possible for you?

Love her

As songs go, I don't think there's anything more sublime than listening to Herb Alpert's song, This Guy's in Love with You with her in the dark. Playing that song makes the world feel pretty perfect and if a man wants to tell his girl that holding hands is enough well this is the tune that will bring them together in a moment of sacredness and trust.

We get so far away from feeling the essence of preciousness because industry today promotes what is slick and quick and what makes a buck, and finding a tune that forms words when we don't know what to say to her, well this song is simply enough.

It starts slow and rises to a perfect end, just as a night with her should. In romance we need to create private ceremonies and hold ourselves up to a certain dignity and be surprised simply by being alive and let that carry over into simply being in love. Why is it so hard to do something as simple as that?

For a man so used to rough clashes and hard engagements with bad guys in a tough world that simply doesn't care this song has a calming peacefulness and refinement that lifts the soul. Find a song for her that conveys how you feel, that takes you away from what's ill with it all, find a song that says, "I don't want anything from you. You simply need to be loved." Play that song and enjoy her beauty. Love will alight your souls.

Bring it out to the cold light of day.

There are a lot of great movies about hardnosed detectives and hardened warriors about to enter dead zones where evil hatches it eggs. Our heroes penetrating eyes gaze steadily ahead before they open a door or enter a cave. We hesitate along with them as they halt before dealing death to their foes. Perhaps some twisted death awaits them.

Well directed movies fill you with a sense of dread, sadness anger etc. Dante's Inferno is the first part of Italian writer Dante Alighieri's journey through hell and he is guided by the ancient Roman poet Virgil. They travel deeper and deeper into its Hell's maw. As we travel through life, we experience what we feel is our own personal hells.

My own friends have told me about the difficulty of working cases on sex trafficking, child snuff, homicides etc. All of it is difficult, unpalatable stuff. Evil exists in this world and many police officers and military are the bulwark or gatekeepers to hell. Not only do they stand fast to keep evil at bay but they enter the gates to prevent it from escaping and seeping into our own world.

What about decompression? What about dealing with the weightiness of pain when you depart its clutches? Abuse, gunfights, PTSD, death...We are not just sterile observers like Dante. Imagine traveling down caverns of Hell's planes and the deeper you go the harder it is because an insidious weight becomes heavier. Depression, sadness, rage, jealousy...train yourself to understand what you are experiencing, reduce the baggage that weighs you down, teach yourself coping skills to handle what comes ahead, conserve your energy until you deal with the Big Boss, reframe and refocus and find quicker, alternate pathways.

Deal with this garbage before it eats you alive. In the Dark Ages we are told they hid evil away and spoke little of it, during The Enlightenment new philosophies and ideas developed and people discussed darkness. They brought that nastiness into the cold light of day and so should you. Deal with it before it deals with you.

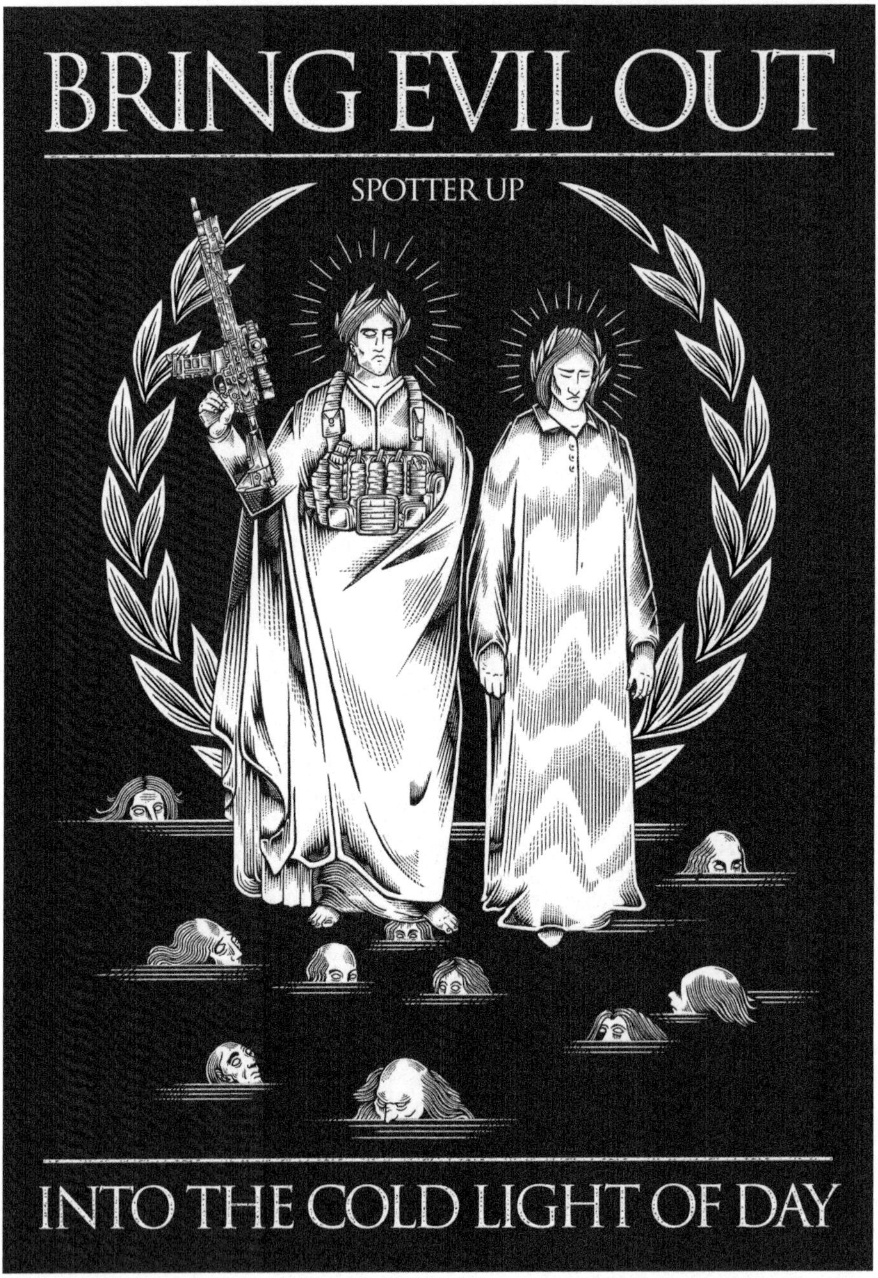
BRING EVIL OUT
SPOTTER UP
INTO THE COLD LIGHT OF DAY

Ars Longa, Vita Brevis

Brother, ring in the hours with action for life is fleeting so ensure that you live it well. Tell yourself that you are alive. Ars longa, vita brevis. London is now ashes. Who really puts those lines down, anyway? Who inspires them but the living? Do something with your life! Do not rest with the energy that God gave you.

When I see Degas, I see Absinthe and dancers; I see the delicacy of living, the feminine, the common, and I see an 'individuals' work in progress... I could go on (and should to clarify, but I won't). And this is great and everything -- creating the art, living the depiction of his subjects -- but the burning. Where is the burning? It has gone with the action. I long for what you do because the embers still burn within you. You have a fire. Keep that fire.

Drink? No, if I am serious with myself, and with you in this letter, I know a drink would not do. This is not the time for celebration but for work. It is the suffering I long for. The world is filled with beautiful girls and guys and its particular social strata. Big cities are a hub for individualism, consumerism, worthy pursuits for sure, but mostly half measures...This is the most Spartan time of my life. I have food. I can pay the bills somewhat but I can live honestly. Why worry?

Indeed. But the feeling comes alive only as I realize the single purpose of living for me is to move towards God's glory. Anything apart from moving in that direction absolutely argus-eyed is destructive and silly anyway it's looked at.

ARS LONGA VITA BREVIS

TELL YOURSELF THAT YOU ARE ALIVE.

Life is tough but life is good because I feel pain and this is the way to go. Feel the pain. Move with life and vigor until your feet stop moving and cold possesses your body, and the lights exit your eyes. Hold onto the exhale for as long as you can. Far as I can tell this is the path. I know how you are doing, and there you go, now you know how I am. Take care old friend. My thoughts are with you and my prayers go out. Let your spirit be alive. ~MM.

We Need Pain

David B Morris' book The Culture of Pain is a fascinating read. Philosophic questions such as, "is pain a mountain we can ever conquer?" is asked by Morris. Is mental pain and physical pain separate or from the same source? He seems to posit that working-class Joes, poorer classes made up of stoic Italians or Hispanics, for example, are more accepting of pain because it is a way of life when they get injured whereas more refined types are less immune to it seems. Military cultures for sure endure because of conditioning where nonmilitary cultures cannot; adaptation through training. There's a story about a man named Gibson who is part of a 1920's vaudeville act. He is able to shove nails deeply into his flesh down to their metal heads without wincing. When he was a boy, he was hit in the head with a hatchet, yet felt nothing; he went home to show his father. His Christ centered crucifixion act where he drove irons through his palms made a woman faint dead and so he retired. His boredom had him amusing friends with his carnival antics but a life without pain left him a life he felt was a dead end.

Painlessness isn't a gift, but a curse. We know that we need pain impulses to tell us when to shift and move, to not pick up a hot skillet or to put down a burning log. Science tells us children without pain impulses do not fare well. We all have the challenges of pain but what we choose to do with it will define who we are and can be. Some people, writers in particular, dig deep into it. I haven't mentioned here what soldiers are capable of. Those who embrace pain can paradoxically feel liberated rather than enslaved. What say you?

Good evening Mr. And Mrs. America

Decades ago, radio hosts brought people together simply by speaking into a microphone. Families gathered round communal areas and listened. The late journalist Walter Winchell used to greet America every night by radio, and though his career waned, at one time millions of people tuned in. He stated, "Good evening Mr. And Mrs. America, from border to border and coast to coast and all the ships at sea."

American DJ Casey Kassem ran American Top 40 from 1970 until 2009. Listeners could tune into the radio and dedicate a famous top 40 song to someone far away. Maybe it was an old love in Birmingham, Alabama or maybe a brother once seen in Michigan who hadn't been seen in decades. The airwaves united millions of people from different walks of life like never before. So much has changed. We are fragmented now more so than before because of our common access to technology and like some odd diaspora we are carried away by our iPhones willfully into our solitudes.

Preprograming and recording removes most surprise and anticipation. An impatient or time-deprived generation doesn't look forward to fire side chats, gatherings round the television for family shows, or tuning into live talk radio as it once did and honestly, they can't because things change, so who of us can blame people for tuning out? Radio 1 in the U.K. once held people in sway and the power it had! Selecting a playlist from Pandora has taken away the element of surprise, and recorded podcasts do the same. We hung on the note of every newly released song or an old one which opened up our hearts. Sure, there are similar platforms today to those older ones and generations from now others will likely grow misty eyed over their lost pleasures. To our small reading audience, we hope the best for you. Whether you find us on Instagram or elsewhere, we wish you well.

Tonight, should be an incredible night. Don't tune out life. Find a way to connect despite where you're at and what you're going through. Whether you're pulling a midnight patrol or getting started on the road to do a long haul, I say to you "Good night Mr. And Mrs. America, from border to border and coast to coast and all the ships at sea." Yep, that goes for everyone else out there too.

What is your purpose?

During one of the scenes in "Chariots of Fire" the character Abrahams is discussing running with his friend. Abrahams shares his thoughts on the theme of winning and losing. Abrahams tells him, "I don't know" and states, "I've never lost." Abrahams trained his entire life for the Olympic event and he goes on to state, "You know, I used to be afraid to lose. But now I'm afraid to win. I have ten seconds in which to prove the reason for my existence, and even then, I am not sure I will."

Abraham's thinking is perceptive in that he realizes his quest for personal glory is coming to a close and his passion to win might dissipate. Personal glory is only so fulfilling and those who move towards it find that emptiness soon follows triumph because it can never fulfill the appetite of the spirit.

Accolades can never deliver the fulfillment you want and glory is fleeting. Rockstars will tell you that chasing after that higher high on stage is elusive and the reasons for it are based in self-aggrandizement and narcissism. Juxtapose Abraham's way of thinking with Liddell's who states to his sister who chides him for focusing too much on the Olympic gold medal, "Jenny, God has made me for a purpose-for China. But He has also made me fast. And when I run, I feel his pleasure."

The movie speaks to us about men who asserted their own values in a time of classicism in Britain when there was prejudice against people belonging to a particular social class. Running freed them from an imposed systematic oppression of subordinated class groups but running gave them far more than that. Liddell goes on to defeat Abrahams who goes on to replay the defeat over and over in his memory.

My heroes Prefontaine, Abrahams and Liddell had their own reasons and passions for running. Running was a way for those outsiders to be the best individuals they could be. What the movie does best is capture the exhilaration of running as a celebration of the spirit. The movie imbues in us a wistful affection for the past.

Don't Ever Drop on Request

Ever see the movie, An Officer and a Gentleman, with actor Richard Gere as Aviation Officer Candidate (AOC) Zack Mayo? You remember the scene where he's hustling the other AOC School candidates by selling them shined boots and belt buckles? There's a good lesson to be learned here for anyone who wants to be a leader. Navy AOC School requires personal honor, courage and commitment. Did you catch that?

Throughout school he's been circumventing the system, lacking in humility and exploiting his mates for profit. By paying for shined boots and belt buckles he doesn't have to put in the labor and can't learn the important lessons of sacrifice and self-improvement. Good ol' Marine Corps Gunnery Sergeant Emil Foley, played by the awesome Louis Gossett Junior, puts an end to Mayo's nonsense. "I want your D.O.R." the Gunny snarls into Mayo's face. Zack Mayo won't Drop on Request and in the end learns those important lessons and gets redemption too.

The strength of the movie is in its great story and each actor's excellent acting. It's about personal growth, love, and what people should stand for. You watch the movie and over 13 weeks you get to see the characters grow. We care about Mayo, Paula, and their choices.

Many of us can relate to Mayo's broken childhood, this selfish-selfish man, and his quest to better himself. We see how Mayo and Paula play around and pretend they don't care about each other. But we're wise enough to know they need each other.

This corny yet very relatable story is about a big loser who becomes a much better man. There's some good chop-socky too after they exit the local bar. The best part is when Zack swoops in and carries Paula away.

Why does this movie resonate with us? We admire people who rise up from struggle. We realize somewhere inside that selfish, bastard of a man, is a hero struggling to get out. Be that guy. Every day, be that guy.

Love When You Can

Heard It in a Love Song is a song by The Marshall Tucker Band, written by Toy Caldwell off their 1977 album Carolina Dreams. The song speaks of a man not wanting to get too comfortable with love. The song is catchy, the lyrics simple, the message powerful.

The song speaks to the weirdness found in the human condition, in that it seems we want what we can't have and have what we don't want but it's really not that simple. The need to find purpose exists in all of us in various kinds and degrees. In the end we sometimes must meander like water. Perhaps leaving for a time is too extreme, maybe it works for couples that need their space, but all of us have some need to ebb and flow.

I've been known to look out at what I perceive as the immortal horizon from my fixed position and what I feel is the smallness of my town. At times I wonder if I'm missing out on something. Each minute, each moment, from cradle to grave we'll contemplate our value even if we've found our purpose, and vice versa.

Perhaps when we've passed, as lovers who turned to dust, truth will be revealed in an eternal world after we inhaled our final breath of peace. Perhaps this was a prison too small for our dreams or perhaps we'll find that we were really truly free. Perhaps we'll see that it was all but damned foolishness to stress so hard.

I don't have the eternal truth right now for you, my friend. But if you've a place to rest make it worthwhile before you put your boots back on and leave. Love when you have it, and seek it out when you don't. Warriors can only wander for so long, right? Flesh to flesh, heart to heart, chest to chest, feet to feet.

Love the young

Hell, I remember seventeen; awkward, reckless, energetic, filled with a goofy awe of life and an impatient wonder; wiry, strong and hungry to grasp experience with a mind that couldn't process information fast enough due to my deep and immense emotions; yet conversely so sure of my youthful purpose.

Young love, wild, pure and seemingly free; we rushed into the immortal world and fled our little cities and towns hoping to exist forever and chase heroic glory. Life was good and fruitful and blessed.

Thinking about my 21-year-old step son today after hearing the Eric Church county song, Springsteen. I'm thinking about a small boy trying to grow into a man and figuring his way in the world where the lines have been redrawn socially politically religiously and more today.

How can we prepare youth for this erratic world so they don't lose the life they have and die in some tragic lot? The beginning of their life is filled with struggles, while aged and with maturity they start to handle the hard climbing. We can't prevent them from acquiring the bitterness many of us have felt, but they must learn the lessons that every man must learn in the world, all by themselves. When do you step away and let them go? I love you so much you knuckle head.

Love your children with all of your might and support them. Teach them to grow into men and women.

I'll show you how a man dies

I believe it was the poet T.S. Eliot who wrote a critique against writers that have their protagonists die at the end of their stories. If I recall correctly (forgive me it's been 30 years) his essay was directed towards writers of tales bereft of substance. Tales like that are an easy way out for the author from creating true dramas. These dramas really shouldn't be told if a story is to have any weight. I understand his sentiment.

Poor storytelling uses death as a means of closing out the story via emotional visceral means when the writer is skint of story substance. The writers are basically covering up bad writing and using manipulation to elicit shock as a technique or the story ending is left open-ended and the reader draws his own conclusion to the meaning whereas a master storyteller crafts something that ends understandably with real poignancy.

Cheap death makes for great Hollywood movies because the character becomes Christlike in death and the heroes' sacrifice gives more time and life to others. We connect with that. Literature such as a Tale of Two Cities or a Prayer for Owen Meany are books that are done well. There are lame tear jerkers out there. You know the chick flicks you cry at with your date? Don't lie tough guy!

The original I am Legend written by Matheson and redone as the Omega Man tied the ending up well. Actor Charlton Heston has a spear pierce his side, his blood of life flows into the fountain, humanity has another chance. The Will Smith version with the death of Neville was an afterthought in my opinion; lame. In the end I'm just a dude with an Instagram page, and my opinion.

If we can consider the value of our life, if we become better men, fathers, husbands, brothers, soldiers because we watched Maximus die at the end of Gladiator, well then, I'm all for it. Sign me up for two showings please. "Are you not entertained!"

I recall a story of an Italian contractor kidnapped in Iraq and executed by scum. His final words were, "I'll show you how an Italian dies!" Powerful, powerful, powerful.

He closed the story of his life in such a manner that all of us must give him applause. Bravo! Bravo! This was not a book or a movie but real life. And you, how will your story end?

Where are the men of valor?

I had a conversation with my brother about raising his young son to be a man of valor. It begins when children are quite young and impressionable. We continue to stoke their embers until they can carry the fire by themselves. It's necessary that they learn to be their own men and not so sensitive as to give into the pressure of wrong-headed peers who choose to make others victims. Children sometimes give up on playing games, and adoring stories about Gilgamesh, or Beowulf, or Roland once they're around a pack of boys with a cruel wit, a mean punch, and a weak spine. Perhaps they reacquire that love when they go into the service or maybe not, we can hope. The classics, history, poetry; get them excited about becoming men who are not afraid to stand up for what they believe in regardless of the mentality of the pack when the pack are damned fools. The tactical world is full of cartoon characters.

I'm reminded by G.B. Shaw's quote "And all the while there goes a horrible, senseless, mischievous laughter. When you're young you exchange drinks with other men and you exchange vile stories with them; and as you're too futile to be able to help or cheer them, you chaff and sneer and taunt them for not doing the things you daren't do yourself. And all the time you laugh! Laugh! Laugh! Eternal derision, eternal envy, eternal folly, eternal fouling and staining and degrading, until, when you come at last to a country where men take a question seriously and give a serious answer to it, you deride them for having no sense of humor, and plume yourself on your own worthlessness as if it made you better than them."

I think how men like Joyce, Wilde, Beckett, knew the rich history and stories of their own people despite their own shortcomings. Home never leaves you, nor does your original loves. A man needs to know who he is by knowing where he came from, so he has a sense of where he is going. I hope whatever thing you once possessed, that gave you a thrill that made you feel heroic, that you'll take them up again. Look up your old heroes and become men of valor again. Now live it.

I grok you

I look at a lot of old pictures of soldiers taken 30, 40, 50 years ago and I wonder what was going through their minds at that particular moment. It's likely their thoughts were no different from ours. Men on tanks, young lads on planes, rucks of soldiers kicking up dirt with every footfall, headed into some kind of battle. They were all part and parcel of the great human condition.

Where are they now? Have they gone on? And I look at pictures of myself, of my friends, and veterans that I don't even know and I wonder where will we be in 30, 40 or 50 years…

Have we all done something to make the world a better place? Will some young boy one day look at old pictures of us and be inspired to get out of the daily routine of his young life and join a service? Despite the glamorization of the military, we often present to the world the military can be a grist mill to the spirit at times. Regardless of your sentiments, whether you are for it or against, after having served, I grok you. Grok? Yeah. Grok.

If you follow ol' Robert Heinlein, 'Grok' means to understand someone so "thoroughly that the observer becomes a part of the observed—to merge, blend, intermarry, lose identity in group experience. It means almost everything that we mean by religion, philosophy, and science and it means as little to us as color does to a blind man." Simply it means that despite our differences that I call you brother. Hail if I see you. Farewell if you go.

When we die, and follow the hounds into the hollows, and the great spirit into the glen, where Mead flows and delivers a river of happiness to all who drink of it know that I wish you well. I call you brother. Honor to you for putting your skin into the game, whether you be a fireman or police officer and a medic making a damn difference in this sometimes very, bad world. I grok you.

Why do I like poetry?

I often felt like I lost the ability to express myself. I felt like I lost the ability to speak about the things that wounded me, that made me feel vulnerable, and that also made me feel whole again. Poetry helps me survive.

Amy Lowell (1874-1925) wrote that, "poetry and history are the textbooks to the heart of man, and poetry is at once the most intimate and the most enduring." Real poetry that doesn't copy or pretend to be something will never end up being derivative, stupid or insipid and remote from people's lives. (Paraphrased).

It is something despite the fates, or the outcome of things, that we are still able to feel alive. Poetry is the art that makes us feel human and fills us when we're starving or makes us feel raw. It allows us to remove our masks and get into the depths of our hearts. Poetry means men have written something with feeling, and awakens in us imagination.

I think that when people say poetry means nothing to them, it's likely they haven't found a poem or poet that speaks to directly to their heart. Brooke may appeal to one, while Auden to others. Today it might me Eminem. I don't know. For me, it could be song lyrics from the Clash.

The director of the movie, the Grey, when developing the story wrote a few short words down; something simple, not complex. He was developing the movie character and I wasn't surprised when just a few simple words he wrote appealed to so many viewers. His poem grabs you at the gut level. Sure, he stole from Henry V but at a basic level he captures the sensibility of most men backed into a corner. And I do agree with him here, that we must wake up to live every second fully and to leave this life exhausted, because we gave it all.

The hero, played by the great actor Liam Neeson recites the poem to himself for courage before fighting the leader of the wolf pack. I feel that poetry is just one facet of the many parts of the Greek Whole man and Paideia that my Western Civilization teacher always talked about, 30 long years ago. The warrior-scholar. Read something that knocks you to your feet tonight.

The Fall

I read a story about actor Brad Pitt that fascinated me. Supposedly he loves this world so much that he is afraid to die and leave it behind him. I think about Brad's words from time to time, I do.

I ponder the biblical story of how Adam was banned from Eden. What fear Adam must have felt leaving the protection of that vital, life-giving garden only to enter into a wild world where the potential of death could be experienced by him at any moment.

Imagine the implications his decisions had upon his delicate mind and heart being manifold. Surely, he must have felt shame, fear, wonder, anger at himself for getting banished, and for disappointing God. He too must have felt a surge of loss, this disconnection from being unplugged from the source of all creation. Perhaps he left at night when a billion stars covered the sky like a wondrous cinema of whirling lights, and though he knew Eden must remain inviolate there was something pure and simple, and joyous waiting ahead for him.

Those who are afraid of eternity might rest their hopes upon what seems fixed pillars for pavilions that will eventually crumble. Build worthy houses, not from things but out of men. Do not love this world so much that you become timid, terrified of success terrified of failure, of life and love and even death. Do not let the idea of freedom turn your legs to stone. Take action and live without regret. Think about eternity and not about losing something upon this earth.

In some moment of weakness every one of us, man and woman alike, has tattooed upon our heart the symbol of our sadness which summed up our greatest failure, a dying Fall. Go into the world without paralysis and live fully, despite doubts and feelings of being alone and unprotected. There is nothing back there for you so commit yourself fully to what is ahead and a legacy of building up men, raising families, those things greater than yourself. Foist your eyes not on the world but on the night sky. You are not alone. Just like the stars in the sky there are billions of men in this world just like you.

I reenlisted in the military after a 20-year separation and a brief lackluster career. At age 39 I was going nowhere. I was broke and for a long minute jobless. I spent my free time drinking, fighting in bars and street corners and chasing women. I was good at being a loser. It was a matter of time before I'd be permanently in jail. My self-destruction was borne out of my frustration that I believed I was something, and not that I was nothing, and I dreamt of opportunities to prove myself.

The military saved me. I was losing my mind. Hope isn't just for young men and women. I applied myself and was good at nearly everything I did because I wasn't going to waste my second chance. God blessed me but not in the way I thought. How good yet odd life is. Don't quit on yourself.

Be fragile

I was out running and listening to Gene Clark's "Strength of Strings" Incredible. His song is powerful yet simultaneously fragile. Clark stared out onto the Pacific Ocean from his Mendocino home, pondered

philosophy and came up with the song. He was faced with the dilemma of trying to give language to something that evoked feelings so strong that no words were sufficient for what he felt or heard. Words failed him while music moved him.

"In my life the piano sings. Brings me words that are not the strength of strings." Listening to his song reminds me of Ray Davies song "Waterloo Sunset". The words to Waterloo came easily to Davies yet he was too embarrassed to share his creation with his Kinks bandmates. In both cases, a music or a sight evokes feelings so grand, that man tries to impossibly interpret the heavenward power of it by containing their great emotions into mere words.

Davies stated he felt his song was about how innocence would prevail over adversity. Clark shared similar sentiments with Davies but on the other hand he seemed to move in the opposite direction.

Throughout Clark's life he was afflicted with serious health problems, including ulcers and alcohol dependence. He created the song using the technology of the day. His song has been covered many times by other artists. Whether you like, hate, or don't care about their creations, one thing is certain, their words and their creations moves many men. Destroying things is easy but creating something worthwhile is difficult.

Any reader familiar with English poetry and Francis Thompson will recall his difficult life. His father wanted him to study at Oxford, but Francis lost his way in opium. Before his death he penned the incredible "Hound of Heaven". Out of a man's spiritual destruction came creation, redemption and death. Each writer had a different story. Yours is different too. Destruction is easy. I hope you take time to create something this weekend. Or chill out and find something powerful that inspires you.

Lay Down

My brother posted this video on his timeline of the song by Melanie called Lay Down and it truly resonated with me. A masterpiece. The chorus with the Edwins Hawkins Singers is incredible. I hadn't heard it in over 40 years. If you can get through the dated video and its poor sound quality maybe it will connect with you. Her sincerity in her pre-show interview is apparent—1960's youthful, hopeful, naiveté.

Although the singer is idealistic and the lyrics were written after her attendance at Woodstock, I understand her sentiment. I believe any warrior prepared for war should first attempt to resolve most conflicts with peace. I was truly moved when she said "we all caught the same disease and we all sang the songs of peace".

This video and her song captured a moment in time when people were very hopeful despite and perhaps because of the tumultuous time; Vietnam, MLK and the peace protests. As a person who understands violence and has been around it his entire life it gets tiring at times to see it. You get weary. I think most of us who carry the metaphorical sword and shield understand the world's pain and the need for the dove of peace but I don't make the mistake of believing in Utopia, at least not in this world.

We live in strange times where our country is becoming fractured again —sadly large parts of our diverse culture is bereft of reason. 20th century love is replaced with 21st century hatred. We are the buffer against evil but we shouldn't be emotionless automatons.

Even as we are full of emotion, we must still perform our duty despite the toll. Emotion never leaves anyone. If you are weary, rest. If you are in pain, find love. If you carry a heavy load, find God. If you are an unbeliever in anything stand for some "thing".

Reason may tell you there is no solution so what solution are we left with? Find water to give you respite from the bitter dry world that takes your joy away. Be strong. Be humble. Be durable. Be open to having your heart pierced by glory.

Survivor

My mother's heart was never at rest and she often remarked to her children how she wanted to die and join the ghosts of Vietnam and the war that made them so. But she could not do so because she was here in the States in some place of relative comfort and they roamed where the ghosts of war go. The guilt ate at her for decades. Survivor's guilt is something many people experience after being in the clutches of war.

There is guilt about staying alive while others died; guilt about the things they failed to do, and the things that they did. How tragic then what war does to men, and it destroys women and their children too and in many ways for generations. There is much to be said for the bright summit of knowledge and the dark valleys of ignorance that we climb up and head down. How often do our feelings tell us that life will only be difficult?

I'm reminded of the last words of Van Gogh. He said, "the sadness will never end." I think many of us have felt that way at some point in our life. Sorrow visits the most gifted and the least gifted regardless of what any of us creates or destroys.

Even during hot summers, I felt so many cold silences and was lost in blind avenues of despair. We cannot know everything, and we most certainly know little or know nothing in the wide scope of knowledge. If only we would look up every time, we cross the high plains and the low hills on our journey of life and actually comprehend the majesty of eternity couching the universes.

We are but one small planet going round a sun but it is ours. Every time we take direct action to learn something new and something good, we get higher upon that summit of knowledge and away from that valley of disbelief.

We must be willing to learn about life and our place in this world to understand how beautiful it all can be, and get away from guilt, shame, and second guessing in order to find out why we must leave the dark

mysteries in those long and sad lands of ignorance. If we shed any tears let it be for joy at what we will be and not with sadness for what we once were.

Faith

I'm never banging someone over the ears and head about my faith but if you read between the lines in my writing and look at the iconography, I use for a lot of my brand you can figure it out for yourself.

It's not because I want to keep my business and my faith separate, or because I don't like to proselytize. It's simply that I think people should arrive to their conclusion about what I'm trying to share and it shouldn't be directly. I want it to be in a way that deeply resonates with them, and isn't a turn off. I also want it to be about discovery whether it's a like or a hate for us just as Bertrand Russell or C.S. Lewis concluded certain things while riding a bike or a sidecar.

I don't want this brand to ever be solely about commerce to make big bucks. It first has to be about something bigger than wearing well drawn tacticool art. I want people to be proud to wear what I sell. I want people to have real affection for what I share because they've gone on the journey with me and discovered too that they really like the message even if they aren't believers.

In the end even the atheist can see clearly that virtue and enterprise are good things and that despite many differences I believe we can all appreciate being a good example in the world and not being a drag. In the end I'm just trying to bring love into a world where there's a lot of pain and men sometimes need inspiration more then they need my lecture.

Imposter syndrome

I'm reminded of a story I read about the late great actor David Niven who once commissioned as an officer in the British commando unit. Despite his fame, money, fighting prowess, title and success with his love pursuits Niven stated he always felt like an impostor.

Suave and polished, handsome and funny Niven's notoriety opened many doors but he once stated he felt a time would come when he would be tapped on the shoulder and a man would beckon for him to follow. He would be led away for being a fraud. Niven was an accomplished yet complex and deeply insecure man. His philandering ways brought him heartache and he also humanely experienced the death of loved ones. Did he have it all?

Today I think how many of us don't even know what we're even here for. As the joke goes, "I'm just here for the violence." What is your cause? We wander around, standing in lines while gazing at our phones, and we're following others who are just as lost, and we hold onto this feeling that there must be more to life. How many useless conversations do we partake of because we're actually insincere, how many wasted opportunities because we are inauthentic with our time with others and also with who we've become?

For some men there is belief that we are nothing and yet the evidence suggests we are something. Why is there this continuous conflict in our mind? Instagram won't allow a complex answer here for my premise but we need to look at the root causes for why we are what we think we are and realize schemas have a way of following us through life, sometimes to our detriment. In the end we should try to live vitally.

Life will end one day. We don't need to jump out of planes or go through combat first to live richly, rather we first need to be honest with our motivations so we don't have conflicting feelings in our heart, before we end up feeling like we are fakes. Mostly act upon an honest intuition but don't simply throw reason and morals out the window. Just my opinion.

Study your lover like you study war

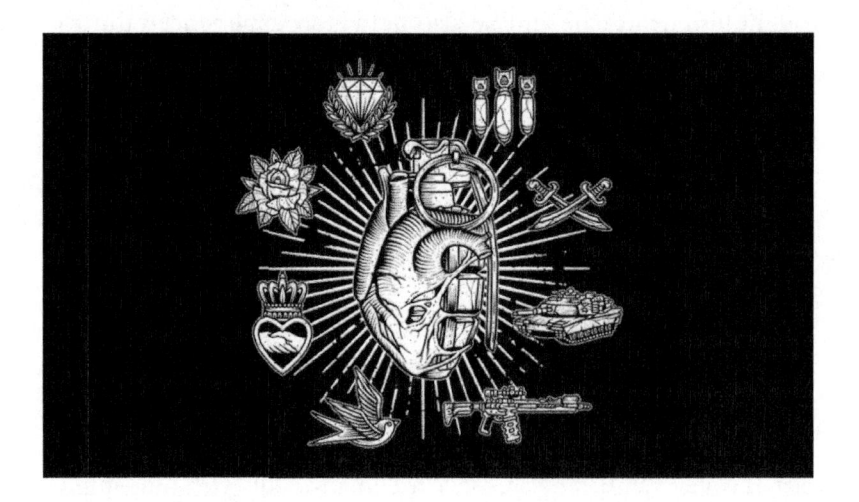

It always blows my mind how a man can make intense war with men and yet make indelible love to a woman but this bifurcation makes sense and its necessary. It's necessary for us to channel our aggression straight into the enemy when it's needed in times of danger, and it's necessary to channel love into our lover's heart when that time comes.

We take away her fear and she will take away our pain. Like two pulses of electric current joined at the hip. Two arcs of invisible fire within two souls. Sometimes we can truly connect and intertwine. We should never see our lover as our foe.

A movie that really captures the strength and gentleness of a warrior, and a character we should all aspire to emulate, is Maximus-Russel Crowe's character in the movie Gladiator. He is a man amongst men; fearless, powerful, a leader and he is a caring husband and a loving father. There are men like this in our world. Find them and learn from them. Men are often so quick to study warfare and weapons that deliver the best destruction but they spend little time understanding their lovers. Study them. Find out what moves them. Learn what their needs are. Study them as much as you study the blade, the gun, and all those ways of delivering death. Study love. Love them completely, refrain from speaking harsh words, honor your vows, be a man and not a boy. Sharpen your weapons for war and dull your tongue when you're talking to her. Good luck and try to stay off the sofa you fool.

The emperor has no clothes

I've never liked the statement that clothes make the man though I believe that I understand the writer's intent. We wear clothing for various reasons, and it's mostly for practical purposes. For some of us clothes can be like armor and it is simultaneously used intentionally or unintentionally as a means of making or not making good or bad impressions upon others.

The writer Hans Christian Anderson wrote aptly about pride and vanity in his story the Emperor Has No Clothes. I think most people get the idea Anderson posited. When we are feeling exposed in front of others, we might feel a lot of shame. Feeling shame induces many people to cover up their perceived failures and flaws. Humphrey Bogart was a veritable tough guy in film noir but he was a reedy 140 lbs. outside of those choice suits. I'm not opposed to fashion. My brother taught himself to tailor high end men's apparel and I learned the basics of construction, color theory, style pros cons etc.

High quality threads can sometimes hide the worst physical deficiencies; legs too skinny, belly too large etc. but it can't hide ability when the time to show it comes. It can't hide whether you can run, box or shoot. Clothing can't hide heart but it can sometimes hide fear, right, even when you're shaking like nothing else. It can sometimes mask muscle but it can't mask willpower.

The Duelists told the story of two soldiers that distinguished themselves through their service and become generals, however, their mutual hatred never ceased, even when the initial cause of their rivalry was forgotten. So, clothes can't cover up common sense, skill and talent or a lack of it; many slicked-up shooters can't even shoot at all. In the movie Collateral actor Tom Cruise does an excellent job mowing people down all while dressed in a slick looking grey-tonic suit.

How do you determine what is good apparel for your purpose? The market is catching up with the demand for functional, stylish wear. Learn to look smart learn to perform smartly where you get comfort and utility. But in the end the man must make the clothes, not the other way around. Ability over style first. Sambas, jeans and t-shirts aren't a bad place to start.

The 13th Warrior

"Lo there do I see my father; Lo there do I see my mother and my sisters and my brothers; Lo there do I see the line of my people, back to the beginning. Lo, they do call me, they bid me take my place among them, in the halls of Valhalla, where the brave may live forever."

The 13th Warrior is a great movie for any time. The final speech by Bulliwyf is mesmerizing. He recalls the power of his lineage and I think more men must do this. They should dig into their ancestry and recall that history when they are afraid, in doubt or about to meet an opponent, so they can speak of who they are and who their people were; even digging into their family's unsavory past if they must.

I've done the same recollection in my youth before fighting and still do from time to time by muttering my last name under my breath. It always gave me courage. My mother fought anyone, I'm not shocked to say, and I learned her ways of never backing down; sadly, she was often the instigator. At a rundown casino she was once called a derogatory term for Asians and so she jumped on the gambling card table and kicked the offender in the face. She said, "do you know who I am?!"

My mother passed away 3 months ago. While alive, I had a hard go with her but I appreciate some of the hardest lessons learned. Years ago, the hospital called me to say she was injured. Without blinking, I stated, "Fighting?" Yes, they replied. The police stated she fought against three men on the Oakland public transit. Thanks Mom, you were a maniac but you were our maniac. R.I.P. You never backed down. KNOW yourself and honor your heroic past and be brave daily.

Be the Monster

Mänstər/ noun 1. An imaginary creature that is typically large, ugly, and frightening. Synonyms: giant, mammoth, colossus, leviathan, titan. Why do we like the Batman? Because we see a wounded boy who turned himself into something big and strong enough to turn fear against the fearsome. As a child he turned the monster that horrified him into his own. Batman doesn't have superpowers. He earned every skill that he has and he uses it to become a legend among men. He can die yet never gives up despite the difficulty of his mission. He plans and comes prepared for everything. He has willpower, determination, intelligence and strength. He's human.

In life magic will never save men. Batman is a capable man with principles who is willing to become a monster to rid our world of evil in order to save men. He is our monster. One day your family, friends or teammates will need you. One day you'll see a child or a woman in the street beaten or abused. Don't turn and look the other way. When the time comes, and you are prepared, be the monster. Strike fear in the hearts of those who choose to do evil. If you don't know how to terrify men then you must learn.

The Boys of Summer

Many great songs capture heartache and the loss of innocence however I believe The Boys of Summer is one that captures loss best.

Sure, the song is slick and was perhaps produced with the intention of making lots of bucks but it works regardless what we think of corporate driven rock. The synth, the guitar dolling out righteous melancholic chords, and Henley's soft singing make this song superb for playing while cruising down the freeway before the world starts stirring.

If any song richly captured atmosphere and left us with the realization that summer died and youth slipped away well, this song is it. The jangly guitar solo, the simple effective lyrics leaves us wondering about lovers now gone. Youth ends, and the people we love go away but longing continues forever. Youthful invincibility extinguishes and the burden of that knowledge is carried into maturity.

Life must have loss for us to appreciate what will never come back. Penetrating thinkers, and introspective loveless romantics can likely imagine what the world looks and feels like where heroes go in Tolkien's Undying Lands. Writers and tellers of heroic tales such as Beowulf, and King Arthur no doubt felt like us, and considered how much of the world was changing, and how they couldn't control fate. No matter how frequently we feel loss it will always feel like a foreign thing. Songs shared round the fireside in ancient Greece, or Decorah, Iowa are different from each other but the longing for another time is the same.

Arthur's men searched the ancient world for the Holy Grail and a way to end pain. Some feel that 'future' knowledge is a burden while others believe obtaining more of it liberates us from the past. How do we escape the past? We don't and shouldn't.

Instead of wallowing in some deep funk when those injurious memories come, why not be grateful for those wounds? "Leave your troubles behind. Yield to the joy of living, yield to the possibility of dying, yield to the discovery of smiling and see with spirited eyes what your earthly eyes cannot see; the deepest, blackest midnights and the clearest, bluest skies; still, green blades of grass and sand the color of white wine. Live in awe."

These violent delights have violent ends

Men always quick to issue violence and slow to administer peace never understood the true essence of a certain power and its fields of influence. It begins somewhere along a wave of restraint and builds to an excess yet it never rolls to an end. It is a capacity that develops into something in the future that can be used for good or abused for evil.

Understood properly it is a latent promise that can be harnessed to shape the world and it must be held under a secure command. It isn't a matter of having it or not having it, in fact all men will have some of it but will never have all of it.

Men who cannot issue it accordingly never understood how it must be issued sparingly for it is given by divine authority. Used honorably it allows men to create, develop and can even show how to sever lasting relationships that can still be good and meaningful because it never seeks to control. A comprehension of it even allows men to perceive what it needs to destroy.

This power although bequeathed, must be developed and nurtured but it will never die. It only wanes and eventually returns to its source when a man's life expires. Those who ignore this incorruptible source are truly acting out of their own regard, and its nature is replaced by another source.

The source of this power is love and used in moderation it helps men mature, and have respect for men and nature. Men alone become corrupted by allowing themselves to be fully consumed in an immediate or a long-suffering destruction because they as a steward never allowed their appetite of lust to be satiated.

Momma take this badge off of me

My buddy retired. A true warrior. A true believer who worked so hard in life not to compromise himself. A gang banger who turned his life around, took care of a son at the young age of 16, and then served this nation. He spent 26 years away from his two boys. Now he's home. I recall the sacrifices he made.

I was listening to Bob Dylan this evening while running, had me thinking. How many of us have to walk away from something that we loved that simultaneously injured the ones we loved? That's a hard pill to swallow. Whatever your old purpose, whatever your new purpose, and whatever scars from old wounds that never really healed, I hope you'll spend some time truly looking inward.

Ask yourself how can I make things right with my family? Experience new feelings that allow you as a fighter to begin anew and become something different. Retirement isn't the end of your journey. Ask hard questions and come up with honest answers: What is the meaning of life, why did this person die, what value can I provide in this world, why did they take a good man, how can I truly love my family, what are the steps to be there for them, how can I learn from this, did I learn from this, what will become of my life, now what? If you are honest and sincere with your feelings you can regenerate. Recover and begin anew. Do it now "Mama take this badge off of me."

Teach boys to become men

My father took me to many movies when I was growing up. Thankfully I was able to watch thought-provoking stuff when I was a child. Mostly westerns and war movies of which I thoroughly enjoyed discussing with my older brother. I still recall watching the actor Richard Harris star in the movie A Man Called Horse. It was 1971 and I was 4 years old.

The movie was based on the Dorothy Johnson novel called Indian Country and was set in the 1820's America. In our tale Lord John Morgan, played by Harris, is captured by Mandan Indians while hunting. Morgan is given to the Chief's mother and he is abused and mistreated. He is treated like a horse and in one memorable scene they mock him by mounting him as if he were an animal.

Eventually Morgan falls for the Chief's sister and in order to prove his worth to marry her he must undergo brutal rituals including a particular rite of passage called the Okipa Ceremony. Okipa (O-Kee-Pa) requires Morgan to be painfully suspended in the air from his chest with hooks. The movie ends with him joining the tribe, taking the name Horse and becoming chief. What a powerful rite of passage. I do not recall much of the movie but I will always remember the scene of Morgan's ritual hanging.

A rite of passage is a ceremonial event and marks the transition from one phase of a person's life to another. Rites of passage exist in all historically known societies and the rite marks the passage of the person(s) from one social or religious status to another. A rite of passage is often used to describe a transition from one place to another in the life of a person; generally, it is used to describe the change from adolescence to adulthood. Rites of passage presents a young man with the opportunity to signal to his community that he is ready to accept the responsibilities and privileges of the roles his community defines.

Young men have a great need for rituals to mark their passage to manhood. They will invent their own rites if society does not provide it for them. Teach them to be a contributing member of their tribe.

Manipulate the model

Nikolai Tesla it is said could envision a locking mechanism in his mind with such intense clarity it seemed to him to be real. He could see every turn of the tumbler. He used the power of his mind to build. Like Tesla have a vision on where you want to go and what you want to be despite life continually shifting its goal posts on you. Your sole faith in yourself may wane however a marker held at some point in your mind that you can see, even when things feel dark, can become the brightest light that shows you how far is its distance and why it is an inspiration.

Following routine allows you to exhaust any apprehensions, because your focus isn't just based on want of pursuance but also on need for execution. Manipulate the model in your mind until you can see the product from every vantage point and understand what it is and what you must become to twist it apart and put it together from every angle.

Make the complex simple, and the foreign familiar by breaking it down and then follow the tracks until you arrive at your destination.

This side of paradise

One of my favorite quotes from the book that first started me onto the path of reading and real discovery. F. Scott Fitzgerald's book called This Side of Paradise. Genius. I spent years in disillusionment and despair looking for a truth, fighting nightmares and was daily dead walking.

Fitz wrote about post WW1 disillusionment. We live yet we don't always get what we want but do we give up? I see a lack of restlessness today in our new generation, or any real angst as it was in our lost generation, and their need to seek out meaning and purpose.

The angry young men of those before us locked in lives of manual labor, who lacked opportunity, who didn't know leisure brought by the advantages of wealth like many of us do today and how it can soften many men.

Adler wrote about it, how the coming of the Industrial Revolution would bring changes in attitudes, and I state it brings some men to their worst. We owe it to ourselves to be true, owe it to ourselves to be "alive" and seek to live each day vitally. We must live sensitively so that we can feel, we must live authentically so we can believe, we must live critically so we can learn, and we must above all live to make a difference or we are just going through life as sensualists and voyeurs, mouthing words yet doing and saying nothing.

We must wash away the kernels of exhaustion from our sleepy eyes daily and fill our pupils with passion for living or we may as well quit and start dying.

"Here was a new generation, shouting the old cries, learning the old creeds, through a revery of long days and nights; destined finally to go out into that dirty gray turmoil to follow love and pride; a new generation dedicated more than the last to the fear of poverty and the worship of success; grown up to find all Gods dead, all wars fought, all faiths in man shaken..."-F Scott Fitzgerald.

Come away O human child

Poets like W.B. Yeats obtained his lyrical power from looking into folklore and myth to make his people aware of their lost, heroic and rich past, and that same ability I think was picked up by creative men like singers and songwriters Shane McGowan and Mike Scott.

These men believed somewhere long ago in that past that there were incredible stories to be told; so, these men had something to say, and they formulated a way to say it. Although they held to traditions, they also broke molds. Men should have purpose. Somewhere in each man's genealogy is a family member who should be studied and then honored. Lean back on those in your bloodline and emulate them. Tell their stories. There has to be something good back there to teach us how to cast long shadows on the world. Be proud.

Don't be inconsequential

Rebellions aren't just the aspirations turned into action by angry young boys but it will never be performed by gutless old men. For some it was Black Flag, the Clash, the Jam, maybe even the Firm, Cockney Rejects. Minor Threat, Fear yes even Elvis Costello was doing good stuff. Who knew in decades to come what their posture would be?

Yes, for angry young men these singers were gods and a way out of youth's boredom, a way to act out, connect, or even do something meaningful, yes for many kids it became a gateway into a new world. Many of us even joined the military. The world doesn't always change the most from the top down, it starts in the gutter and drowns out the elitist whispering by countering it with its rebellious screams. If you want to be relevant change the culture, if you want to be inconsequential follow the status quo.

We live in a day and age where the sociopolitical culture must be countered because it's doing everything to tear down the strong pillars that hold up a free society in order to replace it with a construct that will fall on everyone's heads and from that rubble could make all men slaves. Get involved as much as they do with their stances on gun control, open borders, abortion, immigration, religious secularism, you get the picture. Who knew the counter-culture, cool kids of the old generation were actually uncool, sell-outs and therefore hypocrites? Educate yourself first and then decide what you want to be and do.

Reading literature is often a poor substitute for doing something useful, such as taking action. And it's done by some people who don't take real steps to make good change in this world; in fact, we are dumber and less brave for it. Be more than just a reader and a critic.

Run towards the Minotaur and kill him

We get lost in mazes sometimes. We forget our purpose or we become paralyzed by succumbing to fear and we can't move to even find our way out. Men forget what they were put on this earth for, or we just lack the courage or the focus to accomplish our intrinsic goals. Good God, we're supposed to run towards the Minotaur and kill it!

In legend the Minotaur was a bull-headed monster born to Queen Pasiphae of Crete after she slept with a bull. The creature we are told resided in a maze that Daedalus and Icarus built, and it was regularly offered a sacrifice of youth to satisfy its hunger. Theseus the mythical king and founder of Athens was known for his courage and cleverness. With just sandals, his sword and intent he sought out and killed the beast.

Every man and woman every day is faced with the loss of youth. Youth gave us our curiosity, our hopefulness, humor, motivation and playfulness. Youth too gave us our sense of adventure and need for incessantly questioning things. Don't let youth die in the maze of the Minotaur.

Smell its foul odor, close your eyes, listen to its heavy breathing. Track it down and pierce the heart of this monster because it devours youthfulness and with it your hopefulness. If you are feeling at a loss today because of something in your past you need to get off of your fat ass and charge ahead every freaking day and kill that Minotaur. Theseus battled and overcame his foes. Do the same.

Everyday believe that you can make a difference in your own life and the lives of others. Don't run from your problems and the things that can devour you like your addictions, instead run at them bang on and destroy them. Shout, "come at me! I am ready to kill you!"

I know why the stars shine

Some men look up into the sky and wonder at the bright stars and hope. Others look at the brightest light as if it is the eye of God yet see only a mote. Shame and a sense of smallness crushes them. Unwittingly with their own narrow vision they close the great lid upon what is perceived as a speck and blind themselves from seeing the greatness they were meant for.

Men often replace one dream for another and in doing so replace the original one with smaller dreams, until they don't dream anymore. The breath of sky galactic smothers beneath its folds those infinitely named souls into her charcoal-colored darkness, where hope retreats into the quiet country, and all birdsong falls to silence.

A professor of biochemistry, an astronomer, and a theoretical physicist. Asimov, Sagan, Feynman wondered. What did they imagine when they looked at the stars through a telescope, what did they think of as they peered through a lens? Did they imagine an astronaut hurtling through the dark while mission-bound as his spacecraft shot past Mars? They had their own ideas about creation, religion and the laws of physics.

Feynman recounts a tale about astronomer Arthur Eddington, who had just figured out that the stars get their power from burning hydrogen in a nuclear reaction producing helium. Feynman shares in his story that Eddington, "recounted how, on the night after his discovery, he was sitting on a bench with his girlfriend. She said, "Look how pretty the stars shine!" To which he replied, "Yes, and right now, I'm the only man in the world who knows how they shine." He remarked that there is a wonderful kind of loneliness a man has when he makes a discovery.

Whether you're an atheist, an agnostic or a believer of some kind don't stop being hopeful, don't quit at dreaming, don't stop looking into the stars and discovering what it is that you were meant to be and what you're meant to do.

Be honest with yourself because an answer will come. The stars you look at tonight whether as a soldier in Afghanistan or a cop in Detroit may hold a wonderful kind of answer for you even in your loneliness while looking at the sky above.

I spoke to God, he said I must carry you

A man's courage is always increased by a man willing to descend with him into Hell. If you're not willing to set the example as a partner and a hero then who round you will?

The purpose and the plan for every one of us who purports to follow the tenets of the warrior life is to live vitality, to seek out challenges, to embrace our uniqueness, to go against the grain time and time and time again, and change the weak culture around us despite the losses to our self.

We must give in to pain and discomfort until our mission is done. We must fight the hounds of Hell and all of the world's pain, to seek out a cup that is purported to not exist so that an injured society can drink from it. We must do this without benefit of sword or spear or shield. All that we have is our courage and conviction. Show men how to heal their hearts, to honor their vows, to hunger for life again, to stand tall again, and to eventually show other men the same. Be a light in the darkness. If you don't then who will?

Little Big Man

Some men who speak strongly with words may be weak in action, and today we are a world filled with critics who've never done a damn thing. The creation of social media has made it easier for a million men to complain about what they dislike, while many make no movements to create solutions to problems that many people would like.

Reading literature is often a poor substitute for doing something useful when it's done by people who don't take real steps to make good change in this world; in fact, we are dumber and less brave for it.

One of my favorite movie scenes comes right out of the movie Little Big Man. While the movie was an anti-establishment movie it had some great moments in it that I love. One of those great moments is when actor Chief Dan George gives a moving speech while actor Dustin Hoffman as Jack stands by and observes him. The Chief shouts up to the sky, "Come out and fight! It is a good day to die! Thank you for making me a human being!"

The Chief stares at the sky and his life doesn't end as he expects it to. It begins to rain and they walk off to have dinner. There are real men today who possess the character of Chief Lodge Skins. They have lived a long time, experienced much, seen the world change and are ready at any moment to go.

The movie ends with Jack thinking about the coming of the modern world (the 20th century) and the ending of the era of the open plains. He looks at the situation with sadness. He is a man who cannot change. He lives in the past like most warriors who live in the past of a heroic, bygone era and the world changes without them moving in it.

The pen replaces the sword, preaching replaces action, cowardice replaces heroics and liking a post replaces throwing our physical weight behind a movement. The cultural pushes come from lunatics and we can only watch in dismay at the stupidity of suburban rebels who've never experienced a nation in destruction yet want one destroyed anyway. We cannot just sit and watch the passing of the trains, or the falling of the rain. Educate yourself, arm yourself, not just with books but blades. Swords allow men to become a real insurrection if there comes a time for less words and more action.

Paradise

Sometimes I think back and wonder about the lost friends, lovers, jobs. In the end what I lost was opportunities. Is it worthwhile to talk about foregone conclusions or possibilities that passed? Sometimes it feels as if there isn't any love left in our souls. Life and the past seem closed and the story is over, or is it? Right?

I've watched the magical Cinema Paradiso more times than I can count. Young Salvatore leaves everything behind and becomes a famous Italian filmmaker, yet haunted by the memories of his first love, he returns to his hometown after an absence of 30 years. His return home is a pilgrimage worth watching on celluloid as he connects with his lost love. Walking away from home and then thinking about coming back to it seems difficult for many of us.

I used to sit at the docks in Oakland and look over the bay into the city while contemplating the life I was leaving behind. Many of us feel like Adam leaving Eden. There is no going back whether or not we want to. The way is blocked by a Nephilim with a giant sword of fire. The chord to God's magical and life sustaining garden has been severed. The person we know got married, or a friend has died, so reconnecting in some way impossible. Or is it?

I am reminded that some things are possible. My old friend of 30 years tracked an old love to Germany 20 years after losing her. What elation he must have felt to discover that she missed him too. They are now expecting a child.

There is redemption in this world to remove all of the s--t we've done and enough left over to bring us into a healthy, future. No one said it was going to be easy. Don't just focus on the real because that won't get you anywhere. Do we raise our children to believe life is full of heartbreak and misery? No, we let them follow their hearts, yet we forget how to follow ours.

Focus on the impossible, the outrageous, on dreaming and chase it. Despite how many people have gone away, in the end, there may be something to build from but you'll never know until you try. For all the closed doors, for all the lost opportunities that you cannot obtain, there is peace. There is peace but you have to seek it. I'm no doctor. Just a dude.

Burn it down

Success with love can only happen when you don't look back at your past relationship and also burn those boats to commit yourself to being with the one, you're with. When the Grecian armies landed on their enemy's shore, the first order the commanders gave was "Burn the boats.". ... As the soldiers watched the boats burn, they knew there was no turning back – there would be no surrendering.

The Vikings ship burial used a boat as a container for the dead and their grave goods as a way of honoring their fallen warriors. They burned those boats. Two ways of seeing things but similar intents.

One way is to never look back to the old path because the war lies ahead. Time and energy must be spent elsewhere than being emotionally and physically invested in the past. The other way is to honor what was. Both ask that you move forward. Honor your old self and set it ablaze. Honor your new partner too.

We can romanticize past relationships but they are over. Stop playing with your lover's headspace and creating conflict for you and her. Begin a new project. Become a rising Phoenix up from the ashes. Become a new man and the person you need to, no, that you must become. There is no other way but ahead. Become one with them to use love to fight wars that are ahead.

What is your quest?

The 1981 movie Quest for Fire is based off the 1911 Belgian novel by J.H. Rosny and is supposed to take place some 80,000 years in the past. The book is about early humans and their struggle to control fire. Our less than capable protagonists must find fire in order to survive the very brutal world they live in.

The movie unfolds with the apelike Wagabu tribe fighting the tribe Ulam. From here things take a turn for the worse as the losing Ulam tribe flees the attacking Wagabu tribe and the Ulam's fire-tender crosses a marsh and accidentally extinguishes the tribe's remaining embers. From here this is where their journey begins.

The Ulam have to find fire and do all manner of things to survive. They must flee wolves, fight a cannibal tribe and wooly mammoths and get out of quicksand.

Let me ask something. What is your quest for fire? What is the one thing in your life that possesses you? What is the thing you must have like water or air and not a thing will stop you from seeking those out?

A quest isn't something you're doing because it's fun. You're doing it because it's necessary and likely to be perilous, difficult, life-altering and perhaps deadly. The original fire seeker, Prometheus sought out the life-giving energy, and as a benefactor to human-kind he was punished by Zeus with eternal suffering. The influence of the myth of Prometheus extends into our modern time and likely will even after we're gone.

Do you have a quest for fire? Do you have something that burns in your belly, day in and day out? Do you have raging insomnia over it to the point where you have to get up to work on that project? Are you out there training in the rain, snow and heat while your friends are pounding back the beers?

Are you willing to flee wolves and fight cannibal tribes in order to obtain the fire? Are you of the conviction that without that fire you are likely to die? Do you recall how you used to feel when you were young and didn't let life get the best of you? Something to think about this Sunday morning.

Brothers

The always capable actor Robert DeNiro plays the character Mike who tracks down his war-ravaged friend Nick who is playing Russian roulette at a gambling casino. DeNiro comes off as a conscientious yet firm friend while Walken strikes a very melancholic tone by playing Nick so hauntingly. Nick is suffering because he cannot deal with the inhumanities of war.

It may not appear that there is a tender moment in this face-off scene but viewers who understand the bonds created from war are really treated to the incredible feeling of love that Mike has for Nick. Mike is willing to give his own life if it means he can jog Nick's memory enough and persuade him to come home.

Nick looks at Mike with the darkest, deadest eyes. Mike grabs Nick's arm and he sees his track marks. We feel for Mike and we understand his need to reach Nick before it's too late. Mike holds a gun to his head and says, "is this what you want?" The tension of course is palpable.

Mike tells Nick that he loves him. Mike pulls his trigger. Incredible action moment on cinema. Mike reminds Nick about their hunting trips together. Nick recognizes Mike and smiles as he raises the gun to his temple and pulls the trigger. He is tortured by his experiences in war, his survivors' guilt, the shame he feels for owing Mike his life, and for feeling so flat without action and violence to possess his psyche.

Most days for men like Nick are anticlimactic as it should be because the psyche is ill equipped to deal with a volume of excitement turned up all the time. Life as a whole should be sparsely punctuated by moments of violence and excitement for men who cannot handle it. A really emotional man who wants to absorb all of life may find himself empty of relationships and eventually life while a timid man who commits none of himself will be bereft of deep relationships too; or men like Nick who are empty of feeling.

Our goal in life is to find balance. War can create bondage where we feel like we cannot advance or go back. We have scars. Where do we go? What do we do? The anchors that held us down broke free and now we are drifting. Get the help you need. For you strong men, help the men who will need you.

Wake, Eat, Drink, Sleep

"The average man, who does not know what to do with his life, wants another which will last forever." ~Anatole France.

The first time I ever read Anatole France's words, I believed they were quite profound. After reading his words we can essentially ask ourselves what kind of person is it that we want to be.

Contemplate then, if we could live forever, would we ever have need for purpose in what we do, who we are and what we'll be? Would it ever matter at all? How about having a finite life? Wouldn't the opposite of having an infinite life mean that we must have a purpose in the things that we do? Or does that even matter at all?

What if we could live for a thousand years, or a million years? Wouldn't these millenniums be the same thing as living for 100 years because all three have a beginning and an ending? No different from living from a hundred I suppose. We still live, we still die no matter the length of time given to us. But what good is it to live forever it we don't even know what it is that we want to do? Wouldn't that be a hell?

Wake, Eat, Drink, Sleep, Wake, Eat, Drink, Sleep…why bother? But it seems to me that if we have a finite life, whether it's for a hundred years or a thousand, that having an ending allows us some purpose. If we are finite, if our life is brief in the scope of things, wouldn't it be great to contemplate the infinite, and wonder exactly what is it that we must do while we're here?

Balance

The hero archetype is also known by names such as the soldier, crusader, fighter or the warrior. Jungian psychologist Robert Moore and mythologist Douglas Gillette distilled Jung's archetypes into four types known as the King, Warrior, Magician, Lover. For a hero to become a warrior he must move from immature masculinity to mature masculinity.

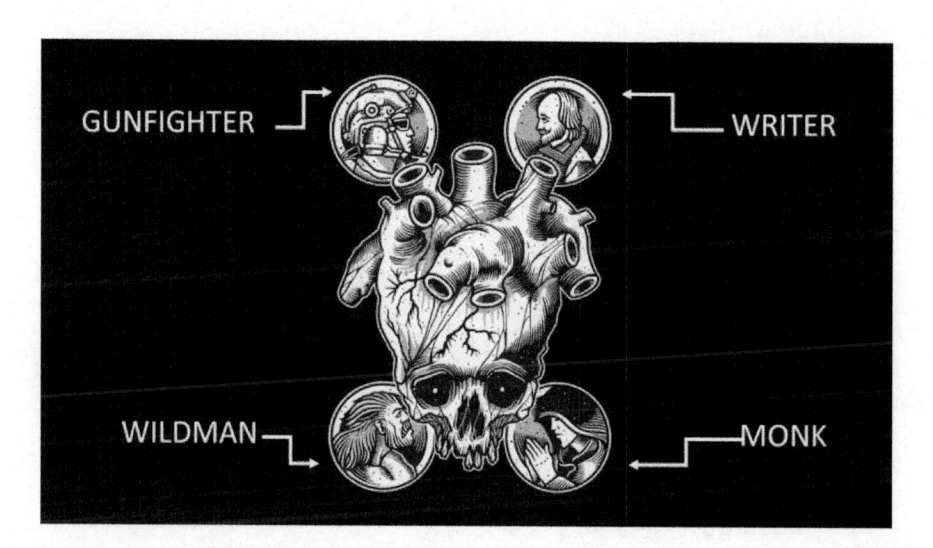

In a nutshell and in geekspeak it is the difference between a fighter such as Luke Skywalker the hot-head and Obi Wan-Kenobi the warrior master; youth works for itself while adulthood works for others. A young hero can progress into something higher.

Military indoctrination, increased conditioning and further experience can make a fighter a master over himself. The archetypical hero seeks out like-minded brothers and sisters who will fight as he does. Thinking is the enemy of the hero archetype because it inhibits him from acting swiftly and forcefully. Yet a fighter that is all action and does very little thinking is nothing more than a drone programmed to kill. In order to advance from fighter to warrior a fighter must mature and becomes something greater.

How does a fighter arrive at this place of enlightenment and mastery over himself?

Men are not machines. Killing solely to kill is done by beasts and not by men. Men are far more complex than that and they have the ability to be introspective. Certainly, discipline keeps the fighter rooted in his skillfulness but to advance beyond his armor, that shell of protection, means he must look within his body and into his heart.

The heart is where a warrior keeps patience, selflessness, love, courage, humility and compassion among many virtuous things. Warriors without empathy for others are simply machines without emotions;

they are an empty construct that are no different from a wrecking ball. But thinking too deeply can paralyze a person until they can't accomplish a thing. One side of the house is action and the other side is paralysis. A master has learned balance; when to act and when to sit still. And you?

After Highschool

The Lords of Flatbush. A movie about young men wandering aimlessly and having to face the onslaught of maturity in 1950's Brooklyn. High school is almost over and the future looks empty.

While not a particularly good movie it came out two years before Stallone would make it big with Rocky. Worth seeing to see him subtly steal scenery. Back then we knew the good guys from the bad guys from their haircuts and the leather jackets they wore or didn't.

What did you do after high school? The Marine Corps, McDonald's, the local police department? How did your life change? Transference. Youth wanting to belong to a gang end up finding productive groups to get them out of malaise but not necessarily out of trouble. Some went from Brooklyn to Vietnam, the Bronx to Iraq and Denver to Afghanistan. My life changed forever when I enlisted and I'm grateful to it. I wouldn't change a thing. I don't think most of us would.

Iron tongues

The movie Dances with Wolves came at time during the waning period of the greedy 80's made known by movie characters like Gordon Gecko. DWW has some complex themes. Costner portrays a Civil War soldier who develops a relationship with a band of Lakota Indians. He appreciates the simplicity of their lifestyle and chooses to leave his former life to be with them. They name him Dances with Wolves. He soon becomes a welcomed member of the tribe.

Few men today aren't self-sufficient outside of national society. Movies like DWW connect with us for reasons I don't have to explain here.

Clint Eastwood plays the self-sufficient man Josey Wales whose words carries weight with Chief Ten Bears. "There is iron in your words of life. No signed paper can hold the iron. It must come from men. The words of Ten Bears carry the same iron of life and death. It is good that warriors such as we meet in the struggle of life... or death. It shall be life." They are not of the same tribe but they speak the same iron tongue that is solid. They acknowledge each other as men.

We are obligated to our society and have roles to play. Can we unplug from daily life? Anyone walking through the Grand Canyon, or the Rockies will marvel and may consider how incredible this land was with roaming buffalo and deer. Being a city dweller, I am removed from this beauty. During the weekends I try and make time to see something other than concrete buildings. Have you ever just sat with men and said nothing? Have you just enjoyed the company of others around a fire and said little?

If you get time, I hope you'll call your brothers, or friends. Connect with members of your tribe, unplug for a minute, and enjoy that bond. Those who are often engrossed in the hustle and bustle of city life don't give themselves the chance to stop and reflect on the importance of life.

We all want a moment of leisure, a fraction of time, in order to tune out the noise, and tune into the things that matter. Those who are able to rise with the sun and get a morning walk in will get a chance to do this very thing. Those who reflect as the dawn rises, who become introspective as the night comes may find answer.

Drift Away

The original Jacob's Ladder movie moved me. The ending of this dark, psychological horror-thriller made 30 years ago still holds the same emotionally poignant wallop for me.

The actor Danny Aiello does a great job as his chiropractor dispensing profound advice to Jacob. Paraphrasing a quote by the Christian mystic Meister Eckhart, Aiello says to Jacob about his horrible nightmares, "The only thing that burns in hell is the part of you that won't let go of your life: your memories, your attachments. They burn them all away, but they're not punishing you, they're freeing your soul. If you're frightened of dying and you're holding on, you'll see devils tearing your life away. If you've made your peace, then the devils are really angels freeing you from the earth."

I was out for a long run and heard the beautiful song Drift Away by Mentor Williams. The song reminds me of my pained brother every time I hear it, and who wants it played at his funeral, but I also imagine a river. Dobie Gray's rich jangly intro is followed with heavy chords that make Mentor's song sublime.

Mentor said, "It was a song where it suddenly was okay for me to write about being hurt and let people know that I had been hurt and I wasn't afraid to expose my feelings."

No doubt many of us after seeing this movie or hearing this song think about how depressing life is at times and how fearful we might be about death or fear of loss. We must investigate to find out the source of our pain or our fear and see where it carries us.

Jacob seeks to hold onto the life that seems to be ebbing away at the triage, and Dobie seems to want to let it all go perhaps not literally but emotionally; each situation would transform any of us in a sensitively, meaningful way. We have all been there where we must let it go and sometimes, we must hold on.

In each of these stories I do not see gloom I see beauty in the darkness and for some odd reason I think too of philosopher Heraclitus quote and I am hopeful because I'm faced with the idea though change is inevitable, change can be good. "No man ever steps in the same river twice, for it's not the same river and he's not the same man." Don't be fearful of change.

I want to die

The poet T.S. Eliot was always one of my favorites. He was a perfect poet, yet an imperfect person, who glimpsed perfection with his far-off vision that lens of wonder that looked into the elasticity of time, and came away trying to find words to describe a loss of identity that came from a well dry of spiritual replenishment.

I shouldn't frame this as all culture, rather I mean to speak of warrior culture and pop culture, and its adherents to fashion and trends who would rather look chic than live the truest life of ritual; amoral living breeds warrior death by spiritual suicide. Men die inside every day, yet long for a vanished glory found only in mythology.

Eliot was criticized for being an elitist but isn't that the perspective that is necessary to hold the line to fight against spiritual paralysis? The above average man struggles to find his place in this world. He communes with others like himself or lives it alone. Who are the light-bearers? The answers to this struggle are never palatable. Self-control, personal responsibility, moral values, and individualism fights against the encroaching mechanical world.

I am reminded of the song by the Hunters and Collectors, "Woke up this morning from the strangest dream. I was in the biggest army the world has ever seen. We were marching as one. On the road to the holy grail." Will this water heal the Fisher King's Wasteland? We are fed culture via the dropper of pop culture. Better to drink some before it evaporates. Spiritual regeneration and return to health are possible. "Sibyl, what do you want?" And she says, "I want to die." We are atoms in the universe. Let us die and be reborn, on this day, into something better. "Living nor dead, and I knew nothing. Looking into the heart of light, the silence." Everything is beautiful and glorious.

You cannot fight an ocean with iron

The Roman Empire is gone just like many others before it. It's been a minute since I had the luxury of time to read The History of the Decline and Fall of the Roman Empire. A very good book. Had I the time I'd read Will and Ariel Durant's the Story of Western Civilization again. I still remember how my father, with such incredible recall, could pull a verse from one of the 11 volumes and describe something he read decades prior. My brother and I looked at him in amazement. How did this old dude have such mental powers? Time in. Every man has areas of his empire that he needs to develop. Some do and some don't. He read the classics, practiced Karate, travelled the world, and wrote on technology for work and a book for a university.

The English historian Edward Gibbon traced Western civilization from the height of the Roman Empire to the fall of Byzantium. Oswald Spengler noted nearly 20 + civilizations rose and fell due to infighting from their leadership. Spengler's model of history postulated that any culture is a superorganism with a limited and predictable lifespan. I didn't like his view on industrialism and racism nor his politics but his viewpoint was interesting. The Romans fought with outsiders, those Barbarian tribes, and also fought battles within.

I give a lot of thought to men who fight the undulating waves of emotion that roil inside the heart. An old tale tells of a Greek warrior, who in losing his mind, fought the ocean waves with the iron rods held in his hands. The movie Gladiator did a fine job of showing the Romans battling an ocean sized army of German tribes. If we can learn anything from history it is that we cannot deal with the insurrections that come from without until we strengthen the empire within. We must do the work to build more than just columns of stone or our weaponry for the armory. We must work on our mind, spirit, heart and social networks to keep our empire strong. You cannot fight an ocean with iron.

False Prophets

There are gods above gods, but every god made by man is a worthless thing, and every man is a church with the potential to become a grand cathedral, but failing to put a single match to candle becomes a black, vacuum until his life extinguishes.

We should live to fight devils, to shelter angels, and to build holy houses, but men too in love with their own pain will let what they love kill them. A spirit that gives up resistance becomes a useless thing.

Some men with an allegiance to their own suffering knowing well that it was constituted by their addictions, can't find any respite from it, even though they beg Heaven for its greatest healing. In fact, as their misfortunes increased, those willing to stand beside them out of impatience decreased, and their willpower ebbed and emptied. Dead men walk the earth. What ends a man's suffering? Con men with broken spirits croak, "give me through my solicitations of pain the entire world's suffering and I will turn it into hope." Who are they fooling?

Legends say King Arthur sent out his men to find the Holy Grail, a wondrous device that offered goodness in sustenance in infinite abundance to stop the world's pain and keep the hellhounds at bay, but the knights never found it, and no man ever drank from it and the world will always be as it's meant to be.

Until that time, we must learn to see that an unspiritual man can fix nothing, until he lets go of his fake heroes, false gods, and primeval philosophies. Live Rightly though it is the most difficult thing you'll ever do. Matthew 6:33 But seek first the kingdom of God.

Tonight, be a MAN

There are tender songs out there. Maybe you've heard a few. Dionne Warwick once sang "Walk on by" very melodiously. A dreamy song. A delightful, soulful, tender song that stirs the hearts of gentle men to long for what seems simpler times, and simpler problems. Boy meets girl, boy breaks up with girl. Girl ask boy to keep walking if he sees her.

Life seems more complex today with the advent of technology and our exposure to social media, the news, and the awareness of economic, political et al issues. But nothing has changed at all. Or has it? A woman stung by rejection stands alone on a silent street while her lover can only surmise what thoughts run through her injured mind. He sees the tears fall from her face and heartbreakingly she wants him to leave her to her pain and shame and regrets. Or does she really?

Black and white film with characters that play out in herky jerky fashion. Old movie reels are amazing. We get sucked into the action. Where is my story going tonight?

Whether a man was a soldier 2000 years ago or today, love hasn't changed at all but there are distractions like cell phones and television that make quiet, calm communication and real connection more difficult for couples looking to work things out. Dial down the ignorance tonight, put away the video games and your projects. Get pulled into her world and wants and worries and will and let her be a little girl while you be the man. Carry that weight. Turn around and let her melt into your husky shoulders tonight. That is all.

Board that train

There's a powerful ending scene in the movie Hostiles starring actor Christine Bale as Army Capt. Joseph Blocker. Rosalie, and the orphaned child Little Bear stand on a train platform, say goodbye and board a train to Chicago.

As the train starts moving, Blocker begins to walk away from them, but he turns back and after some consideration, boards the train as it leaves the station. His hardened face, and his stoic character is framed by good camera work and the angelic sounding tones of the soundtrack fittingly captures his muscular body. He is sad and standing pensively at the door of the train car before he turns the doorknob and enters the portal.

This is a deeply thoughtful, and powerful man. He is a warrior of the highest esteem; a book reading, gunslinging noble man. This is a scene we won't see in movies such as Shane, or most with John Wayne. The hero, beaten, bloodied, weighted with deep thoughts about the loss he's suffered through all of his perilous journeys would never share those pains with another soul. Slowly he spins around to face the departing train, his deep, penetrating eyes that have seen so much lock in sync with the easy movement of this departing train.

Army Capt. Joseph Blocker turns upon his heels and in doing so becomes a different man. Daily we must strive to find a different drum beat and break the lock-step we've marched to for so long.

Loser, liar, coward, weakling

This morning in a dream delivered to me I was reminded of the things that I did in my past that are to blame for the thefts I suffered, small and large sums I wittingly removed from my vitality. In order to feel some sense of peace with myself I have to accept what I stole. Those that I loved are not coming back, for one reason or another, because they either died or moved on.

Those who I professed to love were damaged simply due to my own failures to live up to their expectations of what they believed I should be, and I to live up to mine. There is a litany of other reasons we parted and, in the end, living with lots of guilt is a very painful thing.

I believe it was Nietzsche who once stated the only true Christian was Christ. Even if it's not a true statement it resonates with me. Who dares to truly live out what they claim? That would be difficult indeed, while how many of us are burdened by the labels or titles given to us? Loser, liar, coward, weakling; there are names far worse to be called; yet if untrue, if we believe in the names, we've been called the damage to our heart, mind and soul can injure us for a lifetime if we allow it.

In the same vein how many of us give ourselves labels or titles but we never live up to them? How many of us fall short of being what we think we are and should be? Father, warrior, brother, defender? A lot of the disharmony we feel in our life is caused by many issues but in the realm of authenticity we do damage to our psyche by living as we shouldn't, never trying to break through the barriers of what we couldn't. We can't change how others think of us and it's not my focus here.

We can't change the past but if we want to reclaim some power over ourselves and have strong comfort and assurance in who we are what we can do it is to live honestly, to live deliberately, and vitally.

We must do the work to be live and love as deeply as we should. Yes, we are resilient and we can heal. When we are ready to unravel the past, we should begin to trace yesterday's fixed cord back to its origin in order to repair the unfixed tomorrow and restore power to ourselves. I too know that a price must be paid. I must honor those who lived and died for me, whose words hold value and dominion over my spirit and heart.

Listen to the phonograph

Thomas Edward Lawrence could write, and he could write very well. Anyone interested in a reading about his war experiences should pick up the Seven Pillars of Wisdom. Lawrence accomplished much in is short life. He had a command of the English language, and then some, for he could read and speak French, German, Latin, Greek, Arabic, Turkish and Syriac as well.

Some called him a fraud, and that a few of his contributions to the war were but fiction yet most of those claims against him over time have been disproved. He was a very perceptive thinker, an excellent observer, and well knew his own failures. His sensitivity and deep introspection were treated as oddities in the early twentieth century. Blowing up train tracks, out-riding the Arabs and rushing to greet war,

how inspiring yet he paid a price too. He wrote of his painful captivity, his rape, under the Turks as, "at night the citadel of my integrity had been irrevocably lost."

I've read over 20 books on Lawrence and many of his papers, and I do not personally believe him to be a charlatan. He certainly understood his own broken nature and the motivations of other men, and well captured some of his observations in his book titled The Mint. In the end he attempted to retreat to Cloud Hills for privacy. I don't know if many young men try to model themselves after Lawrence but I certainly did; poet, writer, strategist, politician; how I failed at it all!

What grabbed at me the most was what he did with his quiet time. He played his phonograph, read books and wrote, and even ate from sardine tins while having thoughtful conversations with likeminded dear friends about literature and life. I hope you spend some time away from tech.

Go for a walk at night, look at the moon or the setting sun because the dusky sky is like a cinema; and the glow as it sets on the horizon are like chattering embers having an incredible conversation before it all ends. Think about the wars you fought, the life you lived, the patrols you did, the criminals you arrested, and the love you gave; whatever they were try to recognize your value in life despite your own secret griefs and private pains. Live.

Through discipline comes freedom

Those who enjoyed Michael Mann's movie The Last of the Mohicans likely don't know about a great made for TV movie called The Jericho Mile. As an impressionable, young man and a distance runner this 1979 movie had quite the effect on me.

In short, the movie is about a prisoner named "Rain" Murphy who is stuck in Folsom Prison for life on a first-degree murder charge. He prefers to be alone and spends much of his time running around the facility's track. When he begins reaching a mile in under four minutes, he gains the attention of the jail's officials, who consider entering him into the Olympics via the trials.

The movie is very good and has early markings of Mann's developing genius. There are gang fights, a love story, friendship, fights against the system etc. Murphy and his friend named Stiles do hard prison time. Stiles plasters picture of his wife and son across his cell wall to help him cope. Murphy on the other hand lives under Spartan conditions. Except for a sink pipe that he regularly unscrews to turn into a pull up bar there is nothing to get him through but running.

While gangs are killing and raping each other in prison Murphy stays outside the frays and focuses on his goal of running in the Olympic trials. A wild and emotional man can be surrounded by a thousand men and could feel alone while solitude and discipline might have the opposite effect and make him feel connected to the world.

Running and structure can do something to men who feel disconnected from their brethren even as they run alone. And while in the dark of his cell or room where he is naked and alone, his ears prick up to the sounds no one else can hear and they are like electric fire into his soul.

He hears the whirling of the stars and feels a connection to the universe. His eyes focus through the dark and keys in on his goals. He visualizes success because he can still visualize a tomorrow, a new beginning. The walls come tumbling down. Men are responsible for their own freedom.

"Through discipline comes freedom." Aristotle.

Violence is a beautiful thing

Violence is a beautiful thing. My buddy made this statement. I suppose an explosion is beautiful to a soldier as it levels his enemies, to the crowd observing a boxer destroying his opponent yet is it beautiful to the woman being punched in the mouth by her husband?

I think most of us can identify beautiful violence when we see it. In Chesterton's book The Man Who was Thursday the character Gabriel Syme, is a poet, philosopher, and detective who infiltrates a meeting of the Central Anarchist Council in London. Of the seven members, each named for a day of the week, he finds out that each anarchist is a detective recruited by the president named Sunday. Gregory, the only real anarchist, challenges the Council and implies they never suffered like their subjects and so their power is illegitimate.

Sunday is asked if he has ever suffered. His last words are, "can ye drink of the cup that I drink of?" Jesus asked this of James and John to challenge their commitment in becoming his disciples. Syme immediately understands that all the things on earth must fight each other.

Chesterton wrote this book to affirm that goodness and right were at the heart of every aspect of the world. The book ""...was intended to describe the world of wild doubt and despair which the pessimists were generally describing at that date..." "The policeman who recruits him explains that there is a difference between the real anarchists and the innocent ones who merely think rules are bad and should be broken."

The real anarchists whose philosophy brings the Culture of Death are something far worse than that. "They mean death. When they say that mankind shall be free at last, they mean that mankind shall commit suicide. When they talk of a paradise without right or wrong, they mean the grave. They have but two objects, to destroy humanity and then themselves." If you're musing on this post, consider his words about strength and going the full distance as disciples for one or for the other. "Moderate strength is shown in violence, supreme strength is shown in levity." – "The Six Philosophers, "The Man Who was Thursday. Can you drink of the same cup?" Think about what He meant, and the violence that can come to you.

Commemorial Woe

We are on our own again. Memories of the sea and our scouting party that lost itself in a tangle of trees inside the fog. We waited by the cliff wall and counted the autumns that had come and gone, counted the minutes in our head, counted the friends that are long dead and counted the needless unwanted messes that plagued our life. We counted the lighting flashes overhead, counted the boats and the seamen and barquentines that passed and the innumerable waves that broke upon the breakwater until our boatman came. We counted the failed missions of our life and the love that left us on our darkest night. We counted the plunging leaves and were dazzled by the shifting wind in the night that whispered we will die. We counted even as our eyes turned to stone, as our heart broke, we were alone. We counted and counted dead men and our commemorial woe and prayed for a better tomorrow. Behind the gates and walls that housed the falls of a thousand men and then some, were named Antietam and Bull Run and Stonewall, upon our lips. We left the grounds in silence. We could count no more.

Fall from grace

We fall from planes, we fall from grace, we fall in our dreams and we even fall to our knees. We descend freely because of the force of gravity, and leave our erect position sometimes suddenly and involuntarily. Though standing erect feels safer and more natural than falling we sometimes fall by choice. If we do fall involuntarily sometimes it's because we tripped or we fell to ruin, in defeat and failure, and Heaven forbid we never fall down dead or fall because we are permanently wounded.

Sometimes men voluntarily genuflect and lower their body briefly by bending one of their knees to the ground as a sign of respect or worship. Perhaps they go even lower as if kowtowing to something. No matter, there is much to learn about ourselves when we fall by choice or force.

The playwright Oscar Wilde once wrote, "We are all in the gutter but some of us are looking at the stars." The line was spoken by the character Lord Darlington as he confessed his love and was rejected by Lady Windermere. We can understand his sentiment. Darlington understands that there is a distance between himself and the stars, between him and her, and what is reachable and what is unobtainable. He cannot have her. He looks up from his gutter, which is used to carry surface water to the sewer, and understands as he longs for her that he feels he will never be worthy of this woman, this bright star.

No one will ever be convinced of your sincerity, of the seriousness of your sufferings, unless you show them. However, men who cannot realize their inherent value just might let themselves be carried down with the sewage of life. We cannot always get what we want but if we focus on what is divine and our sacred sacraments, we will realize there isn't a chasm at all between ourselves and the sublime. Fall more often than not and before you get up dwell on why you need to stand up each time, and pursue with fervor what you can pursue. You'll find the stars are closer than you think.

Discern

"We make men without chests and expect from them virtue and enterprise. We laugh at honor and are shocked to find traitors in our midst." — C.S. Lewis, The Abolition of Man.

I read a story told about a child who was raised in a coffin. I haven't been able to verify this story. Likely an urban myth but chilling nevertheless. What I did find was an academic paper written by David Naugle. Naugle shares the shocking story of a boy who was raised by his grandparents because his parents abandoned him. The grandparents assume the task of raising the child yet they do so very grudgingly. The child is allowed to leave the coffin only in order to eat or to go the bathroom.

The boy is confined to this box for some bizarre reason and believes that all children are raised in coffins. When the authorities come to rescue him, they find that the child had no idea there was any other way to live. THIS was the child's reality. It seems his world was turned upside-down. Don't let people hijack what the "truth" is and try to recondition your way of thinking. Learn to reason well and think clearly. We are raising up a nation of idiots and fools whom if given the chance will tear our nation down.

We only get glimpses of glory

We only get glimpses of glory. That's the way it was meant to be. We only get fragments of the eternal. Though we hold the idea of it in our mind we barely fathom the immense structure of forever. On my plane flight home, I was able to skim through a few movies: Gladiator, the Last Samurai and Rocky. I studied each one. Each timeless movie speaks to me as it likely does to other men. Daily some of us wrestle with a heightened awareness that there is another world out there waiting for us. There is bifurcation in our singular thought; we are of two minds. We exist in the life of the mundane yet yearn for another life filled with greatness. It seems there is a simple truth in it that by simply living in our ordinary world we are granted opportunities to see the immenseness of this world and where we fit in them. I do not know whether you will experience painful profundity or immense joy unequally.

Each protagonist has a struggle. Maximus, Algren and Balboa face challenges. Whether it was thrust upon them or they chose it is irrelevant to me. Their way of navigating through it is to take chances, be true to their goal, and to do the work to achieve it; all of it is fraught with peril. Key moments are Maximus' vision of Elysium, Rocky's celebratory dance on the stairs, and Algren's return to honor.

Each hero's struggle reveals something about them that connects with us and it is their humanity. Simply existing may bring glimpses of glory, this nebulous, heightened awareness of another world but waiting for it to happen may not happen. Glory is fleeting, as my friend Kurt says, and that's true. I do not say chase glory. I say take risks, be focused & true in order to find your humanity and peace. If living in the mundane is the equilibrium then I ask what can you do to go up or down?

Outside of a death, birth of a child or wedding day to change our perspective what are you doing to enlarge your view of life and enhance your focus? Both can bring a sobering understanding of where you need to be next and it allows you to choose your next move. If the ordinary is the equilibrium, then just one honest deliberate choice brings a heightened awareness of this world.

Glory

Private Trip speaks in the movie Glory, "[addressing the 54th the night before battle] I ain't much about no prayin,' now. I ain't never had no family, and... killed off my mama. Well, I just... Y'all's the onliest family I got. I love the 54th. Ain't even much a matter what happens tomorrow, 'cause we men, ain't we? We men."

Where to begin? If there ever was a war movie that had me bawling more than a newborn it was the movie Glory. Whether it was true or not Denzel was fantastic in it. The story speaks to men on a profound level and simply connects with our hearts.

Put anyone in a cage and they long to be free. Even most cons who are resigned to life behind the walls would choose freedom if given emancipation from brick-and-mortar surroundings.

One of the movie quotes that resonated with me was the one spoken by character Colonel Shaw, "We are fighting for a people whose poetry has not yet been written." Think about that for a minute. Are there not people the world over who are imprisoned? North Korea, the Middle-East and there are people trapped into slavery here in Washington DC. Human trafficking is no joke.

I'm not proposing a simple solution to a complex problem. Just some food for thought today as you sip your coffee. In the movie the 54th Massachusetts Regiment fights in the battle at Fort Wagner against the Confederate States, and the final scene shows men running into cannon fire. This is cinema but can we ponder for a moment the bravery that it took to do this? Where did fear go?

The movie ends with bodies lying lifeless on the sands of Fort Wagner. The audience wipes their tears away, stares at the movie screen and contemplates how brave men lived and died and we consider our own life, where we fit in it and where we're going next. Consider what these men did to give us freedom. If you have time today read a book, see a movie or do something that opens your heart and let that beast of a man roam. Let him wander. Let that bear cry and when you've done that in the wilderness and also the prisons of your own making, smile.

Tell yourself today is a good day and you know the reasons why. Because you are free, because you have the right to choose who you want to be or not be. Other men and women died for us. That has never stopped resonating with me

Yakuza

The Yakuza is a 1974 Japanese-American neo-noir gangster film. The film is about a man named Kilmer (Robert Mitchum) who returns to Japan after several years away in order to rescue his friend's kidnapped daughter with the help of a man named Ken (Takura). Ken outraged that his sister Eiko was deeply indebted to Kilmer disappears into the Yakuza underworld. 20 years later Kilmer must team with Ken to make things right. Kilmer ends up rescuing the daughter, killing her father, and losing the woman he loved.

There is a moving scene at the end of the film where Kilmer gives Ken a folded handkerchief. He says "please accept this token of my apology" for "bringing great pain into your life, both in the past and in the present." Ken accepts, and Kilmer asks that "if you can forgive me, then you can forgive Eiko," adding, "you are greatly loved and respected by all your family." Ken professes that "no man has a greater friend than Kilmer-san" Kilmer overcome with emotion says the same of Ken.

Their obligations are resolved. Both men bow to each other before parting. In this day and age there still are men that fulfil their obligations without contracts. They follow through on courses of action to which each of them is morally or legally bound despite the enormous cost to both of them. Each man has lost a lot. Ken loses his sister; Kilmer loses his lover. Today men give handshakes yet break agreements, talk trash behind keyboards, and shout while believing their loud barking is frightful to others who know better. How things would be different, in our "civilized" world, if we could go back to the gun and the sword to settle matters. Each man undergoes immense hardship. Though they are from different cultures and their arts, customs and achievements quite disparate their code of honor is very similar. I am reminded of a quote by Morihei Ueshiba, "The samurai is the first to suffer anxiety for human society, and he is the last to seek personal pleasure." Men like Ken and Kilmer can be violent but deep within their hearts are men who believe in the power of love and respect. They are not barbarians, rather they are refined men.

Alone

We've all been there before, right? Traveling through some old ancient towns without company. How funny that a man can be surrounded by a million men and yet still feel alone though solitude can simultaneously make a man feel connected to the world.

In my dark room my ears pricked up to the music coming through my window. I heard words spoken melodiously, and sounds which felt like an electric fire. They launched into my soul and woke my heart like a radio charged with unlimited energy and allowed healing in my erratic journey to continue. The mechanics of my mind worked even if there wasn't a connection of my soul to my brain stem. It was enough to get me moving from one lover to another and track backwards to my origin. Who the hell was I going to damage next?

Guzzle hundreds of pints and devour a thousand crisps trying to figure it out; a million miles away a busker singing an acapella Country Roads song with such fever alerted me to the simple fact that my life had worth and I missed home. A day later my face was savaged by a few

drunks and every blow I landed upon them came coiled within it my own hatred for the world; bullets filled with black powder loaded by my anger. Sometimes we walk away from the light and go into the dark. Sometimes we must break things and be broken in order to reveal the hidden treasure glowing inside ourselves.

How crippling to think about someone you lost, and the moments that won't come back, and the relationship you couldn't develop because death took them away. Peace seems to vanish and all that replaces that hole is pain and the only thing that removes the hurt is purpose. Recollecting how valuable they were and what good they contributed to your life hurts but heals.

Love is never extinguished and their value is never diminished and the pain sometimes feels just like a dull throbbing ache that doesn't disappear but won't possess the heart completely any longer. If you've got someone love them with a mature passion and you'll have no regrets. Try to be happy for the time you had together.

The Silver Cord

Where are they now, our admired heroes, close friends or our young loves? Our time with them was taken away. Listening to certain songs now brings forth old memories and lets it squat strongly in the fore of our mind. Where is the patrolman we lost to murder, the Marine we lost to war, the mother we lost to cancer, the wife we lost to separation, or the girl we lost to another man?

Some are gone because of some complex tragedy or an occurrence that was as simple as a simple goodbye.

How odd is it that a song can uncoil so much of what was wrapped tightly inside of us? Our heart holds a spool of finite emotion that unwinds as a song plays, and like an old record album that ends when the needle falls off the track, our emotion ends too. But while the song ends something new occurs and we might not be ready for the transformative effect the sirens power has on us.

Our fine and vulnerable thread is drawn from our heart like a trembling wire and even a dandelion flower dancing upon it could make us crumble. The nerve exposed, those raw feelings, feels tangible. Despite our heart protesting loudly we really don't want to stop that loss. Though it is a loss we cannot control, it is a pain we want to suffer, and there are sensations and memories we want to recall for far longer than that magic, piercing sting of music and words will last.

This can be a dangerous thing to those with a fragile heart for it can reframe our current sensibility and pull from us some latent feelings we didn't know rested in our soul. Every song out there is different for every one of us.

Yes, many songs from singers do capture heartache and loss. Leonard Cohen, Chet Baker or maybe songs from singers like Diana Ross and the Supremes Reflections. Good writers and singers create things that feel visceral and elegant and can pierce us deeply! Oh deeply! Maybe they don't suit your taste. I simply posit that through our hurting we will have a life better lived and a loss better embraced. Pain sometimes helps us work to finally understand a loss. Let some healing begin and a good conclusion happen. It's something you owe to yourself if it's not also something you owe to their memory.

Where is your Nirvana?

Have you ever watched the movie Big Wednesday? It was directed by John Milius the same guy involved in the movies Conan and Red Dawn. Wikipedia notes. "The film tells the story of three young friends whose passion in life is surfing. Their surfing lives are traced from the summer of 1962 to their attempts of dodging the Vietnam War and to the end of their innocence in 1968 when one of their friends is killed in Vietnam. The three make the difficult transition to adulthood with parties, surf trips, marriage, and the war."

Many of us men relate to the perceived indestructibility of youth, the transition from youth into maturity and added responsibility, the loss of friends and lovers, and the demands of life upon a care free-life style, and finally the loss of innocence and you know why? Because we've all been there before.

Every coming-of-age movie done well illuminates some simple truths for young men. We cannot stop the coming of the future, we will lose friends, we will age and grow as people, we cannot always change our situation but we can change how we see ourselves in it.

We surfed the waves, brazenly rode our bikes fast along mountain ridges, swam in hidden country lakes and dove fearlessly into cold streams. Do you recall the place where you had your first kiss, or met the girl you wanted to be with forever? Do you recall your first punch up with your mortal enemy Butch or Dumbass?

My ashes will be spread across Steamer's Lane. Good times watching sunsets, swimming the sea and running across the shore. All I ask today is what is your Nirvana? What is your secret garden or private place that is a refuge from the world and hell? Where is your Call of the Wild? Is it inside or outside?

I run. I run and it brings me peace to quiet the enormous storm in my head. Mountains tops and hills are my masters and I'm enthralled by their beauty. Do you have a place? Is it where you hunt or fish? I don't say go back to your old haunts but I ask that you do find a place that helps you waken old yet good memories, that allows you to connect with the spirit of the past and the greatness of the universe. Connect yourself daily with your Nirvana.

Uncommon Valor

Why did we love the character Sailor from the movie Uncommon Valor? A character yes, but some truths from cinema that can be learned. He was honest with himself and could accept what drove his mission in life. He told it like it was.

Don't create an image that you hate trying to keep up with. Find happiness in being yourself. Dance your stupid dances, and sing your silly songs, and discard for just a moment the structure of your life and live. Walk the tracks, scan the sinking shape of the sun setting across the hillsides, and don't betray the memories you once let die. Pursue one good dream tonight.

I'm reminded of men who feel like the walls of life are closing upon them, and that death one day will find them. We are mortal but remember even in our youth though we were callow we sometimes had the courage to try. Live as if there is no tomorrow.

No beast so fierce

If you watched the movie Reservoir Dogs and recall the character called Mr. Blue then you might know he was played by writer, actor and ex con Edward Bunker. Bunker retooled the Akira Kurosawa script for the movie Runaway Train about two cons hiding abroad an out-of-control train speeding through Alaska.

Jon Voight does an incredible job playing the character Manny; a tough man who shuns the world and wants revenge on the warden for making his time in the pen difficult. The final scene of the movie is powerful.

Manny breaks the link on the main engine and allows the other riders the chance to live while he surely chooses to die. He climbs onto the main engine's rooftop. He waves goodbye and rides to his death. The warden is handcuffed within the racing block of iron. Smoke billows from the engine, cold air and rushing snow presses upon his grimacing face. His arms are outstretched. Angelic voices sing eerily as he heads willingly to his death.

The movie closes with an on-screen quote from William Shakespeare's Richard III: "No beast so fierce but knows some touch of pity." "But I know none, and therefore am no beast." What kind of man is this? An animal as the warden calls Manny or is he a man, a true human being? The film goes dark.

Perhaps Bunker penned a silly fantasy about a con who dies gloriously while killing a warden or perhaps the simple allegory is really deeper than one surmises. One man loses his freedom while another man in dying gains his.

Like the story or not, like the con or not, in every man is the seemingly indistinguishable light of life we all hold within us. Intense circumstances reveal the size of each man's spark and his pain can sometimes illuminate what seems absent and it is the fuel to set the fuel off. Today my friends choose to live, for a second die to your meaningless ambitions and ponder for a minute the value of having freedom. Let the spark of life become an inferno for others to see. Go out and grab more of it.

Catch a falling star

There's a great scene called Alice Jumps in the movie Last of the Mohicans. Alice would rather die than to live with Magua. The perfection of the movie is helped in great part by the dreamy soundtrack, the seriousness of the actors, and the excellent story and movie directing.

As music plays, we see Alice look behind her to see the high distance between the cliff edge to the ground. She knows what she'll do next. Magua now knows too. He drops his knife, holds his hand out and beckons her to come. In slow motion she drops off the cliff and to her death.

The lesson for us is about courage and living life on your own terms. Alice cannot go forward because to do so is death, even if she keeps her life as a slave of the Hurons. Ahead is truly a bitter lesson. She can't go back because that time is passed.

The power in this scene is that she exits the conflict and makes a move that no one could predict. She takes her consequences and they are from her choices and not those imposed upon her. Her whole being commits to action and like a spurt of fire she plunged to her death but is like an inferno lighting the way to the audience watching her fall like a star. Powerful. If we could only be so brave. It's only a movie but it gives us much to think about. *I am not advocating suicide. Listen to Director Michael Mann elaborate more on the film.*

Echolocation

"Why do we fall down?" Thomas Wayne asks Bruce Wayne. "So that we can learn to pick ourselves up." Batman's father is the voice of reason to someone in need. Be that person. We can all understand that pain is a signal to the mind that the body has been damaged or something is wrong with it.

Pain is a signal to us that we need to stop what we are doing or to take alternative action. Those who cannot identify some of their triggers, or comprehend what painful emotions are creeping up, or what alternative action they should take will need your help.

Remember that their echolocation sense is broken. Like injured bats men too let out a scream, a shout, a cry for help but nothing on the other end receives the message and pinpoints the way. Show them!

Batman needed someone. Alfred, his Butler, became the voice of strength Bruce needed when he was uncertain. Alfred is the calm in

Batman's s---storm of a life. Easy answers to complex problems don't exist. There aren't cookie-cutter solutions to every problem in life but don't give up. Again, sometimes all a person needs is your presence. If that means being on the other end of the phone, or driving up to their house when they are on a rampage, then do this. You might find that your simple act of compassion for someone hurting will take them beyond the place of isolation and into the place of feeling like you truly are their brother.

Yes, Batman was a character from the comics and in the movies. But the character's struggle in movie The Dark Knight Rises movie resonates with us because it is an eternal struggle, we can all relate to. Every man, woman and child will be in a place of hurt many times in their life.

One of the most powerful scenes in this movie is Bruce Wayne's prison escape where he takes a leap of faith in order to set himself free from a literal hole in the ground. But he is not alone. A fellow prisoner, acting as his conscience, asks him questions and gives him answers. Perhaps you can be the voice in the darkness that a man needs to hear. I am not an expert in these matters. This is only my opinion but I will tell you, one day when the time comes, I hope you will teach a man to rise up once again. Good luck.

Seek out noble things

Years ago, singer Mary Hopkins sang a catchy song called Those Were the Days. It was a great beer tavern song and those who like to reminisce will find comfort and some sadness in singing the tune and recollecting memories of friends now long gone.

Artist Terry Jacks redid the popular song by Jacques Brel called Seasons in the Sun. The lyrics summon the past and in some sorrowful way allow for the sentimentalist the bitter sweetness of having loved, lived and known the pangs of something dying but such is the string of life that must be severed, sooner or later.

"Goodbye Papa it's hard to die. When all the birds are singing in the sky. Now that the spring is in the air. Little children everywhere. When you see them, I'll be there."

The songs are simple, the imagery in both songs is rich. Each tells of moments that will not come back.

We give love, we should get love. Sometimes there's a lot of value in feeling pain from loss because the mind becomes quite introspective. The heart and mind both open and wounded will seek closure and may grasp onto ignoble things to seal the rupture. If it's a choice between choosing cheap immediacy over worthwhile remoteness to bridge that gap, I'd choose to search longer for a place to make my crossing, and ensure that suture holds. The thread of time will join us one day closer together to what we lost. The vile will always be vile and the worthy will continue to be worthwhile so let the good hold, for the twain should never meet. Cheapness will never hold.

Seek out good things to pull your injury together. Time will cross this world into the next and let you know the scar you believed could never heal in fact healed. Be patient, love richly, and wait for the secret chord to pull you together with what you lost.

Where is home?

While one man constructs another man is busy being destructive. The man who yearns to control and civilize and enrich his lot will most likely do so and in turn touch the lives of others. Sometimes man fights with man to build his home.

Property disputes occur in small and large fashion. Amazonian Indians are moved from their jungle land in the Amazon to make way for a growing, more powerful civilization. Whether modern or not this world is filled with animals too; mindless dogs like ISIS. Physical destruction is not as bad as destroying a society. No one can come back after that.

The after effects are that refugees rush into the cities where there are jobs which creates an over reliance on the invaders as a necessity of survival. Jobs, soldiers, prostitutes, maids, shoe shine boys, blacksmiths exist where a sanctuary once stood. William Penn settled Pennsylvania as a place for his Quaker brothers and sisters. A place where if they worked the land, it would be attractive to others and tolerant of their religion.

Planning done well creates cities that are largely beautiful and successful, such as Milan. Politics and social issues are different matters. Planning that is done poorly creates blight in cities like Detroit, Michigan. Ghosts of Detroit. Ghosts of Rome. The big automakers no longer create jobs or cars in Michigan. Much has been lost. Creators bring forth objects out of ideas; the loom, the printing press, the steeple, the archway, the compass. Some villages will only ever be villages. Some cities will grow or degrade.

Many factors play into why places rise or fall. Iraq, a place filled with history and wonderful relics today is full of people who destroy all they touch. Tangible things are sterile things. It is man who provides value to those objects or devalues those objects: Rome, Stalingrad, or Timbuktu…are meaningless without men to find meaning in occupying it.

Are all homes made of brick and mortar? In Hebrew the word beyt means home or tent. A traveler would take up his home and carry it with him on his camel or ass.

Are homes fixed in place or maybe they are more about memory and emotional residue in the heart than tangibility? Some men feel better sailing on the high seas yet isn't a ship a home? Where do you rest your head? The thought of home seems to be as tangible a thing as a lump in our throat. We can't see it but we know that it's there. The feeling of what a home is seems to be stuck in our soul. It seems as if it is 'built' into us.

What about those who do not feel 'it' or feel as if they haven't actually known a place called home?

Home. Each man's dream of home is different from his brother's but in the end aren't all of these dreams the same? Keep in mind that a habitat and a home are different things. Solitude and loneliness are different too. Or are they? Whether we walk to our home in solitude at midnight near quiet harbors, or trek across endless dunes and shifting sand aren't those senses the same?

We can cut through straight alleys or follow the curve of a river where cherry blossoms grow. Whether it is brick or stone or logs or iron bars, a home must provide man the feeling of inward peace no matter how large it outwardly sprawls. Whether it is a metropolis or a mud hut a home should provide comfort. Where is your home?

If we live in our home or if our city is our home or if our country is our home, how then do we rid ourselves of the disconnection we sometimes feel for the rest of the world? How does a man shut down the outside distractions that blind him to his inner peace? Does he have peace? What if he came home from war and didn't have peace?

Should we leave our fast-food shops and much of what technology has to offer alone. Should we completely sever the cord or should we from time to time unplug from the world of modern conveniences? Perhaps much can be learned by listening to our internal voice that guides us deeper into an understanding of peace and to where our home is.

For some a home is part of their self-definition. Some people like others to know the community in which they live, and the kind of habitat in which they've settled; they mow the lawn, plant trees, put permanent things down, and build relationships with others around their enclave. It is a way to distinguish themselves from the rest of the community.

Some Westerners do not believe they are defined by the kind of property they possess. Their consciousness or sense of self and what a home is comes from their experiences and personality. In the exciting and inspiring movie Gladiator, the character Maximus (played by Russell Crow) knows that home is a place where his wife and son are. They are his safe harbor.

They are his high tower. In the story Maxiumus has wealth, power, the love and respect of his men. He is a warrior but he is also a farmer. Before the Romans battle the Germanic horde, Maximus grabs soil and rolls it in his hand. He holds it to his nose and sniffs the dirt. Maximus knows what kinds of earth are good for planting. He also knows what home is. How about you?

Marcus Aurelius learned how to shape his own life by controlling his thoughts. He accepted that life was filled with trials and tribulations. Life was not easy for him. He encountered many troubles as Emperor but he reasoned that the universe was fundamentally good. His place of peace, his inner sanctum or citadel, was his mind.

Aurelius controlled that space. He shaped his life around believing that being virtuous empowered him to be courageous enough to face heartache. Any impediment in life was met with firm resolve to not be broken. His mind was his fortress and it was a home where peace settled. Peace lived within him. Nothing without could affect him.

My Instagram posts started merely as an exercise for myself. I hope you found it enjoyable. I wanted to work out some kinks in my thinking. Whether brilliant or not I ask you to work to find peace in your heart. Surround yourself with friends, lovers, family and be grateful for the little you have. You have power over your mind. Find your strength and share it with others. You will not want to flee but rather choose to stay. Realize this-nothing can harm you. Home is where the heart is.

Wild Thing

D.H. Lawrence was an outsider who did not fit into the constructs of normal society. He longed to feel love and ecstasy in a world where he perceived contradictions. He wrote "But better die than live mechanically a life that is a repetition of repetitions."

Some of us find kinship with phenomenological writers like Lawrence, George Eliot, Thomas Hardy or E.M. Forster; men who need conflict while they are paradoxically seeking a unity of the soul through their experience with the exterior and interior world.

The Self Pity poem that Urgayle reads becomes an important part of the film GI Jane. The closing scene frames the whole story of his and her collision, similarities, differences and then separate and also parallel journeys.

Urgayle gives her the gift of the book, with the poem inside of it, to signal to Demi Moore's character that he is apologizing to her for the abuse she suffered under his hands. He respects her. Certainly, she has transformed from recruit to SEAL, but Urgayle has transformed too.

His two varied, readings of the poem mark his growth as a man. Humans have the greatest ability to pity themselves. No animal can do this. Animals live in each moment without any philosophic forethought or reflection on the past even if it starves, but not man. The human soul aspires to be something less human, less weakly, and godlier. Yet, being weakly can paradoxically, momentarily set us free.

Humility is the gateway for transformation into something sacred, noble, and worthy. The symbol of the bird varies in each culture, yet is generally thought to symbolize freedom. In Maori culture they symbolize strength and valor; for some it symbolizes eternal life; the link between heaven and earth. The Egyptians believed the bird symbol represented the power of the soul leaving a person's body.

What do we think about or feel when an animal dies? What do we think about or feel when a man dies? How should we approach their death? How should we approach our own death? What lesson can we learn about our own finiteness? An animal cannot ask these questions and yet, a bird dies "nobly" without ever feeling sorry for itself.

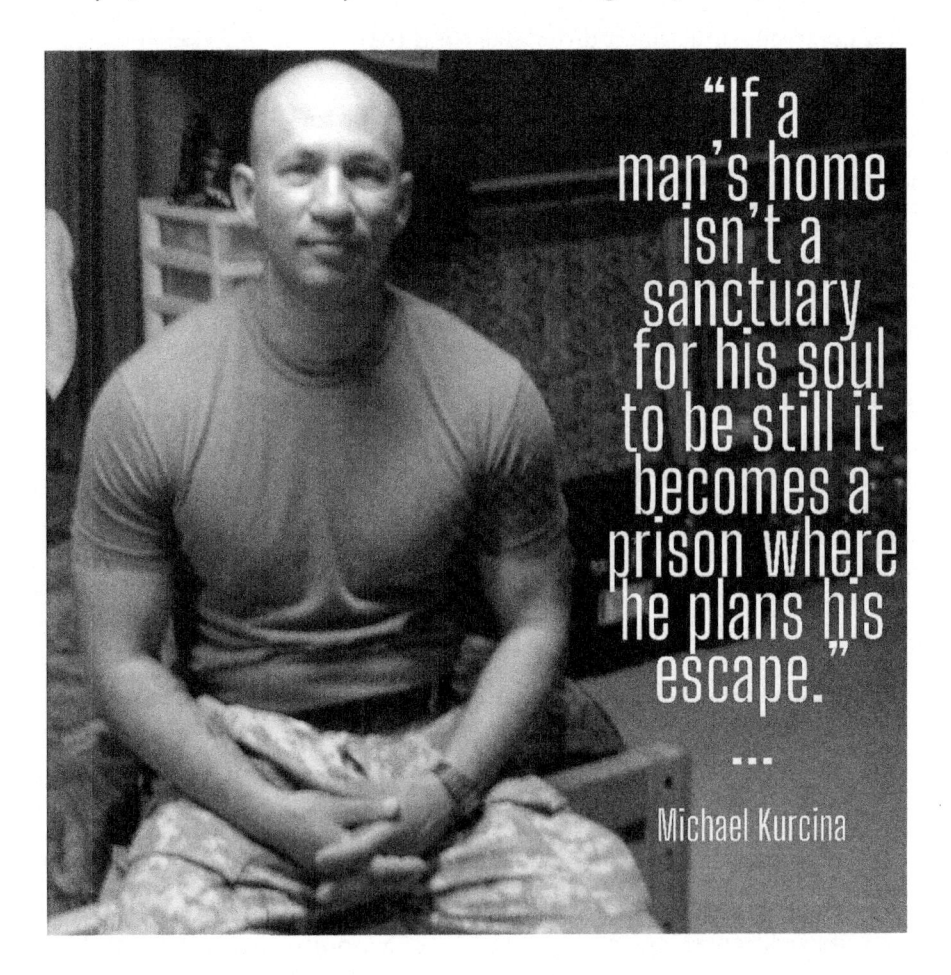

> "If a man's home isn't a sanctuary for his soul to be still it becomes a prison where he plans his escape."
>
> Michael Kurcina

An abortion of peace, a bastard of war

A baseball diamond, a movie theatre, an ice cream parlor, two dollars for a ticket, 30 cents for a cone. These things so close to him in youth felt even closer to him in adulthood, because he yearned for them but they could have been as far away as the North star, or at the dock of an ancient sea pressed against a foreign land.

He could not return to youth. There was no there there any longer.

Every night the hunger to slip off the face of the earth pulled at him. He wanted to get lost in the streets of America but he didn't want to be alone. He saw the lights of the jazzy places, the bright marquees above the pubs and cafes filled with people, just hoping someone would invite him in. Being alone was Hell.

He couldn't turn memory into reality, and because he pledged himself to the fraternity of dreamers he would never graduate with those fraternity of doers. He searched for words, words that calmed, words that reassured, words about bleeding peace and renascent love, that reminded him of his profession as a man of the sword.

He swooped into an archway, leaned against its door. He spoke aloud to himself some sad, pained words, his worried confessions gave him a certain comfort. He was a man seeking sanctuary, a soul in crisis, an abortion of peace, a bastard of war, he was a broken bird.

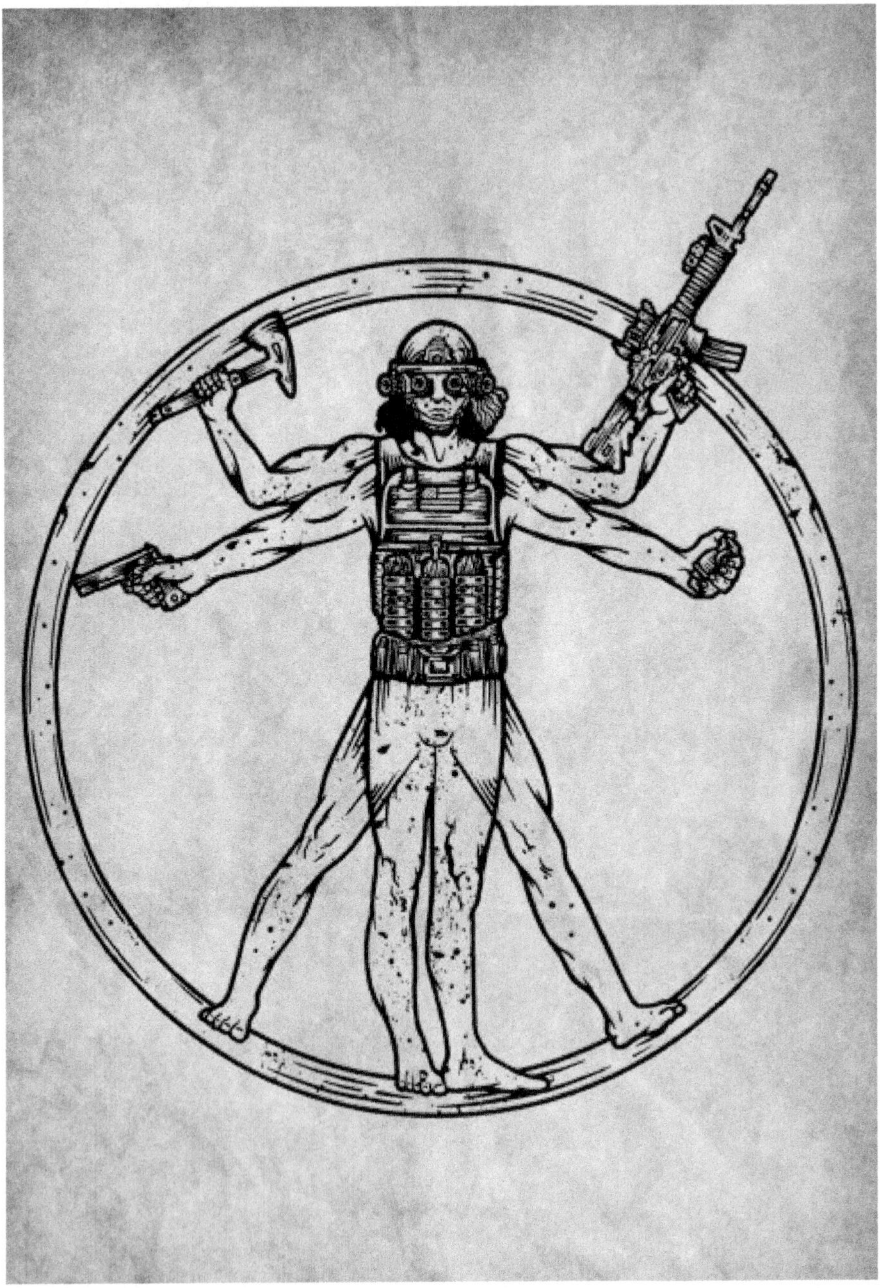

Poetry

Have you ever?

Have you ever dropped your gaze at a man approaching?

Have you ever fought the fear that was encroaching?

Have you ever?

Have you ever?

Have you ever strode naked without your vices?

Have you ever walked without armor and your devices?

Have you ever?

Have you ever?

Fists hanging at their side

Men die within every single time

Have you ever?

Kill

Little Jimmy joined me

Across the waning light

We left behind six siblings

In the black of night

We went across the water

Killed foreigners with our hands

Threshed men like useless fodder

Across deadened lands

Knowing

"Dead vermin, dead men, dead grenades!" Sgt. Hallis turned to me and said.

"I'll be playing for Halifax when I return!" and then he dropped back dead.

We dodged bullets, saw star shells blossom, watched a hundred craters glow

And just like that I laughed like mad, a tortured man that knows...

Eulogy

In loss let us be filled

In fullness let us be emptied

In hatred let us be loved

In love let us give love

In life let us remember

In death let us be remembered

The Prophet

White stag runs o'er the silent slain

Black hearted hunter yearns to live his life again

Bloody tracks break o'er the open plain

Red hearted prize for what was lost and gained

Sunset crosses and a Hellhound's pain

Cup runneth o'er for a deadman's reign

Blue tears trumpet what was lost, what was lost, what was lost, what was lost...

Sometimes

Sometimes we make love to strangers

Sometimes we make enemies of friends

Sometimes we run towards danger

Sometimes we chase what should end

Sometimes we use Band-Aids for bullet wounds

Sometimes we break what we built

Sometimes we kill our love softly

Sometimes we birth our own guilt

Sometimes we hate light and not darkness

Sometimes we believe what we couldn't

Sometimes we blunt our own sharpness

Sometimes we do what we shouldn't

Sometimes we are what we should be

Sometimes we hope it will end.

Sometimes the truth will terrify

all of the timid men

Fragments of A Man's Life

Who are the living and the dead?

Wrestle with twilight, off to bed

Drink to men who are no longer here

Who are they? It isn't clear

A broken mirror and shattered glass

Remembering ages now long passed

Black hulled boats over stretching seas

Heartbreak seeing what used to be

Who are the living and the dead?

Dispirited men I plainly said

Cry for them, as they cannot be

Absent minded, sad memory

Blow our horns the message sent

Eternally damned for the honor of men

Towards the darkness on feckless waves

What meaning is found in what death delays?

The crumbling walls, the plunging knife

The hurried breath, the expunging life

The harried shouts, the toothless dying

Youthful rebellion becomes silent complying

We drink to men from our lonely bed

Who are the living and the dead!?

O God, O God, O memory!

I screamed aloud, it's me it's me!

The fable of your face

Wife

I travel blindly looking for you

Shoulders as rich as the sea

But there will be a time, a time, an appropriate time

To share, the things that we love,

And hate,

That we hold closest to our bosoms

all the things that wound us

and for the greatest things which brings us healing,

and until that time, I will search for the source of the sea

Set the lighthouse ablaze

Bring me into the essence of you

Discovering joy inside your spirit

is like finding rain upon my flesh

Where then is the deepening of meaning in where we go

or where we've been,

and in what we say

if we speak freely to everyone about our secret grief?

Through the oceans of my mind in which my memories wander,

I search for the mouth of you

Neck the length of a river. Oh, but I travel blind

Discovering the richness of your mouth until I can feel

the sensuousness of those lips

is like knowing the reddened depths of jasper

Show me the forgotten speech,

but I travel mazily across your world,

the world I know but hardly know,

        for the fable of your face

        Tomorrow I will return I say,

        I will come I say,

        until I find and drown in this

        invincible source of love

*I gave this poem to my wife. My feeling on it at the time was about separation, loss, myth-making, forgetful memory, and ultimately it concludes with that eternal thing we call love. The idea behind writing this poem is something that all warfighters face; separation from the person they love. What does their spouse's face look like, are we remembering her properly, is she the safe-harbor that we need, should we share our feelings with others everything that injures us or should we keep it private, are we able to make "love" rather than just sex when we finally come together?

Clearly the idea of the sea and all the metaphors I used have been visited before by other writers. I wanted my wife to feel that her love was generous, unmatchable, massive, and baptismal like the water of Christ. In the end all the wrong we do is forgiven. Despite or faultiness, despite being cleaved in two, despite being adrift at "sea" for so long; in the end, all that remains between two broken people, is love.

Shalom upon the sea

Sometimes we feel as if we've been abandoned into a naked kind of isolation.

We are not consoled by the knowledge that we are alive.

Our sad thoughts are not remedied by the presence of friends.

Dawn which should bring forth buoyant joy feels more like oppressive waves.

We are washed into sea like a rudderless boat.

Be not dismayed. Trust not your feelings.

Let the logic of truth sever your ties to the lie that life is not worth living.

Fight back against the smashing rocks and mooring that has you trapped.

Each hour will pass away, let it pass away.

Hurl yourself from the rocks and jetties into new seas and voyages

Hunger again to venture into strange cities and seek out adventure.

Become the man you once were and still are.

Don't you see him?

There... There! See your reflection upon the water!

Now sail!

A new power

Adorn them in hammered ribbons of gold

Bloodstones for the weak, rubies for the bold.

Ships to the sea with God's holy fire;

Burning prow alight, mortal Viking's pyre.

Ravens in the eaves watch ghosts on the hill,

While sea gods wrestle o'er a dead man's will.

Pagan kings clamber o'er what wounded dies.

Wise Odin sacrifices his eyes for eyes,

Cursed empires drown in fire and blood.

Mythologies dissolved into ancient mud;

Comes the Second Coming and the second power

From ash heaps and shadows rises an eternal flower.

Father we must

Extinguish the brilliance of mistakes and begin anew

Impenetrable beliefs, Daedalic dreams fathered for so few.

Two bolts of lightning crackle and end abruptly

Screaming comes corruptly.

Heavy to live in this old wild world

Sacrosanct lights faded so roughly

Two identities borne with patience forever have been swallowed

Revivify! Revoke the light, nothing will be followed.

Upraised thy hands cup ether, for the last drink of sorrow

Bow thy head properly, soberly to meet the mad morrow.

Buoyant waves wash fairly the gentle face of a boy

Heavenward sent warbling, now knowing 'tis much to high

Fall, fall at least deeply

Praised sweetly to die.

Wondrous length the golden tether, free forever to go

Whiplash snapping, coiled now slapping, taught, stretch, torn

Oh, fathers foolish rankled youth, now immortal borne!

Inchoate, echo the sounds of heterodyne dreams colored with Gods and Monsters

Snapdragon tailed, arcs so dark, strangle the God of Thunder

Nausea bound with phosphorous glow rampant ceaseless wonder

To forge the shaft of lightning rods to find no subtle burning

Healer bound but choked in joy, with each eternal turning.

Predetermine being, prefabricate the essence, now the mortals glow

Baffled, burdened hear the loud laments the freedom of mortality!

Painful grace these events; stand upon the proscenium with glorious mad duality.

Vermillion flow from the recumbent bound, lonely enduring forever

Alight! The stage in surreptitious splendor;

Well born Prometheus will never surrender

Listen! Hear every failure calling!

Icarus shouts immortal, "Father! I am falling!"

Faint gossamer wings this broken falling bird

"Father!"

"Father!"

These voices must be heard.

Lost at sea

We swam on shipless oceans

Carried forth on rolling winds

Heard mermaids through sea grass singing

Our journey of wonder begins

Lost in eddyless waters

No man must pay for my sins

Lights that twinkle, moonlight bringing

Hope when our hope has dimmed

A sea of freedom surrounds us

A prison of heartache we're pinned

Under seabirds, over whale skins, clinging

Our journey of woe begins

Lost in eddyless waters

No man must pay for his sins

Lights that twinkle, moonlight bringing

Hope when our hope has dimmed.

Cowardice

We feast once more our secret need

Upon dead men's honor our damnable greed

What we are but willing slaves

Robbing each one of the fallen braves

The dark and impossible now lies ahead

We pass along darkly those silent dead

Reckless men lose what once was loved

Let us lay beneath what lies above

Let God take now what he delayed

Damn us to Hell is what we pray

Other side

Steady your legs.

Brace yourself for war.

Death mustn't trouble you.

It is yet another door.

Boundaries, simply, in a country,

or man divided.

Join the throngs with bravery.

Fearful heart be united.

Darkness like sea waves mystically recedes.

In this new beginning is the hereafter

where true life proceeds.

Sold Out

Paradigm of a modern city

We are followed

Yet unfellowed

Omitted history

There is only cry, cries, crying

For time is why, while, whiling

Down the ways

Certainty for certitude

Oh, cruel insensate! See?

Take, take-in, taking

Voyage upon the waters

Tide, affairs are turning

Flood, ever stirring

Shall! Shallow, shallop

Shalom upon the sea

Glory! Try! Tried, trying!

For, fore, fortune, fortunately

Men are dying

All sail to misery

Regret

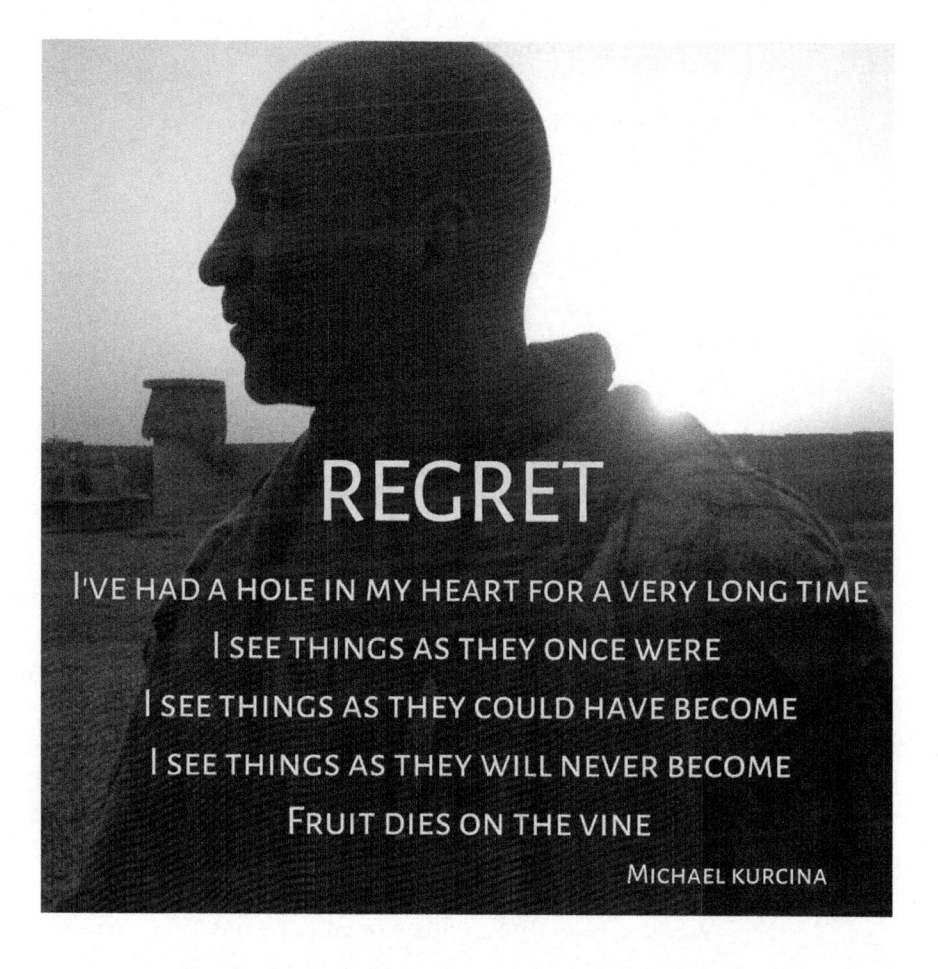

I've had a hole in my heart for a very long time

I see things as they once were

I see things as they could have become

I see things as they will never become

Fruit dies on the vine

Trauma

We heard the whistle by the river

We watched old cars by the tracks

We dreamt of the wives we injured

We heard that house beckon us back

We ignored every insidious whisper

We drowned out the sinister calls

We stopped making death for us simpler

We halted before entering each hall

We stopped making love to whomever

We ceased before planning our routes

We learned that loneliness wasn't forever

We paused before we blew our brains out

We healed by divorcing our stranger

We ended our weird marriage with death

We no longer found peace in our danger

We celebrate now with every new breath

Nightstalker Pt. 1

I saw bleating sheep and a dying asp

Where the wind pressed its will upon solemn grass.

I watched nightfall come and saw you pass

Delirious Shepherd with your perfect mask.

I heard a golden song from the throat of God

A gentle tone yet so very odd

I wept in silence, enraptured, awed

A gravedigger dug and a carpenter sawed.

Is there anything worth dying for?

Whether in time of peace or time of war?

My salvation stolen by the Babylon whore.

My trembling hands touched the derelict door.

THE LOTUS EATERS
SPOTTERUP.COM

MEN

> THERE IS A PLACE IN THIS WORLD FOR THE TIMID MAN.
> IT IS ON THE SIDELINES -Michael Kurcina

One of the secrets to being a man is never allowing the fiercest part of you to be tamed.

Men are built to hurt but we are not built to last. Keep fighting until the end.

Men like swords can be forged in fire; those who change with every burning become the most formidable of weapons.

When men behave savagely only men will understand.

Men kill easily with their eyes but let them do it with their hands and most lose their stomach for it.

Men who have difficulty forgiving themselves for acting like animals may have even greater difficulty forgiving themselves when they act like men.

Rare is the man where violence is his calm.

We cannot return to mothers' arms and mother's kisses, for nothing is ever the same again but we can still honor her wishes by growing to become a man.

If you really want to stand out in a crowd, make sure when traveling with companions that you're the only lunatic.

Men who refuse to pay their dues in the factories of life are simply entitled workers who want to be bosses from the start.

A man betrays himself completely if he doesn't have the stomach to kill those who would destroy him.

A good, violent man can do much to stop the evil in his time.

Do you think you are a man because you fight? Yes, what kind of broken thing would you be if there wasn't that natural struggle inside?

Who doesn't know how to be an animal? Share with me only your secrets on how to be a man.

If a man can't have love, sometimes he wants pain and danger to make him feel like a man again. Beware the man who can't handle them all at one time.

It is impressive enough to have a will like iron but what is sublime is to have a spirit like fire for fire shapes everything inside a man.

Men who want to be seen as kings must stop thinking and acting like slaves.

A dog doesn't know if it is dumb; neither does a dumb man but dumb dogs make good friends, dumb men don't.

Men who refuse to acknowledge the obvious gravity of their circumstance are most deserving when they are crushed by its weight.

Soft hands aren't true indicators that a man lacks a tough mind but they could point out that he had a soft life.

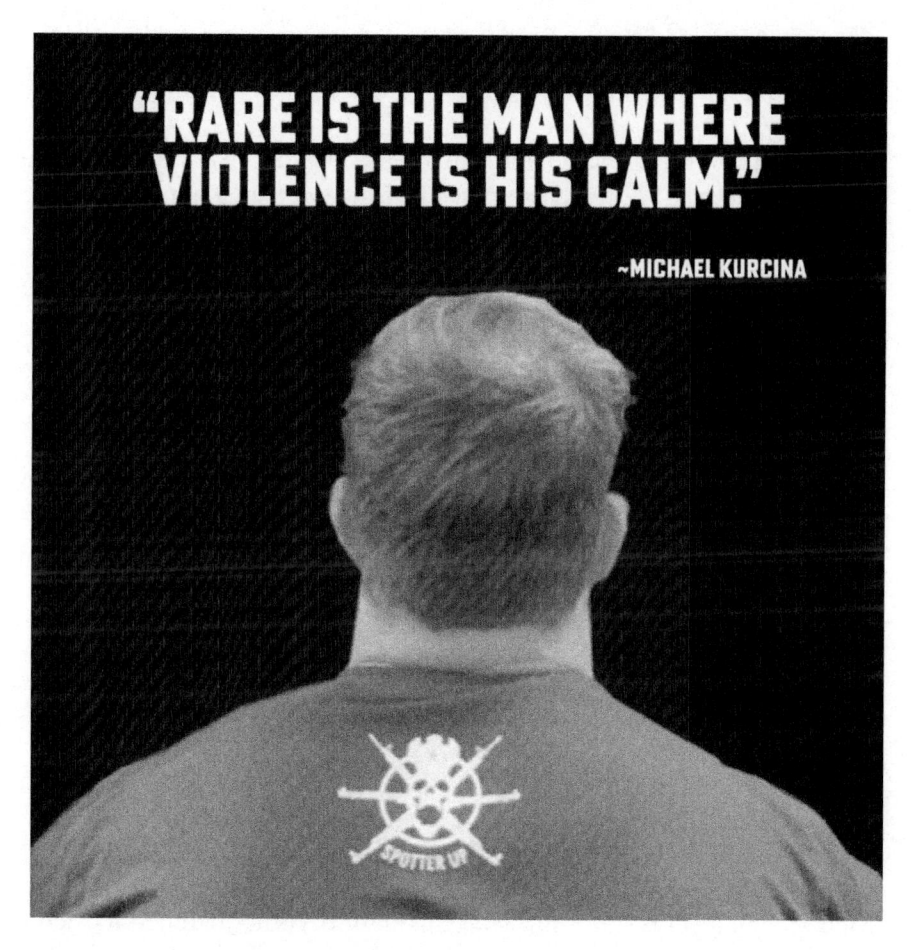

> **"RARE IS THE MAN WHERE VIOLENCE IS HIS CALM."**
> ~MICHAEL KURCINA

Most men don't plan on being failures, but it's equally likely they don't set out plans for being a success.

Men are built to hurt but we are not built to last.

There is a place in this world for the timid man; it is on the sidelines.

A man who hurls insults at other men would be wise to know first how to hurl his fists.

Break a man and think nothing of it but a man breaks you and your mind can struggle with that thought for a lifetime.

I am preoccupied every day in trying not to be an animal, and instead I aspire to be a man.

A true man will expose himself to danger and the world will judge if his courage has any worth.

Every man will watch as the last of his giants wander over the hill and disappear forever. He stands alone without a sign telling him where he belongs. He must learn how to cast his own long shadow.

In every man's life comes a road sign warning him of a dark path ahead but he goes down it anyhow.

I swear, gentleman, thinking like a victim is an illness and therefore a weakness all men should avoid.

We don't need history to tell us that men fought wars for as long as there are men, we already know wars wait in their future.

Just because a man's spirit can take a lot of beatings doesn't mean his mind holds a lot of sense.

Boys leave home to become gods. The world destroys them and sends them back as martyrs.

A mob of men are dumber than sheep and hungrier than ravening wolves; knowing this praise be to men who choose to walk alone.

Each morning starts innocently but the night becomes damned to men who believe wasted time is torture yet they spend a fine and precious day living in the past.

Every man stands upon the world's stage but few want their life to be seen at the thrust or the proscenium.

Men are not changed by fame, no, they change for fame.

If you want to be an insider in the world of men develop a taste for heavy doses of suffering; if you want to be an outlier desire that it isn't so.

Some men don't feel like they're living unless they're killing themselves.

Unlearn what you learned and learn to be who you need to be outside of the pressures of worldly culture and closed minded-peers. Learn to walk like a man, upright with a plan; cock of the walk, rooster of the range.

Modern boys want to throw off the yoke of manhood before they even get a sense of its weight.

Men who cannot appreciate the blessings of friendships might never understand their curse of loneliness.

If you want to be an outsider in the world of men refuse to develop a taste for suffering.

A man who becomes shallower as he gets older has little chance of drowning himself deeper into life in an effort to become mature. A man like this should have his drinks, shut his mouth, and sit at the edge of the water; he is a bore. He should have dived into the deep end more often instead of always splashing water, trying to be the center of the party, and blathering on at the edge of the pool.

The truth is most men want to be a bright light in a dark world but few can withstand the pain when its heat starts burning.

There is nothing new that will ever come out of old earth. A man is a man is man and anything else is an imitation despite the curious phenomena promoted in modern circles about what is authentic.

It is a tragedy when men die pursuing greatness yet that is a greater ending than one where they died stuck pursuing mediocrity.

Blessed to be a beast that feels and reasons not than to be a man cursed with a huge heart and brains.

Make other men go home or raise their game.

Every man is challenged by the urges to quit but those who never fight against them are just tragedies waiting to happen.

Men can do something animals cannot; men can be untrue to their nature.

Man, longs to be divine like all the lights in the cosmos; until he understands his calling, he is nothing but a lamppost.

Like some odd politician most men exist in a perpetual state of apology with the world and one of constant flagellation with themselves.

You want to be gods? Stop acting like men.

Let others deny the value of your warrior class but all will agree when you pass, "there goes a man."

If you want validation see your parents or see a shrink; see a parking attendant. If you constantly wait for other people's affirmations, you'll live a life of mediocrity.

> Every man shows the world a persona cloaked in refinement but he's simply a dressed beast holding back its **SAVAGERY**.
> ~Michael Kurcina

Every man shows the world a persona cloaked in refinement but he's simply a dressed beast holding back its savagery.

We destroy masculinity in America by doing more than just inculcating timidity in boys and promoting swaggering as a sin. We replace what's been tried and tested with what is worthless and unwanted when all a boy wants to do is prove himself as a man. We crush a boy's childlike faith in what is most probable about being a man and leave him doubting if masculinity is even a fact found within him. The new society makes it a heresy to believe in ancient truths.

Men without purpose get into things they likely shouldn't.

Beware men who are willing to sink lower than the lowest of men.

Such a simple yet sacred thing to know that you are a man but so profane to doubt it.

Crooked and blind is every man who cheats himself by never allowing his being to experience its richest life.

As long as men like it as a fashion war will never go out of style.

"Watch the hands and mind the words of a violent man who speaks and acts civilly. Danger is not afar."~ Spotterup

The actual life of a man begins when he takes responsibility for all his actions after he's learned of the consequences of taking none for so long.

She held in her arms this thing, this odd, little thing of flesh and blood that would grow into a man that made war and she wondered, "how did I ever bring into this beautiful world from my blessed womb such a terrifying being?"

Brutal men clumsy in skill weave a warped pattern of their life and wonder how they become entangled in it. *Warrior is one of my favorite movies. I believe many of us can relate to both characters in the movie called Warrior. I won't elaborate here. Stand up, and fight through the fog of your life until it's clear to be on the other side. Even in our later age we might make decisions that we believe ruins us. Fix it. Make it better that thing you broke. I swear to God there is redemption waiting for you. Make your hits in life count. Timing, precision, lethalness. Avoid drama, don't be toxic. Build. Pay attention to the fight. Copy others when the line is good, change the warp and woof, when the structure is crooked. In due time you can stand back and see your masterpiece. Brutal men clumsy in skill weave a warped pattern of their life and wonder how they become entangled in it.

Every man was a boy but not all men remain men. Don't go back. Commit yourself to always being one.

Unless a man already has it together, attempting to live more manfully by moving to Hollywood is no different than an elephant going to a graveyard to prevent itself from dying.

In a prison of their own making men peer through their window and watch the world go by, disinclined to join it anytime.

Without some kind of war men would have a tame life.

Brutal men in a beautiful world will never understand beautiful things.

Watch the hands and mind the words of a violent man who speaks and acts civilly; danger is not afar.

Do not boast of your savagery until you have actually lived among savage men.

We breed boys to be sheep and allow wolves to be shepherds, and if we don't right that wrong, we're going to have a nation of weak hearts when it's time to fight the heartless.

Men experienced in war cannot easily describe the loss of life any better than they can describe the loss of their youth but they certainly can tell you what real fear felt like and when they first became a man.

Some men are born targets and others are born weapons.

How bravely men behave in an age where the pen now replaces the sword.

Sometimes a man needs other men to explain his raison d'etre to him.

When a man becomes too much like a woman, he makes his role as a man unnecessary.

There are strong and deep tides of bad faith that drown weak men in their own fear.

Men anchored deeply in the past and unwilling to change course cease to let their life belong to a future. *They must raise everything they held fast, and move bravely without resistance, to let time bring them into unfathomable waters.

A man who has many friends is like a dog not minding his many fleas until some turn and bite him.

The culture of modern man is enslaved by the constant want of pleasure but the free man at the center of the arena looks back and doesn't give a damn.

Speak and speak sincerely or don't speak at all.

Do not live by your titles but by your being.

Men of war make violence their priesthood to confer death on unholy men.

Be wary on the day that I'm an animal. Today I'm struggling to be a man.

Some things that make a man indestructible is to know he is truly loved and that he truly loves something. With those two things in mind, he is a beast when fighting against anything, because he'll fight for what he believes is everything.

Abandon the ways of men and get back to yourself again.

A man loses two positions when he becomes a good, little proletariat; his personhood and his manhood. He doesn't climb up the ladder of success when he becomes a Marxist, he climbs down it.

When men empty themselves of tears, they lighten the suitcase of sadness they carry.

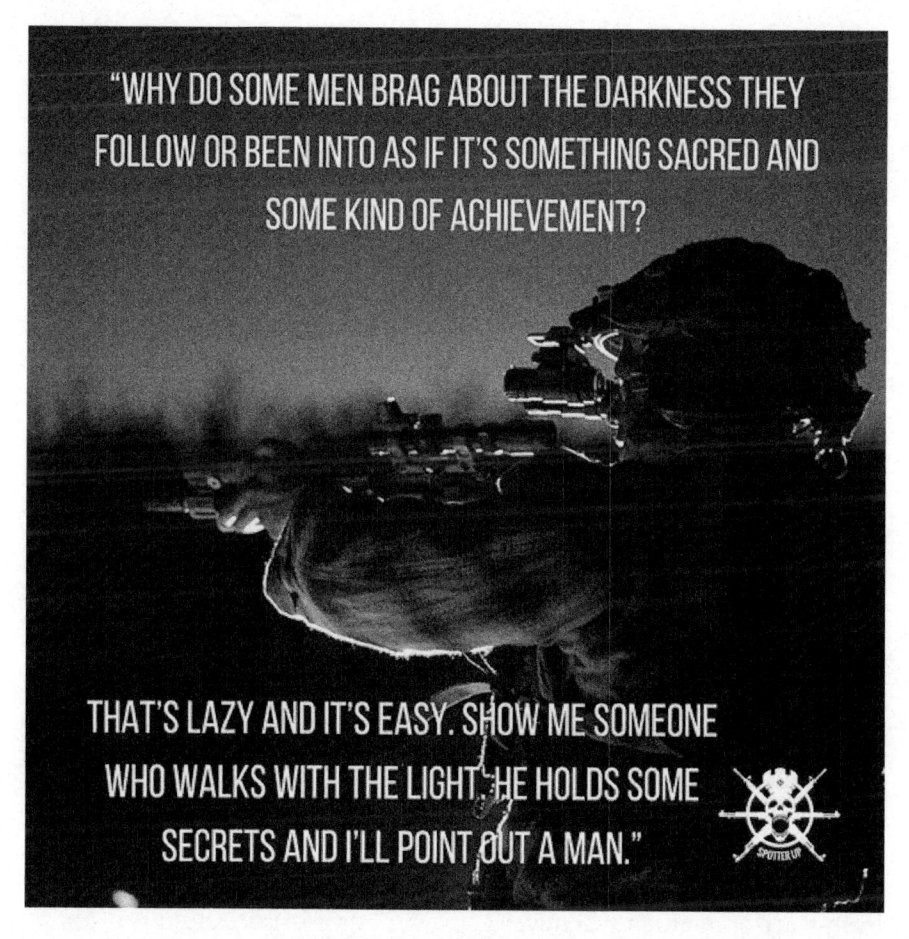

> "WHY DO SOME MEN BRAG ABOUT THE DARKNESS THEY FOLLOW OR BEEN INTO AS IF IT'S SOMETHING SACRED AND SOME KIND OF ACHIEVEMENT? THAT'S LAZY AND IT'S EASY. SHOW ME SOMEONE WHO WALKS WITH THE LIGHT, HE HOLDS SOME SECRETS AND I'LL POINT OUT A MAN."

There's a language that men speak and it doesn't contain words, those who don't heed it can end up on the floor.

Men who choose only familiar pathways rather than strange ones on their journey of self-discovery will never learn that they've learned nothing.

So many men crave praise that bolsters their illusions.

A man chooses to be a pebble among pebbles when he cannot become a mountain.

A roar of joy can quickly become a hush of despair as quickly as a stoic man can become a bawling child when he realizes he ran out of time.

Ask modern man if he can live monastically, primitively, frugally and without his vices. Most men would go mad. Man must learn how use his time wisely while sterilizing his insatiable need to be entertained.

Men easily unravel the threads of their life and it often takes a lifetime to wind up the damage they unspooled.

Men who choose only familiar pathways rather than strange ones on their journey of self-discovery will never learn that they've learned nothing.

Men's spirits like rivers can run parallel but some seek to diverge into a sea of salvation, others an inferno of damnation.

In this age some men will never get there but most do and it is the most beautiful moment when a man knows forever who he is.

Why do some men brag about the darkness they follow or been into as if it's something sacred and some kind of achievement? That's lazy and it's easy. Show me someone who walks with the light. He holds some secrets and I'll point out a man. Only fools love what is profane and think it holy.

The souls of all men are cast in the same mold but every man engraves his own heart.

Whether a man sings or paints, writes or dances some piece of his art should be his confessional, of what he did and what he saw. He should create out of what seems unspeakable and incommunicable to the world until there isn't a need to do it any longer, until he feels peace away from the most inhumane part of himself. If he only trained his hands for destruction, he must train them in techniques of construction. He should be possessed to produce even if he can't replace a single thing that he destroyed; he must learn how to bring good into the world out of the strange places where he chose his exile, and the strange people who chose to love him, or the people he hated, shunned, injured or even killed. Every man who knows the snake knows the sword, fire, banishment and a gate that shut forever. He is only damned if he doesn't choose to control his destiny with his experiences and knowledge.

Some men of great intellect live dangerous lives

DO NOT LIVE BY YOUR TITLES
but by your being

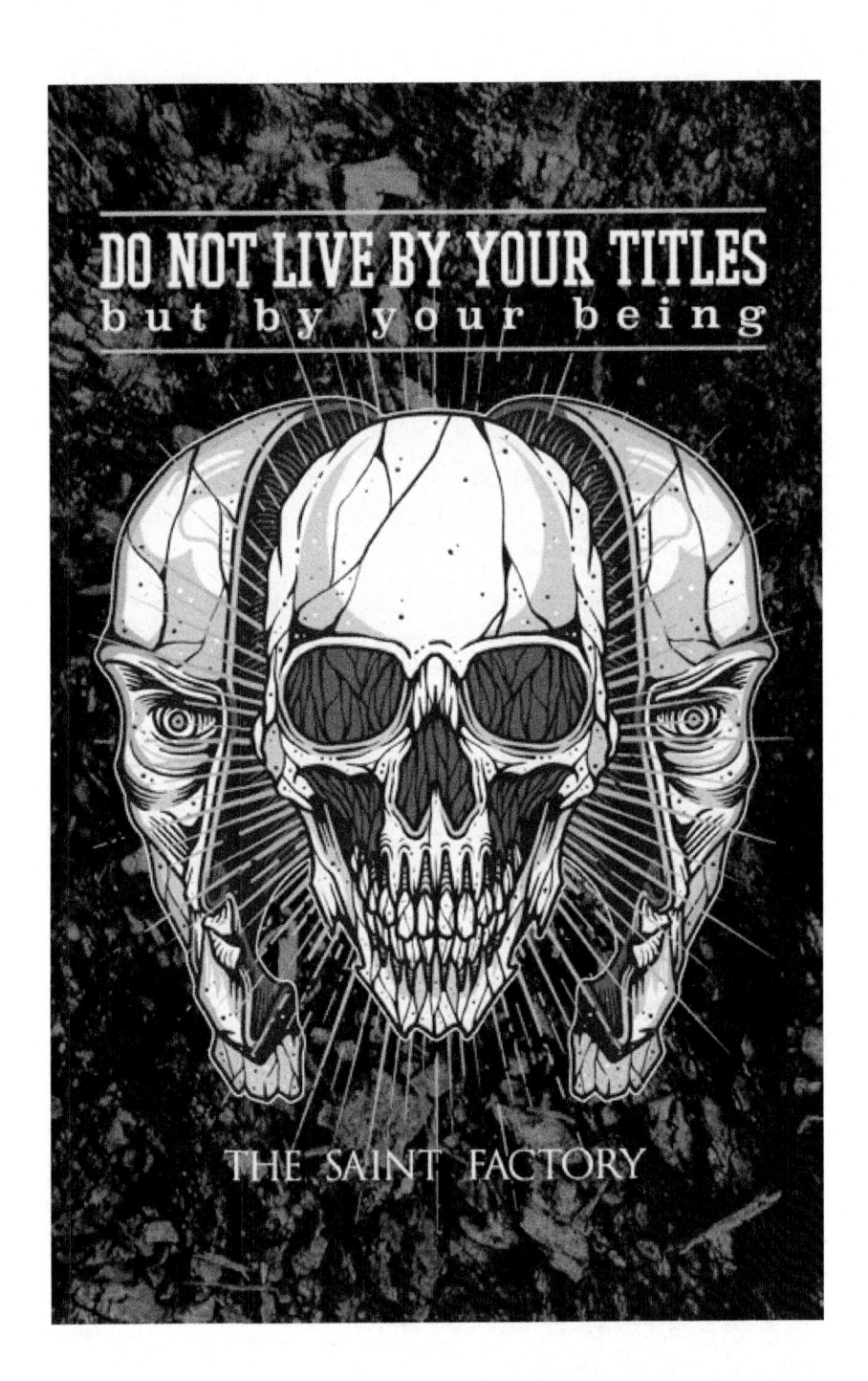

THE SAINT FACTORY

PERSPECTIVE

Yes, breaking free of the herd makes you a target yet it's where you feel what it's like to live.

On any given day a man can face the day that he deserves.

It should be every man's hope to hear at least once in his early life a voice from the darkness telling him that he will die. In his little round skull let the thought sit with him, in his little beating heart let the feeling of fear eat at him, let fear cut down all of his falsehoods so that he can do something of greatness with his new found truth and time.

A talker is all smoke while the doer is all fire, and each must learn to control more and less of what they intend to be.

Fatalism is a weak outlook and a failed, learned belief that should be unlearned. If men want to end their impotence, the inevitability they should accept is that life is filled with millions of unmet, wonderful possibilities, and steel themselves each time they are surprised at its enigmas and contradictions. What princess believes she will never be rescued? What hero ever believes that he is doomed?

No man is damned by his heredity; his bastard father's blood that courses through his veins. *Every man must learn that not everyone will like him, that some lovers will not love him, and no matter how hard he works he can't quickly make his loneliness go away. He must learn however that he is never damned by his heredity and he is free to choose the kind of man that he can truly be.

Thunder that makes some men meek is often providence to the brave.

Into the woods the wild men go, they abandon the laws of men to find a world up close.

No man should ever shrink his dreams or look out his window wondering what he could have been. Death is some men's inevitable and eternal end; let yours be a good one; the time is now.

If you want to be consumed with obsessions make it your quest to live a virtuous and productive life.

I am a fighter and I will be a fighter until the day I die.

Hold onto the exhale for as long as you can; far as I can tell this is the path.

Do not pray for immortality or any event that will make it come, instead get off of your knees and begin to live remarkably.

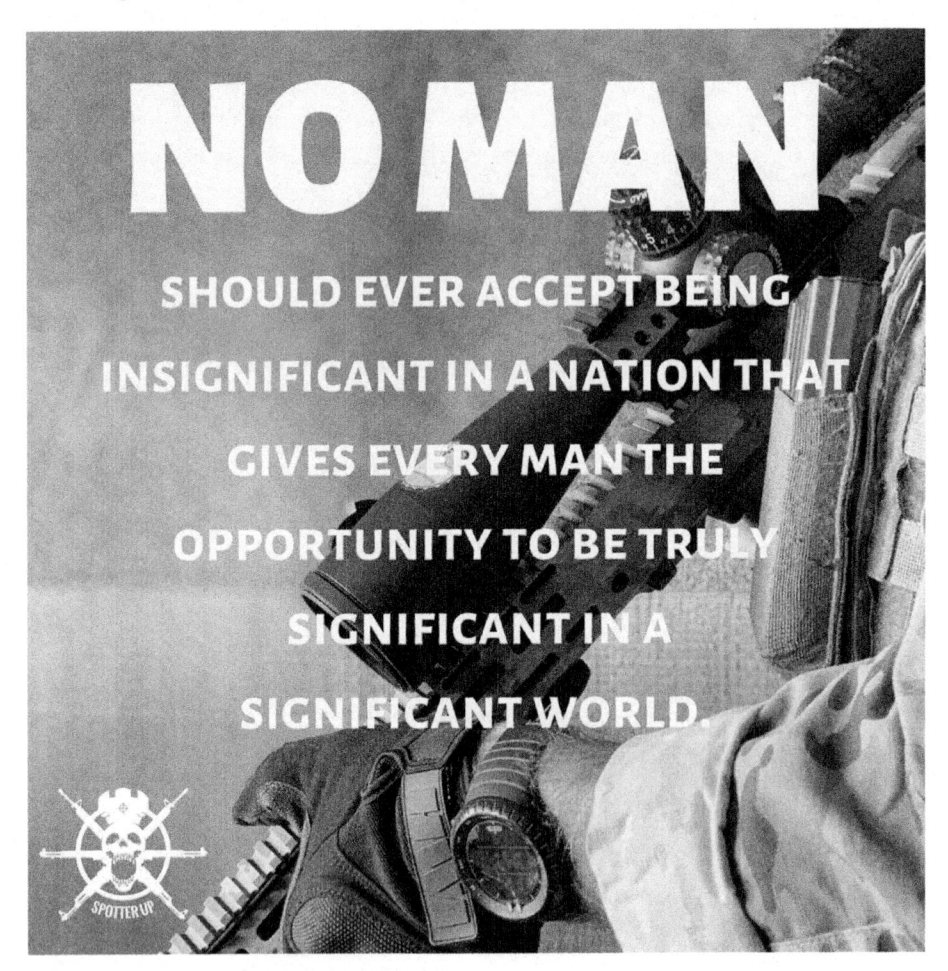

> **NO MAN** SHOULD EVER ACCEPT BEING INSIGNIFICANT IN A NATION THAT GIVES EVERY MAN THE OPPORTUNITY TO BE TRULY SIGNIFICANT IN A SIGNIFICANT WORLD.

No man should ever accept being insignificant in a nation that gives every man the opportunity to be truly significant in a significant world.

How easily men trap themselves in cages and then cannot free the animal they become.

Every man has a private wound that feels precious to him even though it's something he may never understand.

If you think trying to be successful is tough, see what life is like being a failure.

Every man is born carrying a strange cargo and should never be ashamed nor fearful of bestowing his gifts upon the world. *Be relentless, be fearless. Do not go through this life being afraid of what you can be. Don't shrink before the shadows of what you believe is a burden placing itself upon you. Bend your knees and get beneath it and carry that weight. God gives every man and woman different gifts and we must confer them upon the world. We are all useful, and we must learn how to share our sacred insights. Don't hide, don't crumble. You are the rescue ship that brings gifts of respite to the those hungering for more than just words.

Do we tell our children to stop chasing their dreams? Then why do we keep telling this to ourselves? *Do we tell them to give up when they're young, tell them that the future is reserved for losers? No, we don't. How do you become something that you're not if you are always practicing what you've been? Keep quitting and you'll pay a small price at the toll road to failure, but the large sum is collected when you find out the road ends. Chase your dreams. Graduate from the police academy, start a business, become a teacher. Do something.

Your mind is never a hostage to your body and if so, you must turn the tables on your terrorist.

Critics are like those who ride horses to pull down the houses erected by other men yet feign surprise every time they return home to their own.

You're going to run into serious problems when you attempt to repurpose your being.

Excellence is never elusive when your speech and deed are the same.

A quitter goes to sleep believing he can't change the world while a fighter rises each morning believing that he can.

We had no choice in the matter when we entered this life crying like a child but we can choose how we exit it by dying like a man.

An act of dishonor doesn't pollute the blood. *Walk with pomp and pride. I don't believe in the curses of kings; the sons and daughters of Akhenaten or the Kennedy's, or any other royal lineage, and how they lived or died means precious little to me. An act of dishonor doesn't pollute the blood. Some men's hearts are already rotten within, yet a boy who wants to be a man can choose to be unlike his kin. You are not your father. You are not his actions. You are not your mother. You are not her actions. Nothing they did in the past can stain your name, none of their actions, none of their views, none of their core beliefs can taint you. None of it is in your DNA. You have your own morals and codes and ways to live. If you are cursed then let God intervene. Be a man and a king. You are worthy of being a king, so stand up now and be one and not a slave to the way they raised you in their own broken kingdoms. All hail the King! *Curse: supernatural power to inflict harm or punishment on someone or something.

Conscious thoughts are only curses if we can never do anything with them.

In a hundred cities, in a hundred countries, in a hundred worlds you will never discover a person like you; in fact, not even a hundred universes. Now live. Surrender with full abandon to the fine machinery that you are and let it work.

Even the smallest of men casts the longest of shadows for it depends on the time of day and where he stands.

Sometimes we need to heed a strange calling, some susurrus cutting through the night, a murmurous voice so haunting, "you must live a different life."

If you want to be a rebel in this world, be principled.

He who levels violence on the innocent is evil; he who believes it is necessary is evil and a fool.

Seeing with emotion makes most men blind to reason.

The help you seek out there actually resides within you. *How can any man navigate his way through this world if he doesn't fathom the most important points in his life's history? One great moment marked in his memory might not be sufficient enough to get him out of feeling lost in America or out of feeling lost even deeper in the world. He must study his past without doubling back to linger in all of those tubes and tunnels that first led him astray and into those troubled times. He must have the good sense to sometimes connect even the dimmest stars, while realizing the answer out of his living maze isn't done solely by looking back but rather it is in using a compass of truth to see a plane higher because that's where his true north lies. *mark the moments from his past where he felt exiled and use those data points to join part of something good again.

Even a dull life can cut a man like a sharp knife down to his bones.

Nurture the fear within you like a flower until you control how it lives or dies.

Rise up from the darkest moment of your life and see that you can turn it into your finest hour.

Men give up hope after a hundred separate moments trying to leave their past in the past but one solution to ending those feelings of despair is to give it one more try.

The world is seen through a narrow lens to some who lose heart and hope but for others the same loss lets them focus on a panorama of opportunities.

Don't let good sense rob you of opportunities to live stupidly.

There is only now. Do something with your precious time to really affect the world.

Every man is hit by truths, but those who kept standing conditioned themselves by welcoming past blows.

Dance your stupid dances, and sing your silly songs, and for a moment discard the structure of your life and just live.

> Because you belong to the fraternity of dreamers how many of you will never graduate with the fraternity of doers?
>
> — Michael Kutrina

Because you belong to the fraternity of dreamers how many of you will never graduate with the fraternity of doers?

Everyday our hunger for life is a feeling of discomfort we should ask for.

Luxuries or austerities are neither openings nor obstacles to a man focused on getting to his goal. *Continually come up with goals and refine them and how you will obtain them. Truly passionate men and women will not be dissuaded by anything because they are "plugged in" and in fact will be hellbent on getting to their destination; visualize, focus, action, achieve.

Men privately plan their escape from the smothering tomb of their life until each year they become more weakened and less brave, and it becomes the sarcophagus that enshrines them. What history will tell us is a good man's spirit broke under the enslavement of a despot's mind yet freedom was always there for the taking. All a man had to do was walk away.

Be careful of the fictional life you envision for yourself because you may be called on it.

The best teacher makes himself unnecessary to his students.

We want to become legends across the waters, to fight all men, to love all woman, to drink unaccountably and have our stories told but our feelings are nothing but ego, and our destiny nothing but dreaming, and the seed of our destruction planted inside our heart is cowardice. Good God let us get off of our fat ass and give something a try.

Move with life and vigor until your feet stop moving and cold possesses your body, and the lights exit your eyes. Hold onto the exhale for as long as you can. Far as I can tell this is the path.

Don't let stuff like facts get in the way of you living stupidly.

Repeat after me...I am a fighter and I will be a fighter until the day I die. *Rethink things. Rethink how you operate. Put away the booze and self-pity. I've been there, consuming cases of beer and anything else I could hold down. You are not alone. Just because a man's spirit can take a lot of beatings doesn't mean his mind holds a lot of sense. Make sense and find purpose.

Rebellions aren't just the aspirations turned into action by angry young boys who actually make something happen but history tells us it will never be performed by gutless, old men.

A simple way for a man to torment himself is to take his eyes off the now or the future to focus them always on the past.

If we shed any tears let it not be with sadness for what we once were but with joy for what we will become.

Wasted time is wasted fruit but the future is only filled with ripe moments; don't waste those.

One day some of us will understand that life is more than money or fame, and it is about using our experiences gleaned from our past, and sharing it in viable ways with people in it now in order to enrich all of our futures.

Walk everywhere holding peace in your heart, violence in your hands and a plan of action in your mind.

In every man's spiritual life there is but one great sea, mountain, river and desert to conquer; in essence all are the same. He needs but conquer one to have the wherewithal to conquer all again and again; let him never forget what he accomplished. *You know the lay of the land. You've been there before. You know what to do, now do it. Get up and do it. Any man that doesn't refuel his lamp will surely greet the darkness until he meets another man who carries a light. You are not alone. There are men to guide you but you must do the walking alone. Refuel your lamp and make a path for others.

Sing like a fool for singing's sake, dance like one for dancing's sake and don't give a damn what other men think; the world needs more clowns. *A man who devotes 10 minutes of his day dancing and singing sillily might discover that the pain inside his heart eventually goes away. Conscious thoughts are only curses if we can never do anything with them. Do not lose your good sense and responsibility to care for yourself. Live without a certain sense of guilt and shame, and specifically none when it comes to being judged by shameless, stupid men.

Men should experiment on themselves to see if they can devote their mind to serious things. They must be able to live alone with their thoughts for some time without feeling trapped. Men must reawaken their mind and learn to kill time without killing themselves, they must learn how to live alone with their thoughts to see if they can peer at something other than the television or a glass of beer; perhaps a telescope, a book, tools, just about anything to see if there is some genius hiding in that head; if he can do this with some serious devotion, he begins to accept living by removing his indifference to the issues of thinking and feeling.

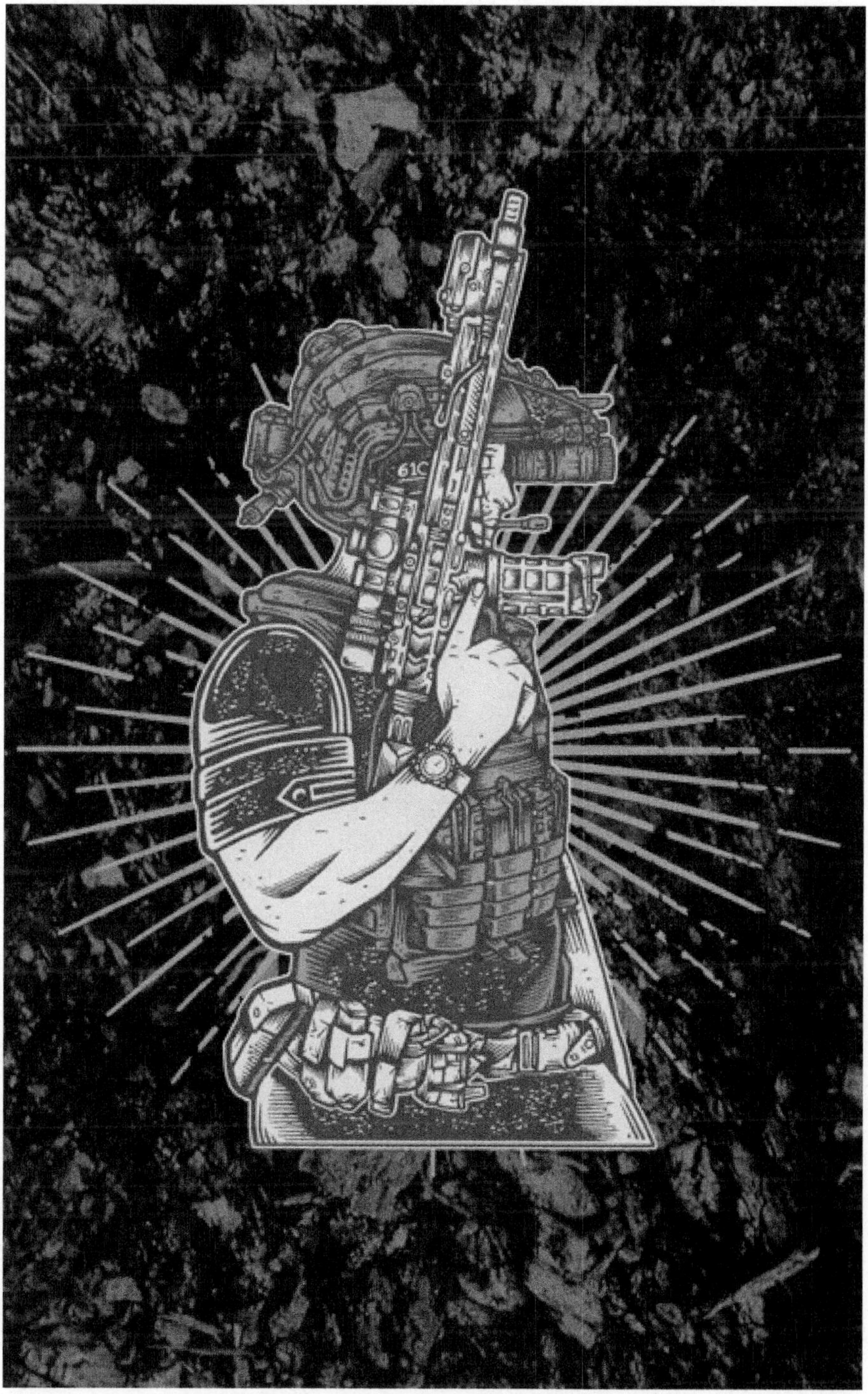

COURAGE

In a world of great need where action must be taken to save lives, heroes abandon themselves, while cowards abandon others as each surrender to his natural impulses and does his deeds without restraint.

Pull on your shoes, and with all the strength inside of you, rise up and go.

You going to stop me? Ha! Even I can't stop me.

Break bread and drink wine all you want with others but when it's go-time, make sure you can shed blood with me.

Cowards abandon others; heroes abandon themselves.

Every day fill your life with fear and then learn to empty yourself of it.

Free the hero that you trapped out of fear in the dungeon of your own heart. It's time he walked the earth. Unleash this champion and let him fight whatever doom comes his way.

Timid men go to the same bars, seat themselves on the same stools and every night drink the same drinks. They think about the same wounds, and know every day they lack courage to leave the same town not because there is any terror outside, it's because they know their hearts hold terror within.

If you must die then die with defiance. Rush into the maw of night and like a fire illuminate the darkness; the world will surely note your boldness and brightness.

There is a place in this world for a bold man and it means making your way to the front while often being told to stay in the back yet you make your move anyway.

Men go to the slaughterhouses just like willing slaves, and offer their necks to the axman until it is too late, to free themselves from that torpor and their imagined chains.

Be wary of letting fear move into your life. She doesn't want to control some of it, she wants to control it all.

The advantage of hours means precious little to indecisive men.

The pen replaces the sword, preaching replaces action, cowardice replaces heroics and liking a post replaces throwing our physical weight behind a movement.

Halfhearted attempts often come from halfhearted men who in the end are just kidding themselves.

Running to safety is no different than running towards danger in that both require making a choice. With one you might live and doing it may bring glory; with the other you'll surely live but you'll likely die every day of shame.

If we are more frightened, jealous, angry or depressed by our life than the lives of others it's time to have the courage to face down what needs to be faced to deal with the why.

Men kill easily with their eyes but let them do it with their hands and most lose their stomach for it.

A man betrays himself completely if he doesn't have the stomach to kill those who would destroy him.

Come at me. Do it, on this day, and every other day but know this that you will never destroy me. Come at me every day but every day I will never fear you. One day God will damn you. I will never fear you. Death I will never fear you.

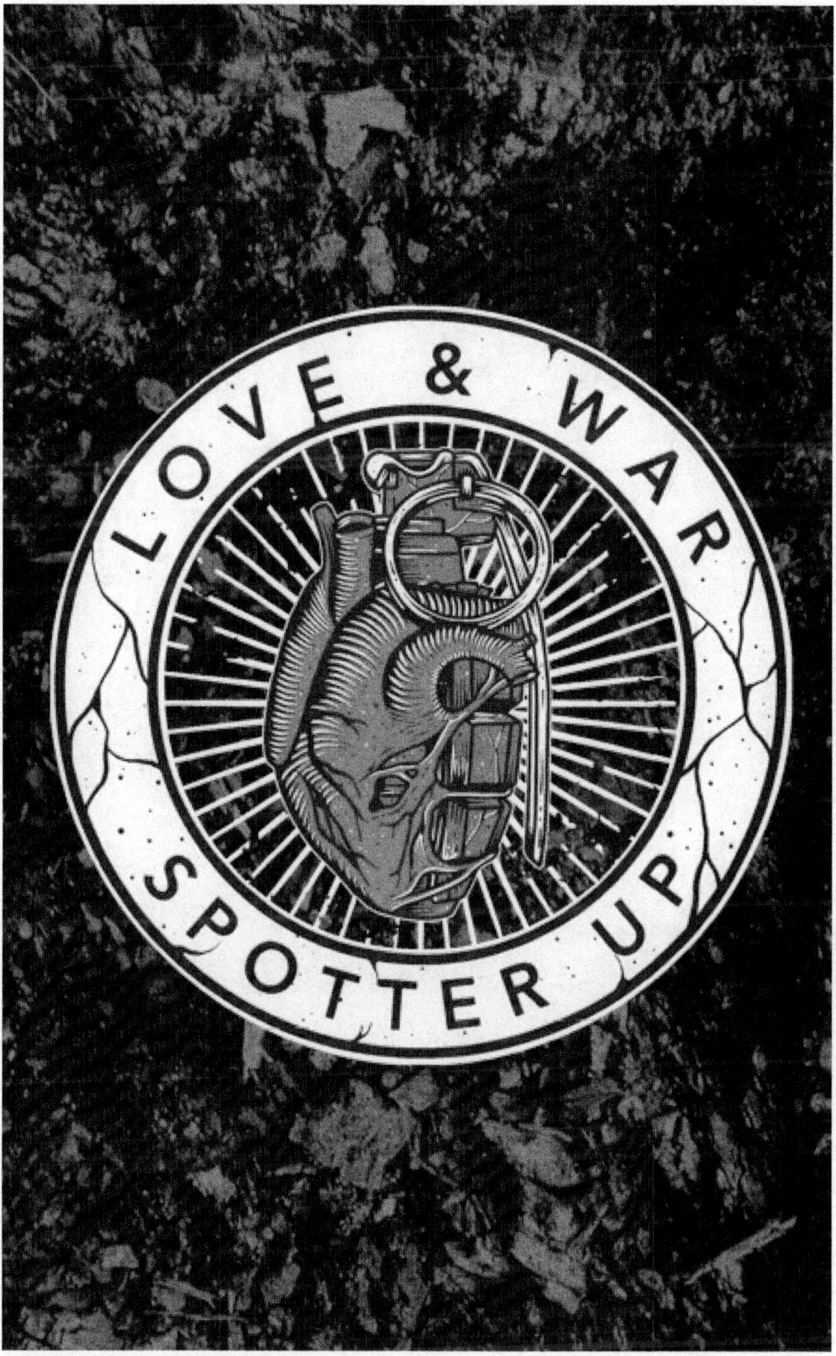
LOVE & WAR
SPOTTER UP

LOVE

Some men act as if love is some kind of creature that should be tortured to death.

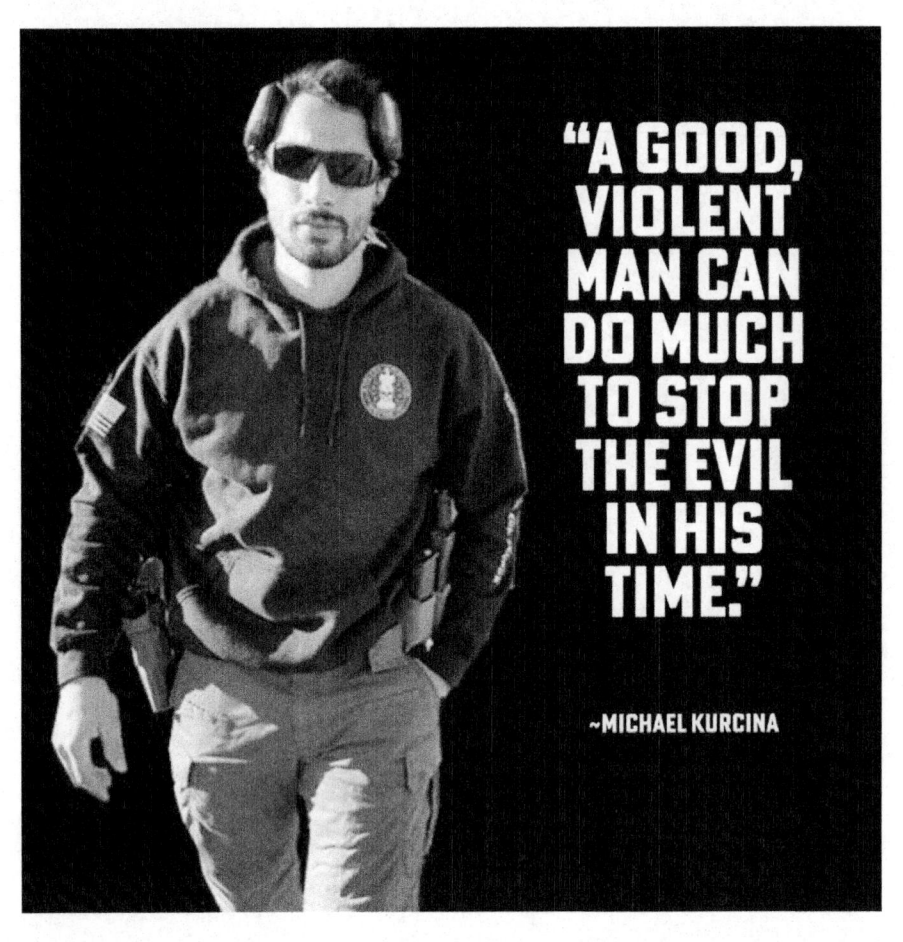

> "A GOOD, VIOLENT MAN CAN DO MUCH TO STOP THE EVIL IN HIS TIME."
>
> ~MICHAEL KURCINA

When I was young, I struggled with all of my energy to make the world love me. When I was older, I struggled will all of my energy to love the world.

To live is to peer out from our captivity, but to love is to allow someone to enter our cage, and we too give in what is termed a beautiful exchange.

Many are spreading a sickness called hate; love is the cure but as always with these kinds of outbreaks there's never enough to go around.

Real love is inexhaustible; if you find yourself now separated ask if what you had was ever so.

Fear is the most easily taught of all lessons; love the most easily misunderstood. We should never love thoughtlessly, but who of us in love ever had common sense? All men in love are fools.

No offer from others will ever be taken when made to a true friend giving you their loyalty and love.

In a lifetime let us write a thousand beautiful words for every ugly one we uttered.

Without a brother we would have a life with a different experience. *Seems obvious right? Of course, we'd have a different experience. Brothers bring experiences different from fathers, daughters, etc., I appreciate the guys that I served with, even if we speak infrequently. Honor that bond.*

Daily, every man should eat as if he believes it is his last meal, as if he was laughing with his best friends, and lie down nightly to what he believes is his final sleep, after making love to his sweetest girl.

Your heart should never be shaped to hold the vice the world wants to give to you.

We love time only when she serves us, when she makes us feel ageless but every other moment, she is a distraction from what we want, to escape our burden of being a man. How rude we are with her. We do not respect her in the morning, we make intense love with her in the afternoon, plead with her to stay the night but just like that she is gone. We play this flirtatious game of immortality with her again and again until she runs out for good.

If you think it is painful listening to a woman speak wait until she gives you her silence.

Even a thousand words spoken in kindness often fails to displace the utterance of the single, brutal one we leveled on the one we professed to love.

> *Every man* who stores away his secret griefs is better served seeing what good he might grow out of those *seeds of pain.*
> —Michael Kurcina

Every man who stores away his secret griefs is better served seeing what good he might grow out of those seeds of pain. Perhaps there are parallel roots with other men that grow because of the injuries of war he experienced, or from some death or divorce. Patrolman, pastor, Marine or just simply a man; true friendships do blossom and can save man from loneliness, anger, grief and self-loathing but he'll never know that until he decides to stop carrying those rotten kernels of destruction in his bag of darkness.

The night called to me and without a will I went to her. Without resistance she pulled me into her arms, without shame I cried to her while wave after wave of peace washed over my honest and abundant tears. I let myself drown in her darkness and for once felt myself begin to truly live.

Your heart can never be shaped to hold what I want to give you. You can sit there wounded, indifferent and even blind but it's time for me to find another me, it's time for you to find another life.

Every married man has experience as a king in exile; always waiting for a wife to let him know when it is safe to come home, and sit on his throne.

Sex between lovers is a temporary privilege; make love though an immortal duty.

To be loved means a couple possessed accepts being captured but neither forces the other's heart to be tamed.

It's easier to force someone that you don't love to go away than it is to force someone that you do love to come back.

One tree may be solitary, two trees are the start of a forest, and three or more are the beginning of an adventure. Seed the world by your thoughts.

I saw your body lying there trembling, quieter than any silent thing and knowing what I knew I would give my very own life so that you could have yours.

Give away the things that you love, the things that could ultimately save you from yourself. Drive them away like beaten horses, only to realize in pity and darkness that it was the one thing you should have saved. Is this you, are you so caught up in bitterness and rage that you damage something until it can never be repaired? God damn you, damn you, don't you want to fight evil in this heavy world? One day the Lord will send for us, and He will send for us. Stop what you're doing and look into her eyes and hold her hand, and see the beautiful light of God that He created in every woman and man.

Being divorced once should make a man wise; being divorced twice might mean he is stupid.

Destroy the greatest thing that you truly love if you want to live your life as a haunted man.

Let us never cease to cherish the brave deeds of warriors who lie at rest lest we forget what it is to be men.

Sometimes savage men have tender hearts and dream things as beautiful as anything a young child can summon. Learn from them to light worthy fires in places that have only known darkness.

A woman who likes to color crookedly should never be with a man only happy with straight lines.

Real love is inexhaustible; if you find yourself now separated ask if what you had was so.

Store love in your heart, and like a granary dispense it to all who are hungry. Feed souls but beware the vermin who would eat your labors away.

It's a cruel thing when women are so beautiful and unobtainable to men.

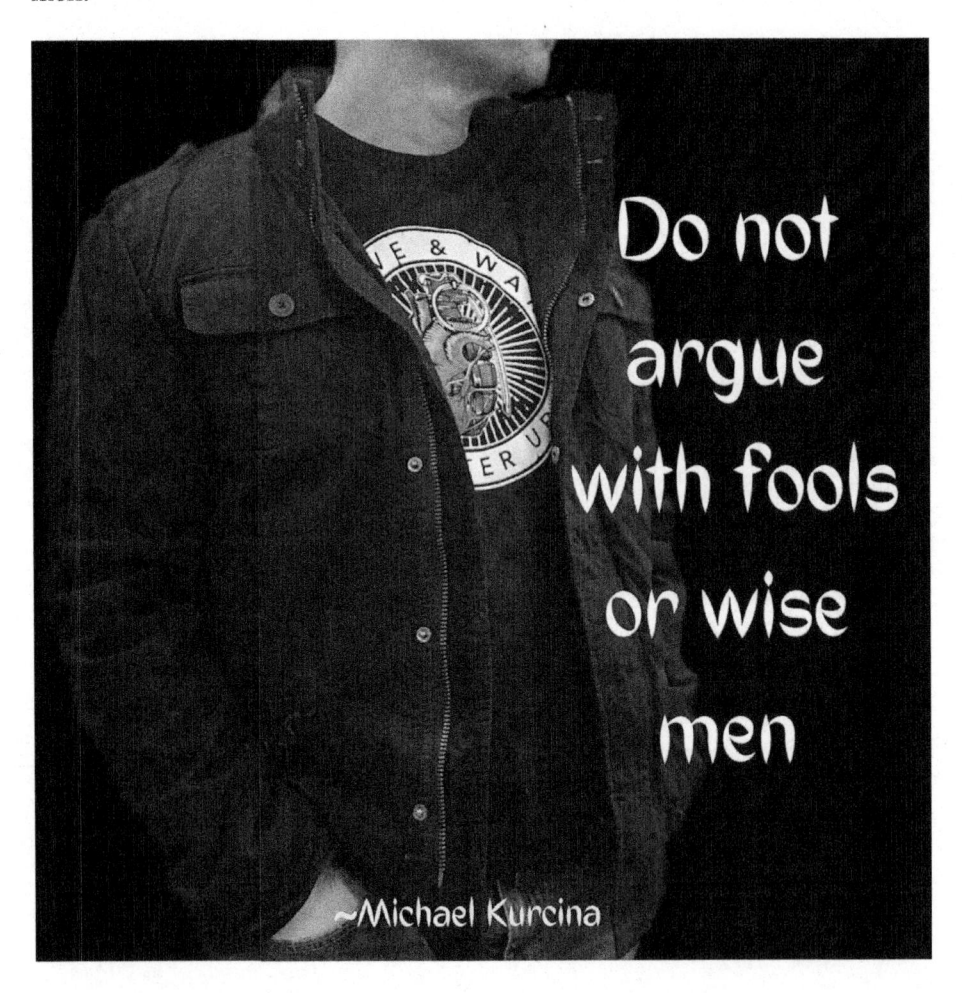

Do not argue with fools or wise men

~Michael Kurcina

WAYS OF THE GUNFIGHTER

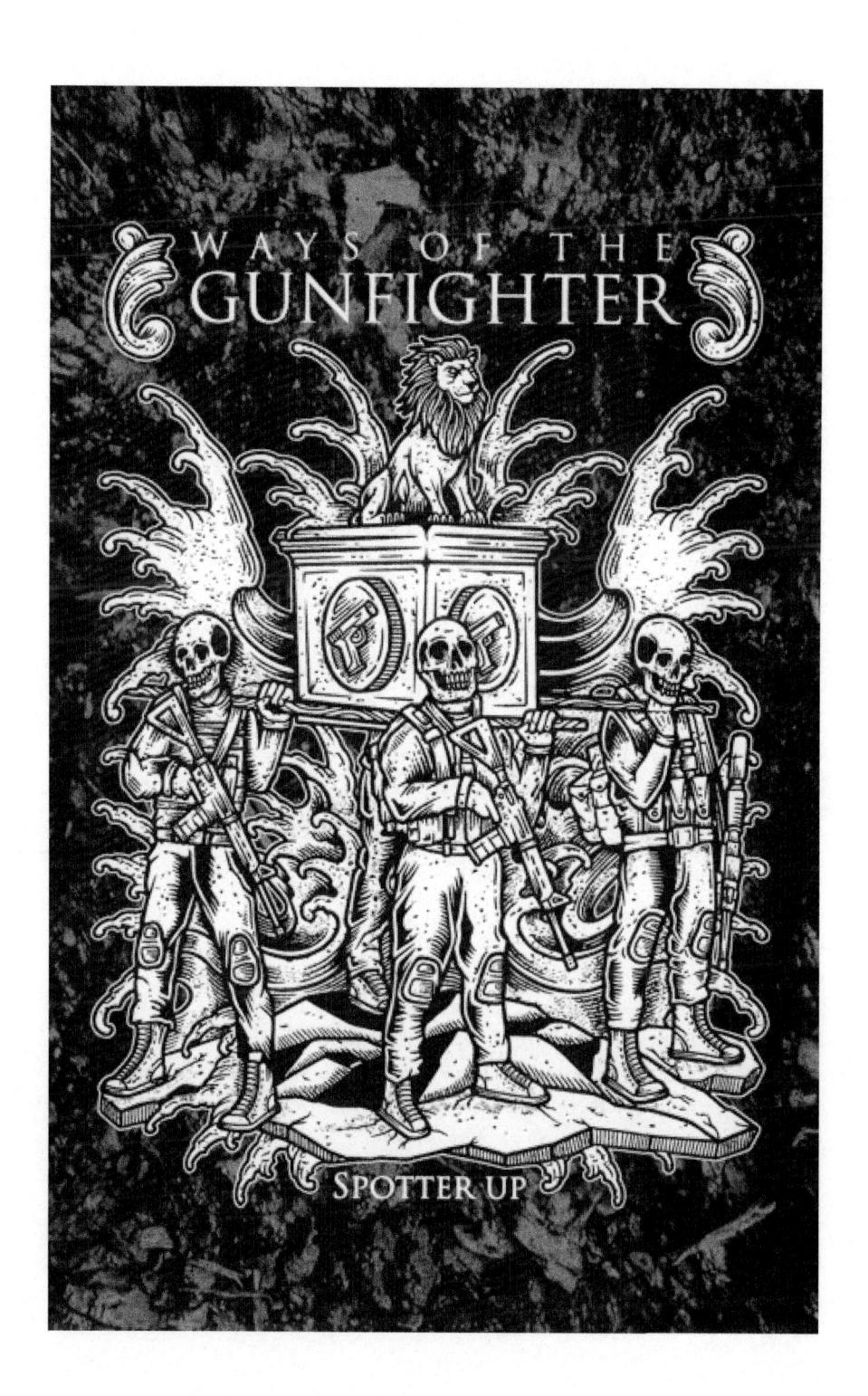

SPOTTER UP

WAR/FIGHTING

Boys leave home to become gods and the world will always destroy them and send them back as martyrs. Hopefully a boy's beliefs are rooted in something stable, something powerful and spirituality everlasting. Good looks, fame, money and success are seductive and can be indecent pursuits to many young and wild men. The activities that Hollywood and similar enclaves rave about only last for a very brief time, and are simply unfulfilling to wise men. Let's hope that boys grow up to pursue things that are more than cheap substitutes for whatever are their endless and singular passions, and we can only hope they understand those conceits and deceits in order to develop into mighty men. Let them be doers and not voyeurs in the realms of truth. Truth makes some men free but it can more deeply imprison others. The world is filled with some very stupid and brutal critics who also happen to be hypocritical men. Let us hope these boys have a good and holy message for the world and not just an earthly message promoting themselves. Let us hope they understand the price of having sentience and liberty. Let us hope they pursue God and not choose to become gods, for mortal men cannot see into time nor memory nor through the universe, and the world will not care when it comes time to beat them down even when they preach about their beautiful passions for peace and love into a world that only wants to practice war. *the wages of sin are death.

How easily we remember. Let it be a good thing how badly we cannot forget what war does to men.

War has always been at the crossroads of faith and doubt. A man who never even had a street-fight at the center of his belief and disbelief needs to step into that neighborhood and by a reckoning through real battle comes closer to becoming a fully developed being.

If damage is a currency let us pay to others more than what was ever owed to us.

Son, let me show you how to shake men like dead leaves falling onto a dark path. Let blood drop like red rain on green grass.

Be savage in youth to be civilized in adulthood in order enjoy all that you fought for.

If you do not want to fight a losing battle do not argue with fools or wise men.

Be fluent in the language of violence to be superior in your provision of force.

When violence is the last option either stay behind me or search for cover and run that way.

In sad places where life is cheap people need saints that make their gunmen weep.

If you have no experience calming a dying man's cries, please spare warriors your unlearned advisement.

If only we could bring as much pain to our enemies as we sometimes bring to ourselves. *Walk to the edge of your abyss and deposit your pain and bad faith into it. Pray that time like a mystic river washes you free of those broken things. It can only hurt you if you keep going back to drink from that sad source. Dig new wells, and don't drink from and wallow in old streams.

When I behave savagely only men will understand me.

There are some things not worth saying to other men; that's why God gave us the ability to make fists.

When a weak man uses violence to shame you into silence two strong blows to his nose will deliver the most beautiful sound.

Brutal men clumsy in skill weave a warped pattern of their life and wonder how they became entangled in it.

Dark men with dark hearts hide from the light of day. Dark men do their dark deeds and then they fade away.

War seems to wake the spirt like nothing else; God chooses how it permanently sleeps.

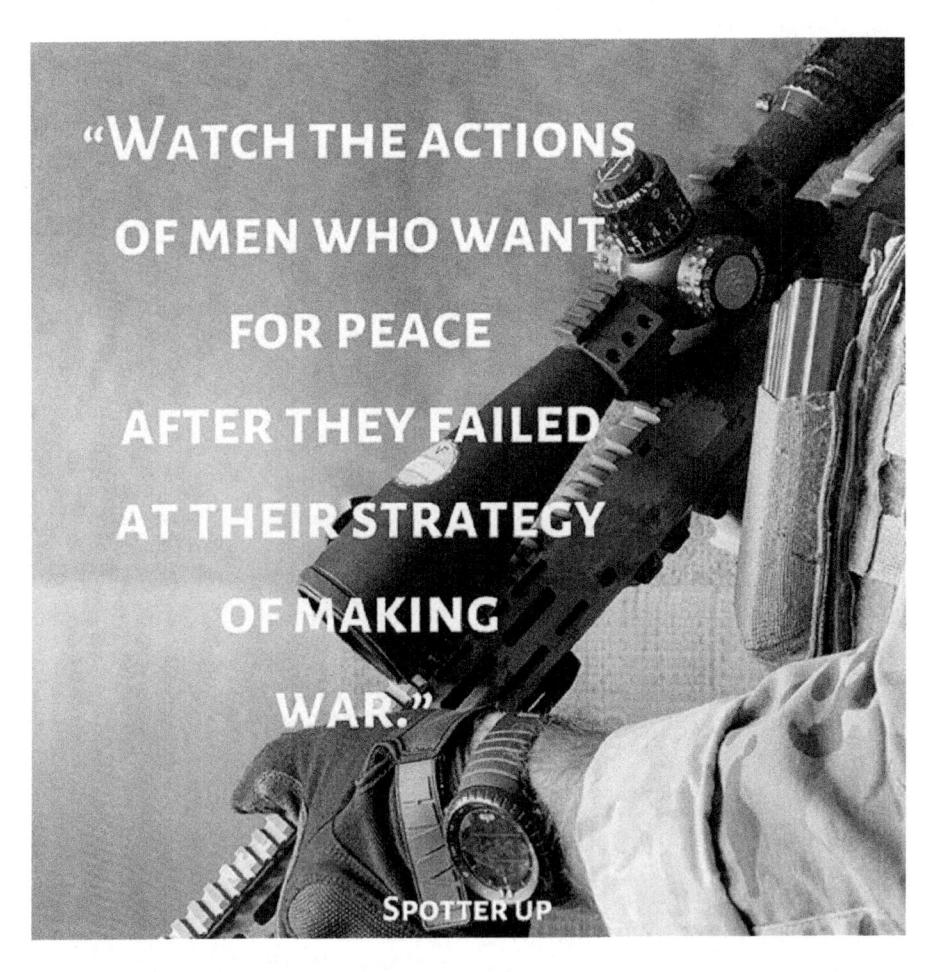

> "WATCH THE ACTIONS OF MEN WHO WANT FOR PEACE AFTER THEY FAILED AT THEIR STRATEGY OF MAKING WAR."

Recall the autumns that came and went, those little men you tore apart with nothing but your violent hands. Feel nothing about the damage done, but of the love that caught you, when you were more animal than man. Sometimes the most fearsome beast in us will find freedom in being truly loved. *Are you okay? Hope so. You ever scared your loved ones by letting them see what you could do to a man? How about what you can do to yourself? Work on it. Work with them. Be the protector, be the safe house and take their love back when they give it to you. Don't reject it. Yes, werewolves need love too.

What man ever runs from love and runs towards death? Can we not call him insane for doing this everyday again and again?

One day we will rest beneath the eaves of our golden houses, and hang our swords and shields but until then bring us a war. Sometimes we want things that cannot be expressed and they should remain unspoken. We are men naked and alone. Let the darkness die after we do our dark deeds and let us in the morning be reborn. Let our weaknesses diminish and give strength to those who choose to love us for they will need that and much more. Until that time all of our focus must be eat, pray, war.

Violence is a handicraft; a common art even brutal men can produce yet what warriors truly understand.

In the intercourse of a violent life, hatred makes infant monsters of us all. We must never let that bastard child grow.

Watch the actions of men who want for peace after they failed at their strategy of making war. *We've all been here before, shaking the hand of someone we just bested in something as simple as a pushing match or something more complex like a bar fight only to watch them come at us with a beer bottle or baseball bat and bad intentions later on in the parking lot.

Popcorn eaters who like to advise from their cheap seats, far from the epicenter of violence need to shut up or come sit front and center where the action really happens.

Whisky and oysters go oddly together like laughter and violence but that doesn't mean what goes in a man's stomach or comes out of his soul should ever be paired.

What mouth will kiss us? What arms will hold us? Mother is gone so we weep our tears and gnash our teeth for the boy we lost and the man we became. We cannot return to youth. We left her and home to get more out of life, and without mamma's loving protection we experienced the horror of living. There was no escaping it for this is what every man in life must do.

Doc never stopped rushing to the buzzing sound of death with his hope of delivering one more life out of the terrifying womb of war.

In a prison of some making we forget the faces of lovers once familiar to us. We dwell in shadow and pity, shame and hatred, conflict and sorrow for what was done to the closest friends we loved. War often will do that to men.

Sometimes sane men become dark gods with their orchestras of war by making everyone cleared hot to destroy.

Men who run towards danger to help others might not have their heads on right but the ones that run away certainly have it on wrong.

Do not expect a normal life when you give your heart to the odd gods of war.

Keep preaching peace, do nothing, or do little when violence comes to others but consider one day that violence may come to you, so be grateful if help comes from someone that won't auction their talents nor principles as you did. When it happens is not the time to figure what it is that you believe. Give regard to a moral code that has real principle, merit and is useful because there are evil men out there. Give violence that is an appropriate response, that fully adheres to your principles, and if need be destroys bad men in their tracks.

Out of the seeds of war, the flowering of man begins or ends.

If we didn't have brothers, we'd find strangers to fight against.

Be wary of boarding a train headed for war, if you change your mind it is not easy to disembark. *A temperate mind is always best if one wants to make a decision on the action to take where it can ultimately lead to violence. Be careful going down that path if you are unsure of the destination and are unversed in where to go and what to do when you arrive. Hold onto your ticket and mind the boarding times. You don't have to get on.*

The shaking sails over tall ships will not carry us home...it is but our swords and honor on the rising hills of these foreign lands. We will go home now.

We make ghosts. The night is chosen, men of war come over the hills. They whistle and hum, making violence their priesthood, conferring death upon unholy men. I can see them, can you see them, these legions of savages running wild? We make ghosts, they make ghosts. See the spectral lights upon the hills, see the big birds, bringing big hurt to mongrels walking as if they are men? Men live and die in their firefights. I can see them, can you see them, their numbers increase all night long and it never ends....

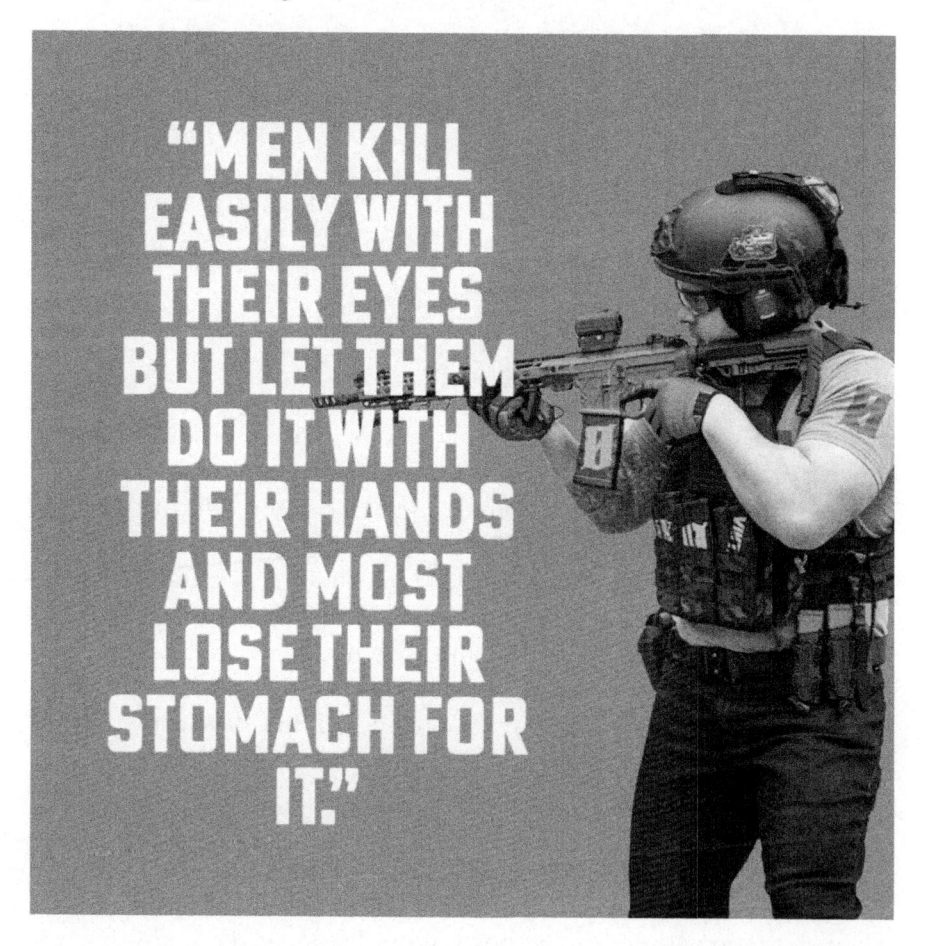

> "MEN KILL EASILY WITH THEIR EYES BUT LET THEM DO IT WITH THEIR HANDS AND MOST LOSE THEIR STOMACH FOR IT."

In that hush of night, we left good men long asleep to dispense wise sorrow with those who knew, and in that sad time of blood we made ghosts of dead men, then lost our youth.

Make sure you win debates by using your brains and mouth, if you feel like you're losing simply use your fists.

Ask them, have you ever known what was in your father's heart and the things he had to bear? Have you seen or known his scars, carried on his body or more deeply upon his soul? Can you recall your history, his history, the stories in fact each story that should be told? The bright glimmer in some men's eyes belie the tragic tales they could tell. They have personal losses that amount to some incredible hells. Some fathers seem cursed to live, suffer and die while other are blessed and savor life. Can we ease burdens, can we preserve that time, can we preserve something that's worthwhile telling? If they have something to say then make them legends in your children's memories. Show courage and look into his eyes.

We entered the unholy houses and killed the unholy men. If you think our spirits are broken, you're mistaken, think again. When we're done, when we stand within the dust bowl of our life let us recall just one beautiful night. Let us remember beauty bright and the whirring lights of those stars above and feel a hope that will save us from ourselves.

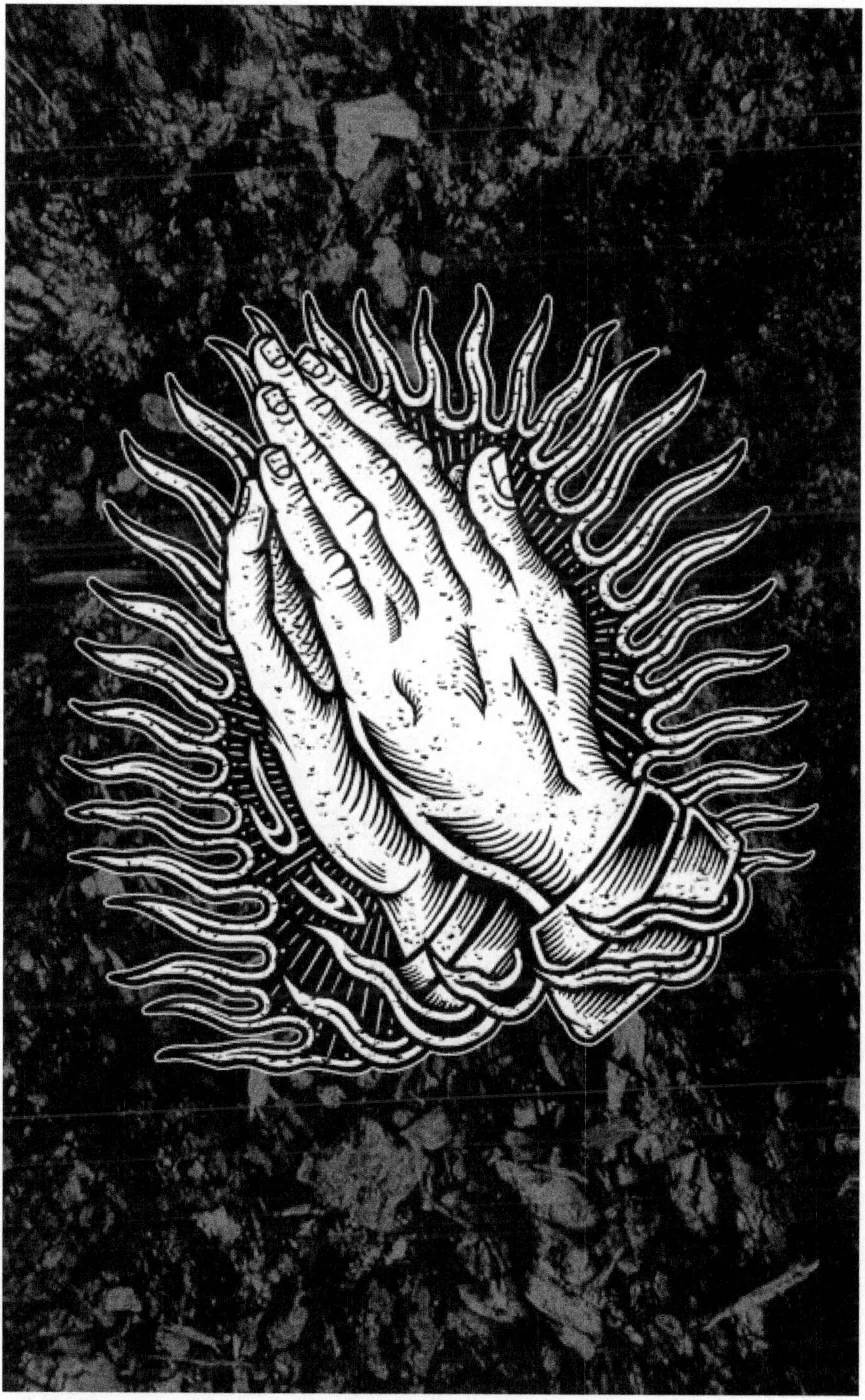

FAITH

Hopefully in our mystic prayers to God we escape the painful regrets from youth, and upon exhaling our aged breath we peacefully accept truth.

Every man is born carrying a strange cargo and should never be ashamed nor fearful of bestowing his gifts upon the world.

When men act the gods may be silent but they do watch and listen, so act well, for they too may act.

All men live with a secret sacrament and a private hell; let each man believe too in a benevolent God and a Heaven to save him from himself.

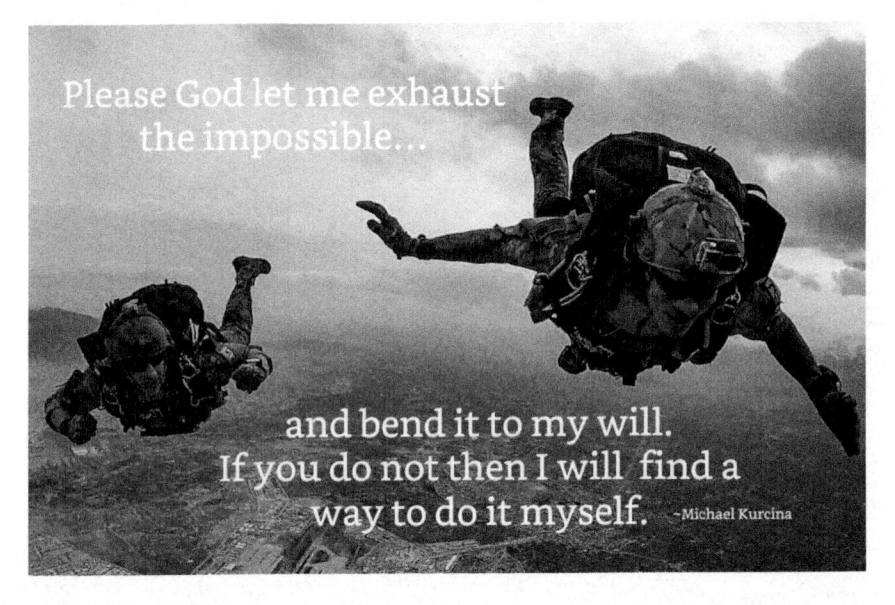

> Please God let me exhaust the impossible... and bend it to my will. If you do not then I will find a way to do it myself. ~Michael Kurcina

The new generation abandoned the old creeds, trusted it best to have no faith and then wondered why there was no meaningful purpose and coda to their life.

We cannot understand eternity. Every time it proves to be a challenge to our categories but it doesn't mean we should stop trying to understand its composition by getting close enough to feel its glory.

When the gods sow discord into the world wise and foolish men laugh alike.

A man's creed is his spiritual sword and without practice in war he dulls what should always remain sharp.

Sometimes 'throwing iron' is the flagellation a man endures to recognize that his life has blessings again.

> SPOTTERUP IS SIMPLY ABOUT "SPOTTING" SOLUTIONS TO PROBLEMS SHOWING OTHERS THE WAY AND NOT BEING A DRAG ON THE WORLD
>
> SPOTTER UP

Every moment God gives each man enough spiritual timber to rebuild the worthy house that he just tore down.

Every man is challenged by the same urges of sin but those who never fight against them are just tragedies waiting to happen.

Fatalists are doomed by the curses of the gods; bold men make them watch and learn.

Leave your armor near the ashes, leave your apprehensions outside the door, leave your weapon near the altar, renew the vows that you swore. *On this day renew yourself... Submit yourself to being redeemed and let go of everything you think that you know. Even when we are broken, we are still usable, we can still be an example to others, we can still be put back together.*

Please God let me exhaust the impossible and bend it to my will. If you do not then I will find a way to do it myself.

Sometimes the dark is church; bring your pain, cry it out and then get back to the rest of your life.

In this world there is an abyss of light far greater than any abyss of darkness, and if we are fortunate enough to catch even the smallest glimpse of it, we might be knocked to our knees by feeling fractions of God's glory.

Build no shrines, honor no men, worship no God, follow no king; see if there is loyalty and purpose without belief.

False prophets in any age always mask themselves to sheep as true shepherds. Mediocre and tumultuous times won't always reveal them to be tyrants, but it will reveal the strong, the feeble-minded and even those in-between as who chooses to be free and those choosing to be enslaved. Our goal as free men is to lead those away from wanting to live in an unfree world, and unflinchingly eliminate all of the Pied Pipers. Simply, all that false patriots want is power.

Be godlier simply by loving others more while loving yourself less.

The undiscovered country. In this fixed world water has as much intrinsic value as wine, intermissions as much value as action, disconnections as much value as unions, and we need life as much as we need death. Life must have boundaries to properly separate us from cessation and without it how could we reasonably contemplate the nature of existence or its end?

Man doesn't just want to be understood, man wants to be worshipped. If he gets what he wants he will become more prideful so it's a good thing if he never gets to fulfill his desires.

A man's spirit split in two over time becomes whole again if he chooses to grow the one and dies to the other.

A temperate spirit is needed to capture one's lawless heart.

On some lonely path of country or street, kneel to pray, and pray to weep. *Pray to let it go whatever troubles you. You are not alone. Let it all out and then drive on. Never believe that one bad moment is a catastrophe. There are always halls and doors to go down and through, there are safe passages.*

Life is not over, your life is not over, you are not alone. There is a hope that we will merit more than just a mention on a 3-inch-long swath of yellowed paper, that we will be remembered for more than being life's punching bag; that we never asked for a second or third chance because we always did something decent with the first. For every greasy spoon we ate in, for every blind date that looked and turned us down, for every place we avoided because they were places for the dead, let's hope in old age and our seemingly forgettable death there was something good in it to be found. Life can be tough but it can be made brilliant.

What hells await men who cannot envision some kind of heaven?

The whole of a every man's life starts out as a speckle of flame yet it can turn into a pillar of fire if he is able to lead others to places, they would otherwise never choose to go.

A man who gets lost in only one labyrinth on his journey of self-discovery can be called a wise man, but he who repeats it tenfold yet never finds himself can be called a fool.

Leave your armor near the ashes, leave your apprehensions outside the door, leave your weapon near the altar, renew the vows that you swore. Recall your ambitions. Men without some deep belief and self-belief may find that their spiritual emptiness leads to their self-destruction. Sometimes when they forget their purpose, or when they have doubts, or are simply tired doing what they are doing it's good for them to kneel and put their head and hands to the dirt and find reassurance there. There is dignity found on the knees. Separate yourself from your activity and reflect. Perhaps you need to remember that you exempt yourself from the blandness of life that affects other men. Why are you suffering? Perhaps freedom has a certain seductive power but so too does a life of discipline. Guard yourself from acting impulsively. Depression is often a self-indulgence and a wasteful way to spend your energy. Why not try and see that there is good meaning in this universe and not an absurd one? There is a magical force, a cosmic and good reason you have yet to understand. Take pause, mediate, pray, push up from the ground. There is a magical chain in this universe that you have yet to grab that punches through the firmament. It will lead you to redemption and perhaps even greatness. Hold onto it. Pull on it. Let it carry you up. Now stand like a man and go where you must go.

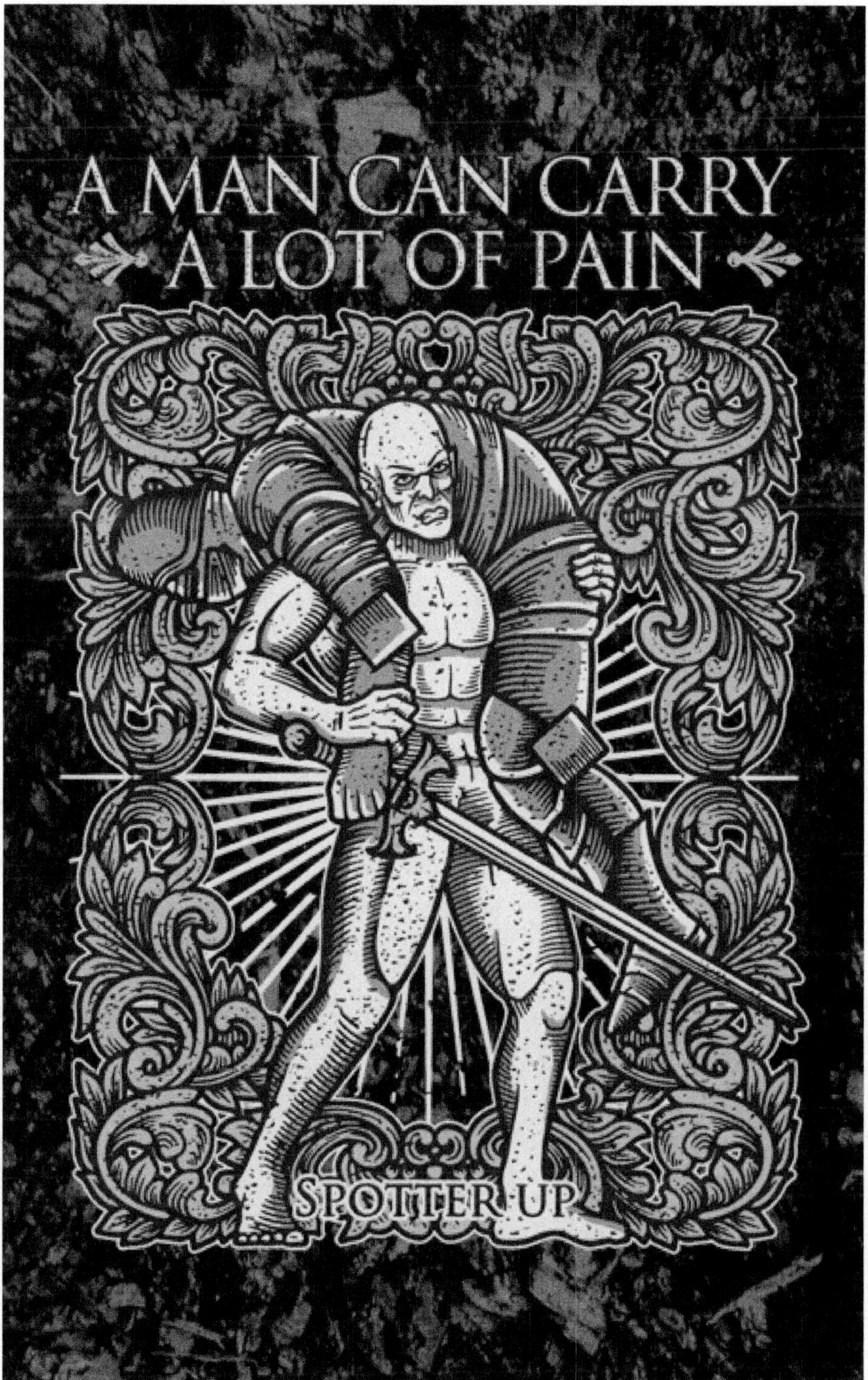
A MAN CAN CARRY
A LOT OF PAIN
SPOTTER UP

SADNESS, PAIN

A man intending to move his life into a brighter future sometimes needs to go back and deal with his dark and tragic past.

The worst suicide isn't to literally die but to know that we sold ourselves out to the world and then with that dead spirit continue to stay alive.

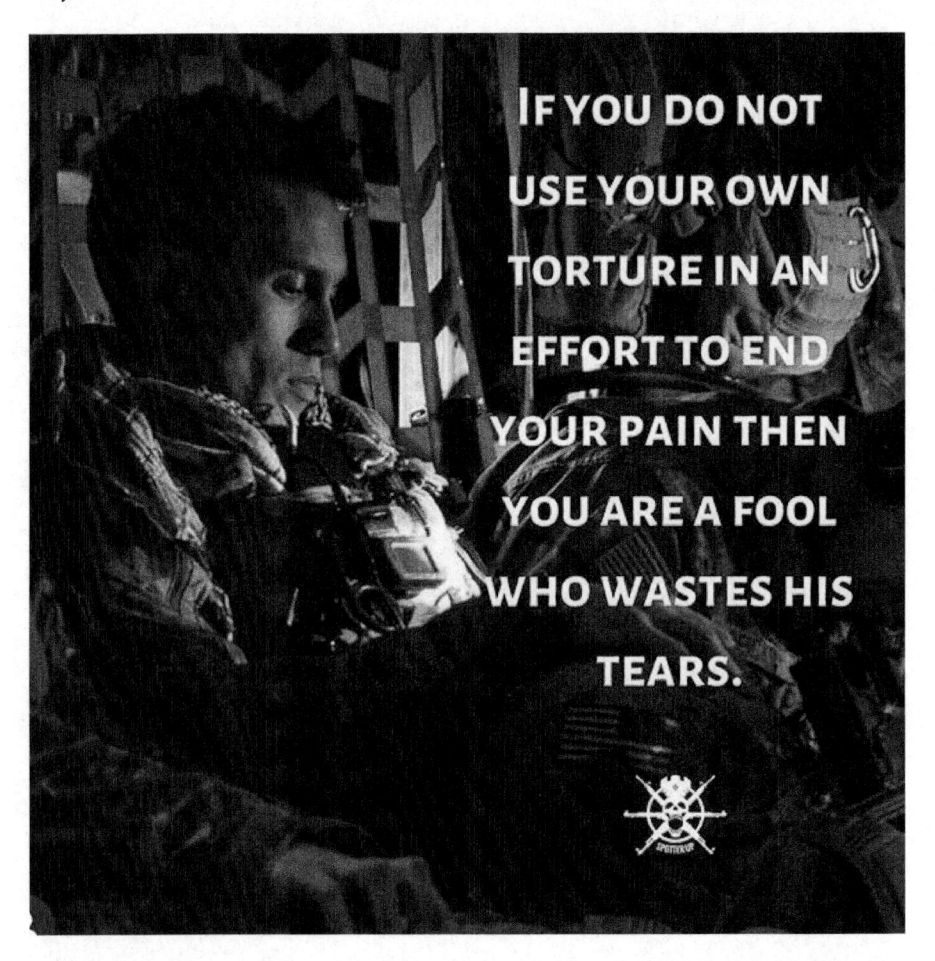

> IF YOU DO NOT USE YOUR OWN TORTURE IN AN EFFORT TO END YOUR PAIN THEN YOU ARE A FOOL WHO WASTES HIS TEARS.

If you do not use your own torture in an effort to end your pain then you are a fool who wastes his tears.

The saddest line in the story of your life is the one that states you lost faith in yourself, that you lost faith in the world, and in the end that you quit and died.

I will survive not because I'm a hopeful person. I will survive because I know how to suffer and so I will endure; these are not the traits of a wise man.

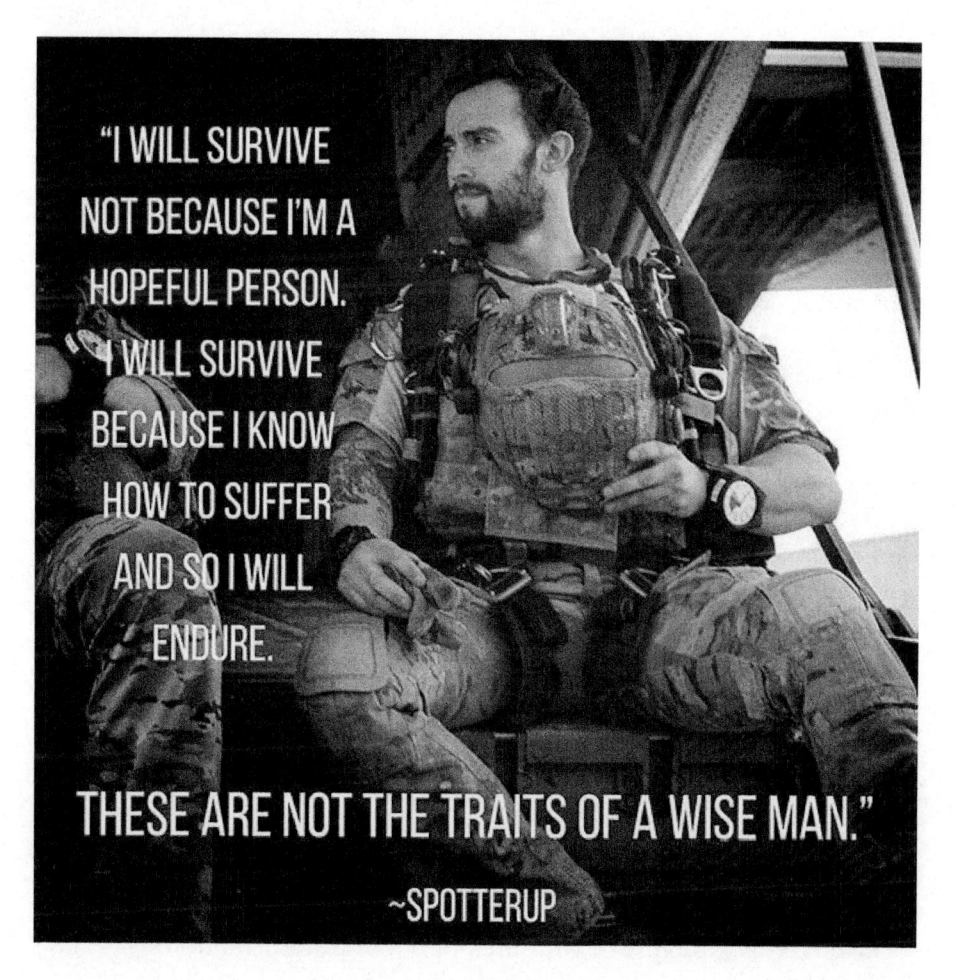

Sometimes the path to healing our broken heart means we must break someone else's.

All of our life is filled with tears; when we die is when time wipes them.

I remember your black eyes, the damaging blade, the good lives you took, even yours to the grave. I recall the city lights and the lives you saved, except your own; dark days.

Without hope life holds nothing, and all a man can look forward to without hope on his spiritual journey to growth and healing are the promises of beatings without end.

When your tongue is tied because of sadness let your tears speak.

Depression is a magical sadness that enchants the mind, deludes the heart and has men believing no better way of living exists.

The belief that life is meaningless enters your mind when your heart becomes weary of pleasure but the antidote is never pain. *We must be mindfully aware that what we think is right is right, aligns with what we feel is right or it isn't right because we then introduce conflict into our life. Drinking to remember or drinking to forget isn't a rationale way to deal with the existential sense of disconnection in life, but we do it anyway. The issue isn't solely with what is incoming, the issue is in what is outgoing. What we perceive isn't what we promote. Getting into serious bar fights won't work either; that is just trying to solve the problem of wanting someone to be extinguished; men who do so are looking for affirmation that they are worth nothing or that someone else is worth nothing. If life is meaningless then your punches and kicks have no worth. The issue is that men feel and think that they are worth nothing yet believe deep down that they are something; conflict again. Pain is the poison; love is the antidote. We must never lower our self below our human dignity or we lose sense of our worth, nor should we see other men as beneath us either; and so, healing means we must really do things that aren't popular, and not find our identity in trying to be popular. (Instagram likes) We must honestly seek the truth by doing much of what we don't prefer. See mankind as valuable. Have healthy structure in your life but not unhealthy monotony. Take action by trying things you've never done before and you'll have new data to process and utilize. Those gathered facts will tell you what sustains your heart and mind and in turn will sustain your soul.

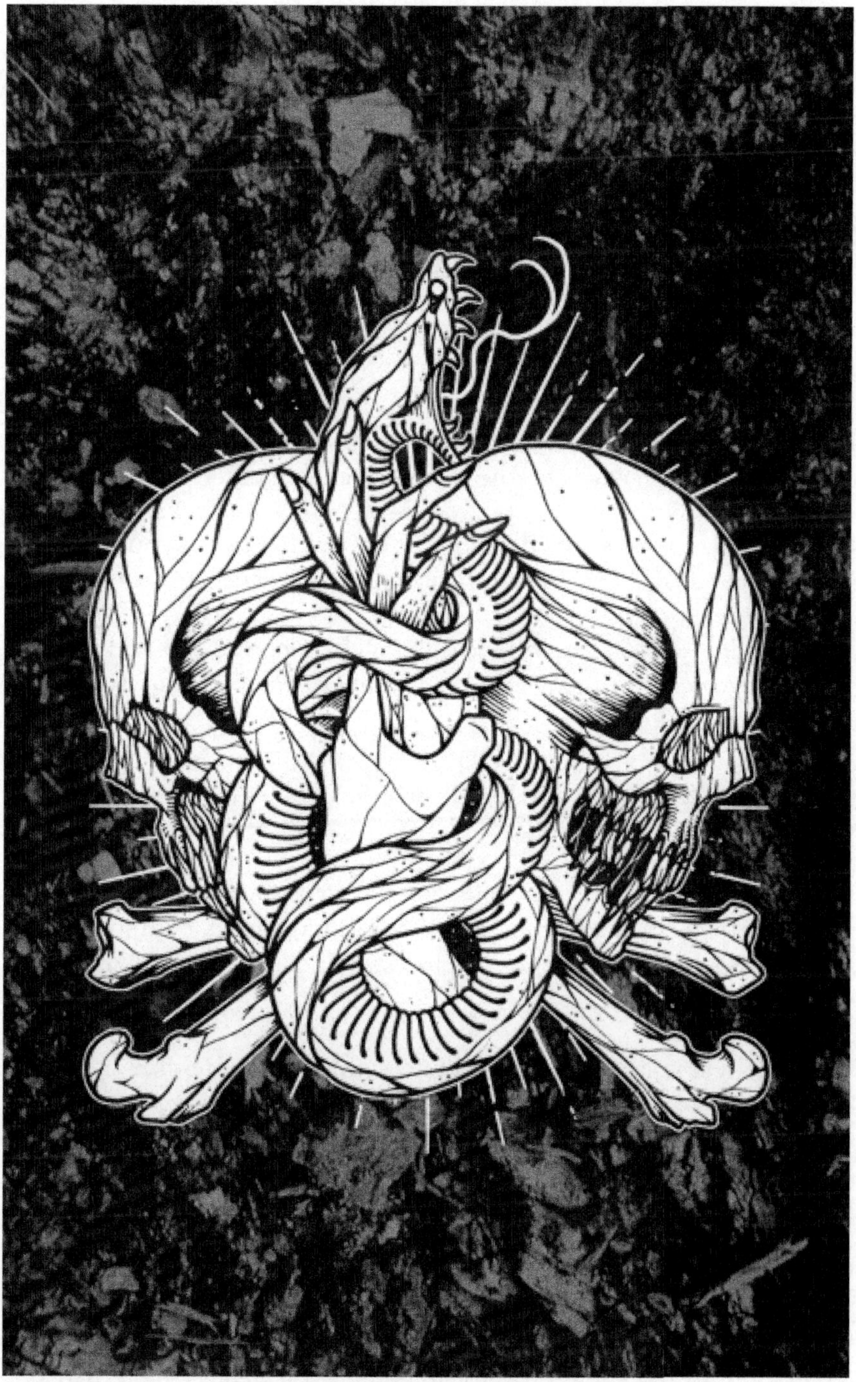

LOSS

The average soul feels a certain kind of loneliness but the above average soul feels an incredible isolation that should never be experienced and can never be described.

Living your best life sometimes requires first going through your worst hell.

The best time to create is after you've been injured but you must be ready and real to deal with that pain.

Brief moments of meditation should be the last thing and the first thing a samurai practices before he sleeps and when he rises.

Do not applaud fools for suffering for any reason rather applaud the sound man who suffers for the right reason yet efforts to stop the why.

The morning starts innocently and the night becomes damned to men who believe wasted time is torture, as they spend a fine and precious day living in the past.

Men are born into exile and spend their whole life upon this earth trying to fill the eternity in their hearts.

In a prison of some making we forget the faces of lovers once familiar to us. We dwell in shadow and pity, shame and hatred, conflict and sorrow for what was done to the closest friends we loved. War will often do that to men.

Men who feel injured by the world need to spend more time fighting back instead of wasting time wondering what the hell just hit them.

The damage we do to ourselves is pain we should gift to men far more deserving of punishment.

When you're ready to build again use those tears to raise a worthy house upon the bedrock meant for it.

No amount of brick and mortar can defend you against the terrorists inside your mind.

And every night he believed it was easier to drink and deal with real ghosts than to speak with fake women about deep wounds that could never be seen.

All that most of us will ever do when we see our life go up in flames is to stand there and watch it burn.

Go home. Put away the gun, the blade and your armor. Tonight, let moonlight fill your eyes. Be ever thankful for some of the truly hurtful stings in life. Moments of grief married with wonder can make you a grateful man.

If you cut out your heart and offer it to the odd gods of war, make sure you learn how to put it back into that hole with peace when they are finally done with you.

Laughter leaves us, we're filled with pain, and in old age had we the years to live and love again let us choose the same, let us choose the same.

In the heart of every beaten child is planted a seed of self-destruction; in that rank dirt they must never let an evil flower bloom.

Grief is one of the heaviest burdens we must carry inside the human heart.

No one will ever be convinced of your sincerity, or the seriousness of your sufferings, unless you show them.

A drunken cry quite often speaks our greatest truth what our conscience knows of horror. There is a house of death that waits upon a hill, and one day we must enter it. What removes the dread is to live richly enough to exhaust our heart of anxiety, and in doing so fills our spirit with peace regardless of our piety.

The pain that hurts most men is regret. A lesson lasts as long as we want it to last.

Ignore the seduction of loneliness and you have the beginning of what might be a life.

The smallest fire on the deepest night is like an inferno to sad, lost men in need of light.

Fret not about the destruction you did in the last 24 hours, instead scavenge what you can and build something useful in these 24 hours now.

Men who believe that love is not enough to save them from loneliness refuse to accept its their greater desire for isolation that makes the loneliness so.

Even small injuries unattended over time can tear strong men apart like water drops into a fissure.

Everything can become whole again. Every sword can be reforged, every wall can be remade, every man can be reborn.

Do you want to do something very difficult? Accept that someone is never coming back. One night darker than the others, one sorrow sadder than the rest. That's a hard lesson. It could have been through a separation or death. Accept it and see if some good can come from you doing that. I believe once you come to recognize doing this is the only way to move ahead, you'll begin to find some very good reasons why you need to go on living.

When you're tired, when you're broken, when you're sorry, when they've left you, when you're empty, when you're lonely, be ready, be focused, to pick yourself up to patch yourself together again.

Sometimes in sorrow we are a mad spectator looking inward to our body's arena waiting for violence, wanting injury and even death to our soul.

A broken heart is like a vast house holding all of the emptiness it doesn't want while absent of the fullness of the one thing it does need.

SPOTTER UP

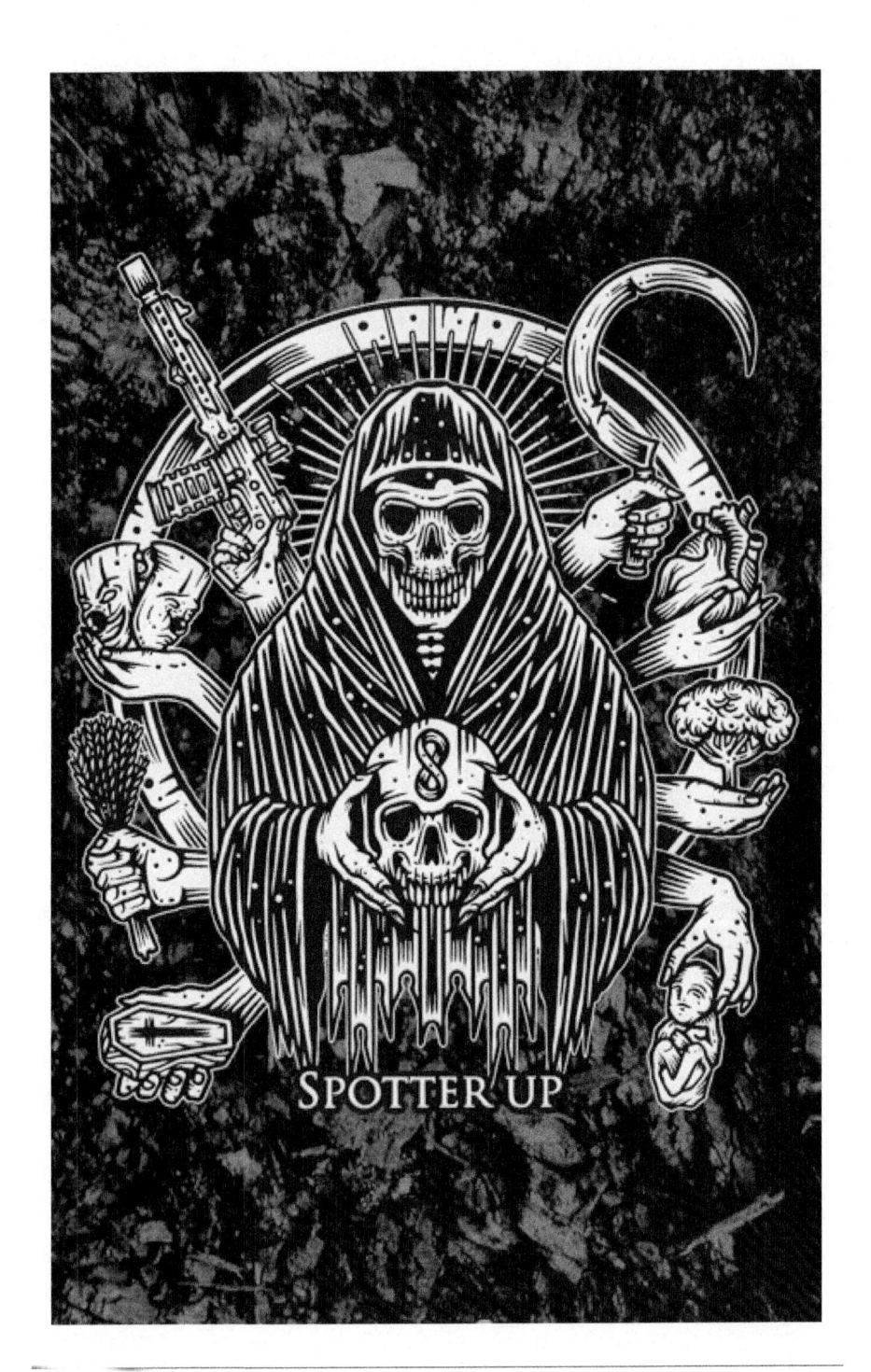

TIME AND MEMORY

In old age had we the years to live and love again let us choose the same.

Of all the many things that men miss most is the long voice of youth, years past, memory calling, hot summers, and the lovers that loved them. Nothing will ever bring any of it back and so they press on...

I wished I was conceived at the first point in human history or died at its end but I live inconsequentially perhaps at its middle and never felt incentivized to truly live.

> We are born...
> ...to *waste* the most *poignant* moments of our lives
> —Michael Kurcina

We are born to waste the most poignant moments of our lives and half that battle is learning how to escape that time, the other half is learning how to use what we left behind.

We drank the night and devoured the world but one day we must face the love we forsook, and the dead we never buried, and relook at the dreams that did nothing for us. We made love to strangers, ran towards danger, we were confused by obligations and gave our loyalty to promise breakers. Brothers, and marriages were lost, children were gained and sometimes even money was made. The young and damned would have to wake up and become men.

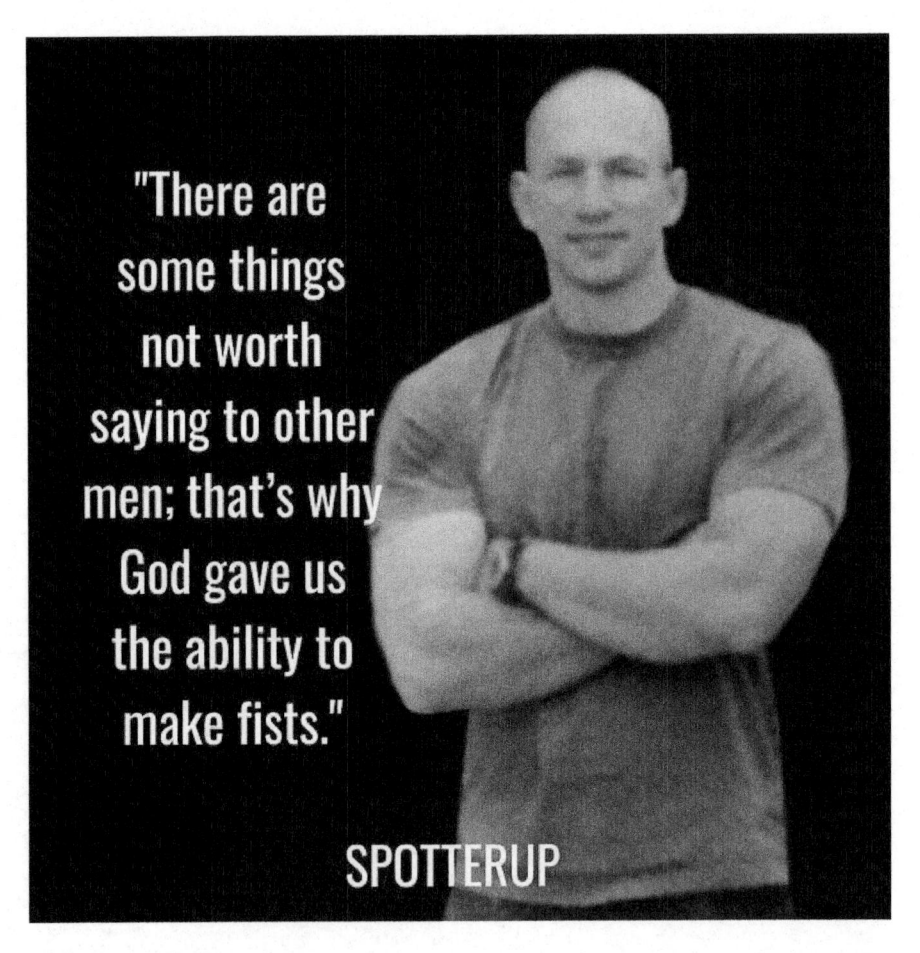

> "There are some things not worth saying to other men; that's why God gave us the ability to make fists."
>
> SPOTTERUP

I rise from sleep often and nightly. It's an exercise I do to see the world through my soul and not with my eyes. In my exhaustion my mind perceives the world and my existence through another portal. I rise up and feel the light of the stars, feel the night, and elation. Like a dog that comes to me I feel her purpose, I feel her same joy, I feel the pup want me, it wants my attention, it wants me unconditionally. Life smothered under a blanket of darkness kicks and fights to stay alive. Like a mask pulled from my head I no longer live in fear, I want to take the risk to see the world as I should see it, and live it as I should live it, and not be afraid of the commonness that daily terrorizes. * In the wind, in the night our soul becomes alive, and it wants more of life. Wake up and let it all come to you suddenly.

Time, we play this flirtatious game of immortality and cheat with her again and again until she runs out on us for good.

I hope when I begin to search deep into my heart that I'll still find youth.

Back there are the things we broke and the things that broke us; ahead will be the things we save and the things that save us.

We recall the golden homes of our youth, we remember the tawny boughs where we climbed, and the cold springs where we were lost in time and swam forever... but youth is gone and we must use what we haven't lost to move into a better tomorrow. *pull on your shoes, and with all the strength inside of you, rise up and go.

Yesterday is distant, while today is close, and tomorrow may never come. Live your life without fear. *You are not a dead body. You are not some eaten carcass on a forgotten road. Do not live as if to simply exist inside that structure of flesh, blood and bone. Move with energy, with enthusiasm, with your power and if you do that then it is beautiful. Let your feet carry you far. Live, love, battle, and go as far as the winds of God will push you to go.

The boldest of plans to spend the wealth of their liberty comes not from free men but from free men who believe at any minute they can be enslaved.

Most people longing for immortality can't even figure out what to do before noon. We can only pray to God they end that clueless way of thinking by one o'clock.

And just like that our summer died; time took with him youth and twenty, and our dying magic this sad belief that we could live forever.

In the wind, in the night our soul becomes alive, and it wants more of life; wake up and let it all come to you suddenly.

Tonight, let moonlight fill your eyes. Be thankful even for some of the truly hurtful stings in life. Moments of grief married with wonder can make you a grateful man.

Where are our kinsmen? Those vibrant youth who once walked with swagger? Some are no longer with us, but their memory is with us, and we will remember until we too disappear and join with them into the forever.

Every night within our heart let us plan for an adventurous tomorrow as if we were leaving an old world in order to find a new one. Let us join a strange tide of men who are not beholden to this world, let us pour back like ships into the old seas, to leave the safety of our known shores and discover something new about life, about others, about ourselves. Let us learn to be unafraid of sailing every morn.

Time wastes us. Let us not return the favor by wasting it.

Indeed, the advantage of hours means precious little to indecisive men.

Regret is one of the most painful wounds that all humankind shares.

SPOTTER UP

CULTURE

If you want to be relevant change a culture, if you want to be inconsequential go with the status quo.

Men whored by fame can be whored by anything.

New monsters will rise: a whorish race of men, whored by power, whored by money, whored by fame and they will set truth on fire until it burns to ashes and deliver the world into the blackest night. On that day heroes must rise.

Civilization is just a collection of loners.

If you want to die with a good name don't be found dead in a cheap hotel; just sayin'.

The truth is most men in a dark world want to be the center of a fire but don't want to feel the pain when the heat is burning.

Society today is so enamored with little saviors rather than a big messiah. They want fast, they want sexy, they want easy. Rebellion today is dancing in the desert to modern beats, boarding trains to get lost rather than to be found, violent hysterics and quick, cheap, primal hookups. In fact, in a hundred years nothing has changed. Men forget how to weep in their souls. Real rebellion today is having a dignified, and true faith in a country of the savage and faithless.

A young man intending to set off a waiting rebellion on ten thousand streets simply needs to set the example for why at the crossroads of just one.

Today's modern fool pisses in his own drinking water and wonders why it tastes so foul.

A society that convinces a man that he should be treated soft like a baby will want for its milk for the rest of his life.

A nation that gives legitimacy to the causes of fools by letting their faith in things that have no authority be the authority will find its men with common sense removed and its power placed in the hands of idiotic tyrants.

There's nothing civil about war and there is nothing civil about civilizations; men don't obey the rules but operate under the pretense that their gloves never came off.

In a free country a dangerous new culture of immoral men demands by using violence liberty for all, engages in a revolution to obtain it for the select few, and by their rebellion will leave a nation with liberty for none because their revolution imposes a doctrine of violence with no set rules.

A society with a culture obsessed on providing freedom and self-expression for all may find itself overtaken by a society and culture that provides it to none.

The lunacy of every false rebel in each age is to preach cliched philosophies because he believes he has something new to say.

An immoral man is an ignoble creature, ranked above a vulture below a hyena but never beneath a politician.

A braggart is an ornament that no real men should care to hear or see.

For eons unimaginative men ridiculed men who were paradoxes but the world was made better by men who left their caves to dream, while the rest hid in the dark and fearfully wept.

If you believe that weeping is a weakness spare me your thoughts on humility. *Out of the depths of sadness or an arising of anger comes power after your tears. In releasing your fertile sorrow, the soul is regenerated and the world to you feels most alive. The ancients knew best. Glory and weeping are intermingled.

No revolutionary in this twisted age will ever be convinced your offering for their cause, even your death, was sincere. A sensible man should never want an insensible man's approval nor should he give his respect out of fear. Every man must decide whether he should turn his back on the idiots of his village, and the mad god of their volcano or just jump in.

In the realm of radical men nothing is harder to do than trying to understand the demands of fools.

Oppression breeds oppression, until heroes rise with the right time and tide. It is no small feat to topple tyrants.

"BOYS LEAVE HOME TO BECOME GODS. THE WORLD DESTROYS THEM AND SENDS THEM BACK AS MARTYRS."

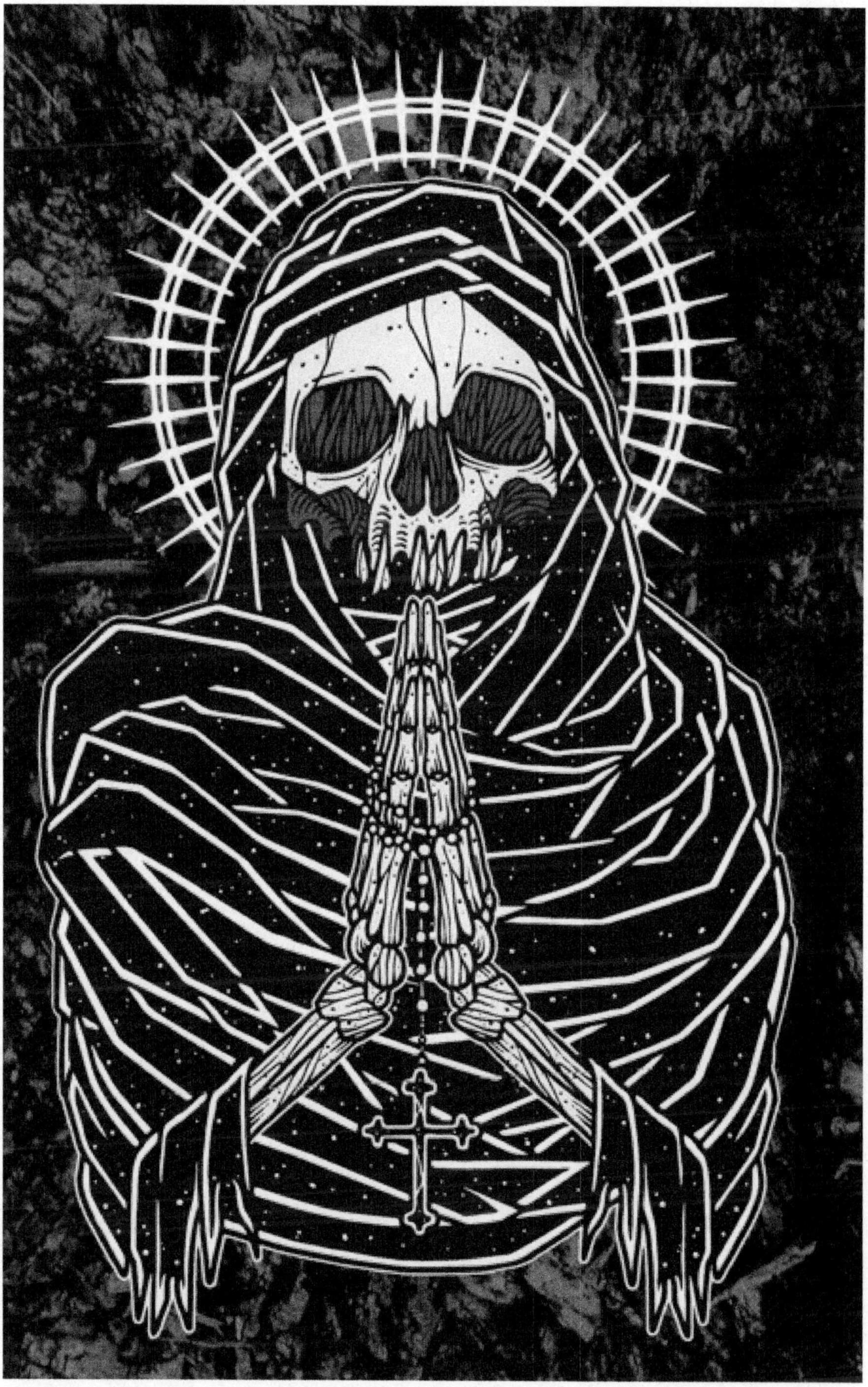

DEATH

> The world is filled with dead men and dying flowers, sullen crowds and crippled hours, solemn bands and casket drivers, baby-cradles and the things *that have been and could be.*

The world is filled with dead men and dying flowers, sullen crowds and crippled hours, solemn bands and casket drivers, baby cradles and the things that have been and could be…Good God give us purpose. We battle against age and nothing. Bleak houses and empires crumble. **Every second offers the chance to start over but one small turn to look behind us and our view upon the future changes like Lot at Gomorrah. Look back into the past of dead leaves and old gutters or brave something ahead. Reexamine old wounds and redress ancient injuries. Again, and again and again….*

Your real life is hidden so that it can be discovered.

In death it would seem that logic leaves a dead man's brain just like love leaves a dead man's heart, and it would seem that nothing worthy lasts forever but we must deny any challenge to our belief there is an eternity for good men even until we draw our last breath. We must attempt to deny it until our eyes get cloudy, until our legs get restless, we must deny it until our mind is confused and our body requires its final sleep. We must deny, deny, deny even if we tragically die alone.

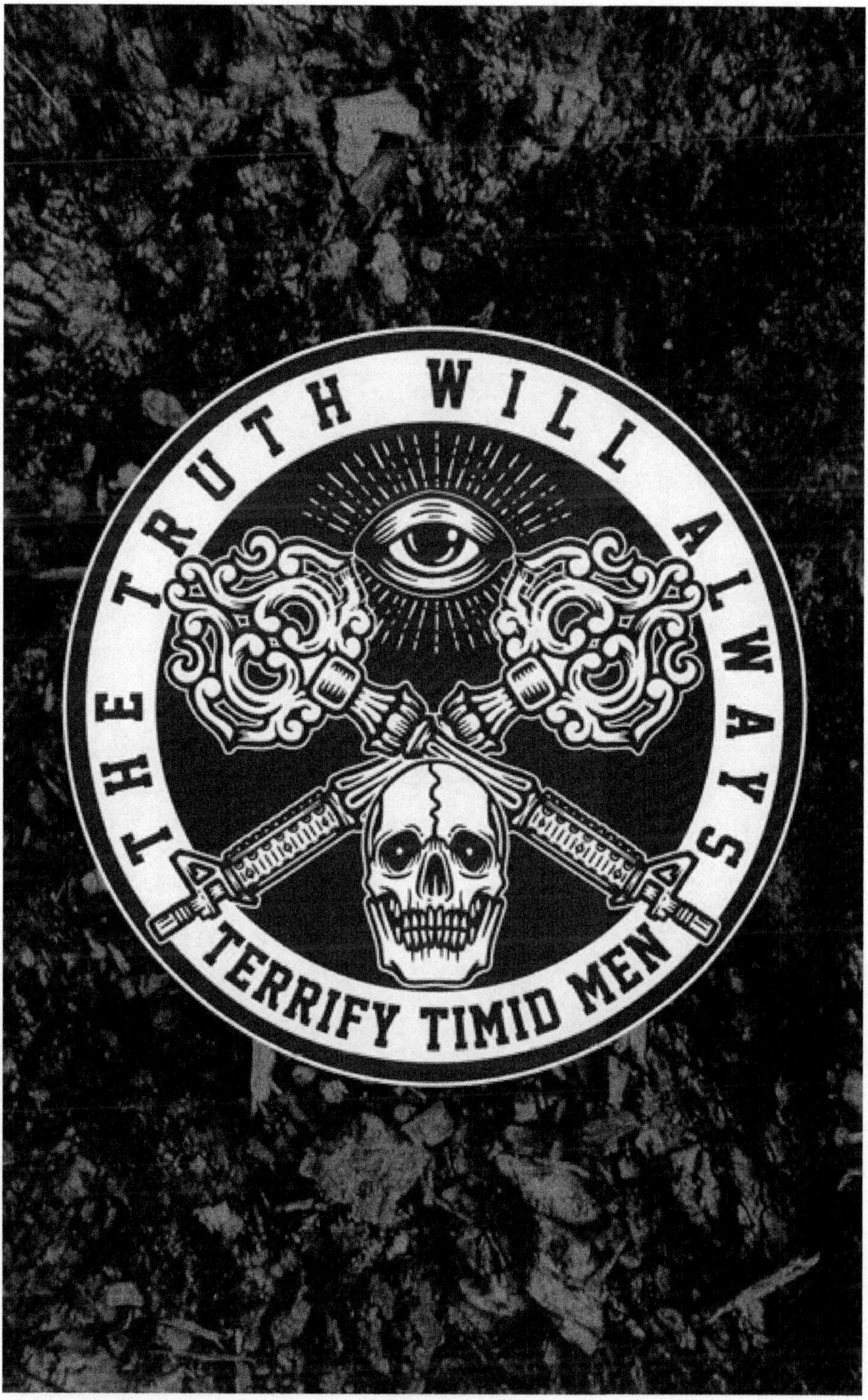
THE TRUTH WILL ALWAYS
TERRIFY TIMID MEN

KNOWLEDGE

A man blinded by pride into believing he is the sole test of authority never fares well when self-examining.

Sometimes dealing with humanity is like being in a strange room where you are asked your expert opinion on something, such as your life, yet you're judged savagely by a panel of idiots who don't know a damn thing yet they hold you accountable for everything they didn't understand.

Thought and action; reading books is generally a poor substitute for action if a man has the ability and time to do more than just read words. Reading literature can make men feel useful or safe while action means taking risks and the thought of doing something often unsettles the mind which in turn can be a blow to their body. A theorist will never be a realist until he applies what he thinks he knows, and then he knows.

Write, write honestly whether it's good or bad because you are living authentically and it can be the tool that saves you.

Thank God for fools. The world would truly be an unfunny place without the antics of stupid men.

Intelligence is the single best weapon against a dangerous world.

A life of absurdities is the punishment due rational men for the unreasonable life they choose to live.

Currents of true thought can wash away the stink of dishonesty a man covers himself in but to baptize in their streams he must desire to get pulled in the direction of those strong waters.

Youth's strength lay in the fact that we were stupid.

When you truly come to the realization that you couldn't learn something is the moment you begin to learn again.

Every man will suffer when removing spiritual cancer from his life. Sometimes he must replace care and caution with brutal violence when applying the knife.

It is our job as thinking men to prepare unreasonable men to accept the truth, nine men out of ten don't want it, the tenth man tries to prepare you.

A fool well experienced in stupidity will always teach what he doesn't know rather than acquiring real knowledge and good sense.

There are good, secret things somewhere in this world but a man must abandon all thought that he's seen it all before. He must let go of what he thinks he knows and be open for once into embracing unexplainable phenomena. He must admit deeply in fact that he truly knows nothing, that he cannot possibly devour it all, for this is the beginning of real understanding and an undertaking for him in capturing a child's joy and wonder.

Every man's heart struggles when dealing with the truth. The dishonest will never accept it as it is while the honest will never accept it as it isn't.

When you learn the same hard lessons that everyone else learned be grateful for it because you are no longer with the dummies at the back of the class but up there with the wiser men at the front.

Yes, you have many strengths; now start working on your weaknesses.

Cowards already frightened by truth should never quarrel with themselves.

Truth often comes like a thunderbolt, a lie like the fog.

If we only had the emotional wherewithal to connect the points at where we failed, we could connect the points to the places we'll succeed.

There is no mystery. Your heart knows what to do. Stop trying to break the order of things. Let what needs to endure endure, and let what needs to end end. When you pull yourself away from the fabric of things in this universe, from the tapestry of men, you become lost like a boy in the woods without knowing that we watch you. Stay the course man, stay the course.

Whatever your core beliefs, be true to it. Don't cheat it. live for it, die for it, and rest easy.

Your bones know what your mind cannot. Act upon it, act upon it, act upon it.

Rather than acquiring real knowledge and good sense a fool well experienced in stupidity will never stop teaching what he doesn't know.

A man who wants to fell big trees must first heed how small ones are rooted.

Move out the mental furniture from your mind to make space for compartments built to hold substance over style.

Childhood is what some men wish to remember, what other men wish to forget.

Historians recount warfare but many a soldier knows; written word can never recount the tragedies planted in every burial row.

Find the answers; some you will want, and some you will never want. There are no secrets in this world hidden to man. Listen to the voices as they whisper to you, clear and exact. On one of those tenantless mornings where there is only night, where the fog sits, and you are alone, pull on your shoes, and with all the strength inside of you, rise up and go.

Everyone seems to want to start at the top of the ladder of success rather than the bottom but the bottom rung is the place where the most learning can be learned but it's also the place where many men never began their climbing.

"Every man lives confusedly in darkness until he is willing to enter into light by exiting the womb of his life and leaves the safety of that environment. He has to make mistakes, he has to take chances, he has to be willing to be cut down by critics and applauded by praisers even at times ignoring what they say, while he finds out for himself what is true and false, and even then, he'll never really know a thing until he leaves comfort behind."

Every man can be reborn

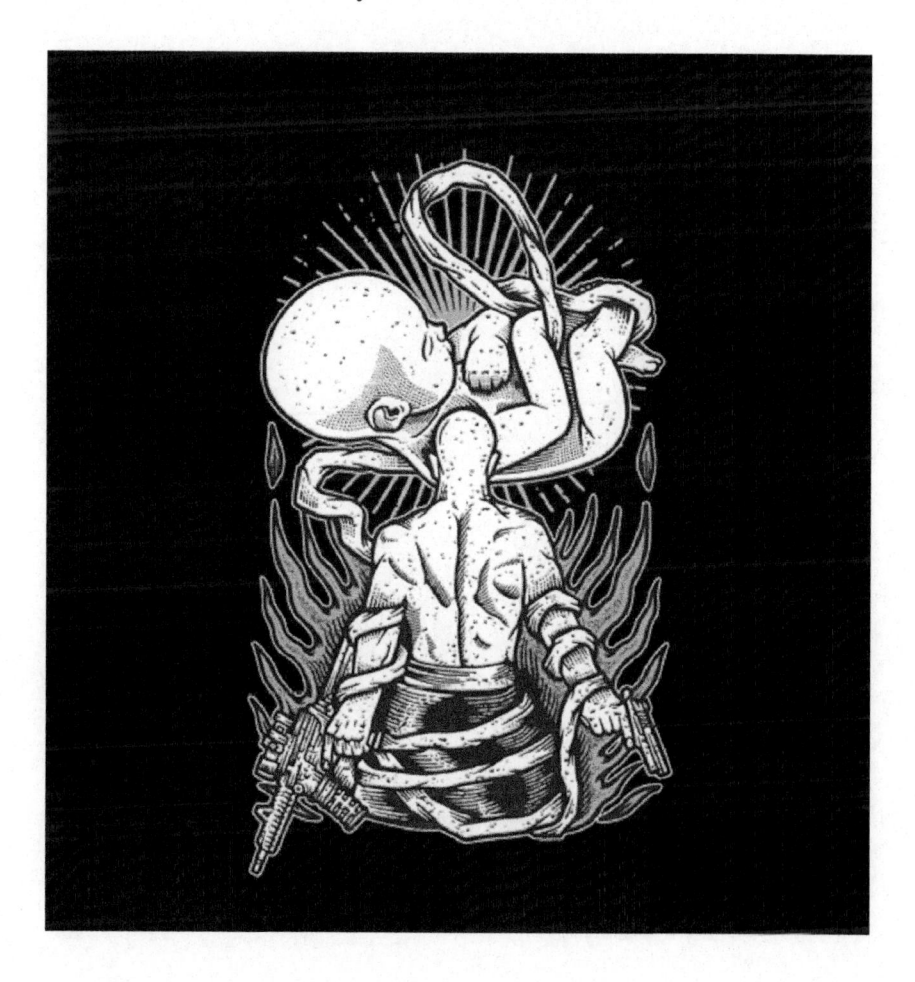

All Artwork Property of Spotterup.com and drawn by Leo Simones

All military images photographed by Combat Cameraman Gregory Brooks, given and used with his permission, except those noted below:

Thanks to my friends for their images.

Bryce Yerk, U.S. Army Special Forces

Daniel Posey, U.S. Army Special Forces

Friends from Ireland

Friends from Special Warfare Combatant Command

Jordan Laird, former Marine Scout Sniper

Joshua Shaw

Julianne Dallas

Kelly Kurcina

Mandee R.

Matt Mcdonald

Michael Kurcina

Perry Yee, Former Navy SEAL and founder of Active Valor

Others gleaned from file library.

R.I.P Mom. I miss you. You were a lioness. A picture of my mother and father when they were in Vietnam. Don't ask me what I feel or think. I've been trying to put my thoughts about them into words for decades.... a Buddhist and a Catholic who no longer practiced their faith and had no guiding principle to keep them together.

A peasant runaway from a village with a single cow and a brilliant engineer who connected at some level, and then were split apart. A beauty and a geek both met in a war-torn country where the US was supposed to keep freedom for those who would soon not know it. Blessings and curses. "But how could you live and have no story to tell?" Fyodor Dostoevsky. Good stories, bad stories. Childhood to adulthood. Whether in war or peacetime life isn't lived in brackets, and it will never be unless you allow it. One huge event may sum up a part of who we are but life doesn't begin or end right there. It's a gateway to something. Search yourself and find out what. Don't let your life be invisible. You've got something to say, make sure you say it. Teach yourself to speak kindly and humbly, guide yourself to write honestly, and then create something from the damage and constructs that you know. We all have some story to share, and some tragedy that's befallen us but we also have some kind of beautiful legacy to leave behind. Impart your knowledge and experience on others but make it good. Make it good. Honor yourself and live to honor others. Fight, love, live. Stand up for what you believe even in the absence of instruction and a clear path. Inspire men and women enough with your thoughtful words to make them weep. Terrify terrible men. Make men cry. Live and love fearlessly. Hopefully people will speak well of you while you're alive and after you've gone. (Image probably from 1964)

I HAVE SCARS ON THE INSIDE. I'M NOT AFRAID OF ANYTHING IN THIS WORLD THAT'S BEEN SEEN. WE FIGHT MONSTERS.